Preserving Cultural Landscapes in America

Center Books on Contemporary Landscape Design

Frederick R. Steiner
CONSULTING EDITOR

George F. Thompson
SERIES FOUNDER AND DIRECTOR

Published in cooperation with the Center for American Places, Santa Fe, New Mexico, and Harrisonburg, Virginia

Preserving Cultural Landscapes in America

EDITED BY

Arnold R. Alanen
and Robert Z. Melnick

FOREWORD BY

Dolores Hayden

The Johns Hopkins University Press

BALTIMORE AND LONDON

© 2000 The Johns Hopkins University Press
All rights reserved. Published 2000
Printed in the United States of America on acid-free paper
9   8   7   6   5   4   3   2   1

The Johns Hopkins University Press
2715 North Charles Street
Baltimore, Maryland 21218-4363
www.press.jhu.edu

Library of Congress Cataloging-in-Publication Data

Preserving cultural landscapes in America / edited by Arnold R.
Alanen and Robert Z. Melnick.
    p.   cm. — (Center books on contemporary landscape
design)
    Includes bibliographical references (p.   ) and index.
    ISBN 0-8018-6263-9 (alk. paper). — ISBN 0-8018-6264-7 (pbk.: alk.
paper)
    1. Historic preservation—United States.   2. Landscape
protection—United States.   3. Cultural property—Protection—
United States.   4. Historic sites—United States—Conservation
and restoration.   5. Ethnic neighborhoods—United States—
Conservation and restoration.   I. Alanen, Arnold R. (Arnold
Robert)   II. Melnick, Robert, 1948–   .   III. Series.
E159.P746   2000
333.7'2—DC21   99-38598

A catalog record for this book is available from the British Library.

Contents

Foreword

In Search of the American Cultural Landscape

Cultural landscape history enhances the possibilities of creative practice in preservation, design, and planning. Rooted in both research and practice by landscape architects, planners, historians, and geographers, the chapters in this pathbreaking volume suggest new ways to preserve and interpret American places. Their reach is broader than traditional architectural preservation, the founding discipline that has expanded in recent decades to include more emphasis on context and vernacular buildings. The authors grapple with the complexities of preserving places where landscapes—designed or natural—intersect with built forms and social life.

In the last two decades, scholars creating the field of cultural landscape history have defined a fresh approach to American landscapes, towns, and buildings. Working within groups such as the Vernacular Architecture Forum or the Urban History Association or under the auspices of material culture groups in geography, anthropology, American studies, or history, a new generation of scholars has connected cultural history to spatial history. Cultural landscape historians situate the construction of places in complex historical contexts involving economic development, land-use planning, building design, construction, occupancy, and demolition. They engage many actors, such as public and private developers, workers in the building trades, and residents, as well as architects and landscape architects. This vibrant new scholarship has nurtured a broader approach to preservation, one more attuned to the unique complexities of places as cultural resources, be they urban, suburban, or rural, built or natural, evolved or designed.

We have all cheered as architectural preservation has energized citizens to appreciate and protect historic buildings, to study their styles, to honor their fine details and materials, and to develop sophisticated plans for reuse that are both socially and economically feasible. But at the same time, architectural preservation has often limited itself by a focus on buildings as architectural objects. Neither the city, as a human creation, nor the natural landscape has easily been accommodated within it. With a model of connoisseurship derived from art history and survey techniques wedded to the materials and proportions of certain types of historic buildings, architectural preservationists have often lacked the tools to cope with the challenges of protecting wonderful places lacking architectural distinction, such as gardens, parks, and settlements in unusual natural landscapes. Architectural preservationists have often done valuable work in protecting elegant older districts of cities, hand-in-hand with homeowners and developers. Often left unsolved were the problems of renters or the interests of ordinary citizens, especially women and people of color, in seeing their own pasts reflected in designated historical landmarks. As a result, cultural landscape preservation has emerged, led by practitioners with strong interests in environmental, urban, and social questions.

Cultural landscape preservationists enter the terrain of practice committed to connecting nature and culture, wishing to reengage basic questions about the relevance of past cultural landscapes to present and future Americans. The diverse essays in this book suggest that contending aesthetic and political points of view have not disappeared. Indeed, the National Park Service definition of *cultural landscapes* differs from the UNESCO definition. Some of the authors emphasize the protection of parks and gardens as historic designed landscapes. Others focus on vernacular settlements created by ordinary people's activities over time. Many of the authors are particularly involved with the question of where nature meets culture. Others research the history of cultural landscapes as products of particular ethnic communities, such as Asian Americans in the Pacific Northwest or Puerto Rican immigrants in New York City. Others ask about the role of authenticity in an era when landscapes are routinely created as commercial attractions.

None of these issues is easy to resolve. They echo the complexities of many of the debates about popular culture that have taken place in American studies and within architectural preservation. Whose history is represented when you preserve a mansion and its gardens? Or a tenement? Of course, the answer depends on the context and the possibilities for public interpretation as well as the artifact itself. At the mansion, curators can tell the stories of the owners, or the carpenters, or the kitchen staff, or the gardeners. These days, they usually tell all four. Most visitors find it more interesting.

Public interpretation—creating a context for the viewer to understand what is being preserved and why—is the key to achieving substantial funding and audiences for the diverse cultural landscape projects analyzed here. In many ways, interpretation is easier for preserved cultural landscapes than for preserved buildings. Landscapes are more often public places, as well as spaces understood on a larger scale. Ordinary citizens often have more access to them than to the interiors of many designated landmark buildings. For this same reason, however, the public interpretation of cultural landscapes is more complex. There are many stories to tell, research must be excellent, and the commitment to public interpretation must be high.

As ever, commercial speculation and exploitation lurk as enemies of the unique, the authentic, and the local. Commercial imitations of historic vernacular landscapes are everywhere from Disneyland to Las Vegas casinos, from local amusement parks to shopping malls. They may be fun, they are often profitable, but they are private commercial real estate projects, not public spaces illuminated by public interpretation. Such entertainments often offer stock characters straight off the movie lot: uniformed war heroes, deferential schoolteachers in long dresses, brash gun-toting cowboys, machine politicians buying votes from workers hefting drinks in a local saloon. Whenever these cardboard characters turn up, they steal attention from what is local, unique, and irreplaceable.

The cultural landscape is by definition unique—that combination of natural landforms and buildings that defines a particular place or region. It is the creation of the women, men, and children who lived their lives within that landscape. Preserved and interpreted for the public, the cultural landscape tells us who we are, as Americans, far more effectively than most individual works of architecture or exhibits in museums ever can. Main streets and mail-order houses, *casitas* and steam baths, small towns and big parks, Pueblo Indian kivas and Midwestern flower gardens—all convey the specific traces of American material life as generations of diverse peoples have lived it.

As ever, resources are scarce and priorities must be selected, which is why Arnold Alanen and Robert Melnick have created this important book. The authors propose new ways to think about places and aesthetics, maintenance, and care. Ultimately, they suggest new ways to recover the historic American cultural landscape as part of larger, ongoing processes of architectural preservation and urban design. Every scholar and practitioner in the design fields with an interest in history will gain from reconsidering what Americans should preserve, and for whom.

DOLORES HAYDEN
Professor of Architecture and Urbanism
Professor of American Studies
Yale University

Preface and Acknowledgments

Although we were not aware of it at the time, the seeds for this book were planted when we first met at a conference some twenty years ago. The occasion was the 1979 meeting of the Alliance for Historic Landscape Preservation, a fledgling group organized in New Harmony, Indiana, just one year earlier. In early June 1979, we and some twenty other individuals from the United States and Canada who were interested in landscape preservation and landscape history gathered at The Clearing, located in Wisconsin's scenic Door County. The Clearing was and is an appropriate place for the meeting of such an organization because it served, from 1932 to 1951, as the home and school for Jens Jensen, a Danish immigrant who played a major role in the development of a distinctive Midwestern approach to landscape architecture. The meeting at The Clearing was organized by one of the founding members of the alliance, William Tishler, a professor in the Department of Landscape Architecture at the University of Wisconsin-Madison.

We especially acknowledge two individuals, both of whom attended the alliance meeting in 1979, for their influence in shaping our subsequent attitudes toward cultural landscape preservation: the late Thomas Kane and Hugh Miller. Tom, long noted for his considerable humor and aplomb, was a Vermont landscape architect who had been engaged in landscape preservation projects since the 1960s; until his death in 1995, Tom was the only person who never missed an annual meeting of the alliance, and he was a key figure in identifying and promoting the field of cultural landscape preservation among his fellow members of the American Society of Landscape Architects. Hugh, who at the time was the chief historical architect for the National Park Service (NPS), had an uncommon concern for the cultural landscapes included within the boundaries of many new parks authorized by congressional decree during the 1970s. Indeed, with Hugh's early encouragement and recommendation, both of us, over the next two decades, have participated in NPS-sponsored activities and projects throughout the United States. We also acknowledge the other members of the alliance who provided us with so many insights and ideas, several of which served as inspiration for this book.

Four individuals graciously agreed to review two or more chapters of this volume and offered invaluable comments and observations: Lynn Bjorkman, Karin Hertel McGinnis, Michael Koop, and Barbara Wyatt. Others who provided information and assistance were Susan Haswell, Kenneth Helphand, Eric MacDonald, Nora Mitchell, Linda McClelland, Holly Smith-Middleton, and William Tishler. We are, of course, indebted to all of the contributors who found time in their busy schedules to prepare essays for this volume, but Gail Dubrow, Donald Hardesty, and Dolores Hayden deserve special recognition for their additional comments.

Finally, this book never would have seen the light of day without the direction provided by George F. Thompson, president of the Center for American Places. It was George who encouraged us to pursue our interests and to put this volume together, and it was he who facilitated the publication process from conception through production. His assistant, Randall Jones, also provided ready follow-up to our many questions as the book neared completion. Linda Forlifer, manuscript editor for the Johns Hopkins University Press, patiently oversaw the transformation of the manuscript into a book, and Alexa Selph developed the index.

To our readers, it is our sincerest hope that you will find new understandings and appreciations of our nation's cultural landscapes.

Preserving Cultural Landscapes in America

Why Cultural Landscape Preservation?

During the mid-1980s, the Statue of Liberty was dressed in unusual garb: from the base of the monument and continuing upward to the torch and crown, New York City's famous lady was encased in hundreds of tons of scaffolding. As disappointed as many visitors undoubtedly were by this encumbered view of Miss Liberty, the need for these restoration and preservation activities was understood by people throughout the nation; obviously, both the skeleton and skin of such an important national shrine and icon required attention as she approached her hundredth birthday, in 1986. Most of the $300 million expended on the project, which also included funds for the restoration of several buildings at Ellis Island, was provided by corporations, although more than $2 million was raised by American schoolchildren.[1]

About the same time and only some six miles to the northeast, another major preservation endeavor was under way in midtown Manhattan: the rehabilitation of the Central Park landscape that had been designed by Frederick Law Olmsted and Calvert Vaux during the 1850s. Unlike that of the Statue of Liberty, however, Central Park's rehabilitation was not readily appreciated by many New Yorkers. As rehabilitation activities progressed during the late 1970s and early 1980s, numerous groups expressed vociferous opposition to several proposals, especially those that called for tree and vegetation removal or the restoration of open meadows in areas used for such hard-surface activities as basketball, tennis, and baseball.

Some smaller modifications were undertaken quietly "for fear of stirring up opponents," but other changes did not escape the scrutiny of a vocal and observant public. Opposition to the resodding and reseeding of Central Park's Sheep Meadow in 1979–80 was expressed by individuals concerned that the

The Sheep Meadow in New York City's Central Park in 1985, five years after restoration of the landscape had been completed. After its reopening, Paul Goldberger wrote in the *New York Times* (5 June 1980), the meadow now appeared "for the first time in many, many years as it was intended to look—like a great, rolling, soft and brilliant green lawn." Photograph by Alanen, 1985.

brown, worn, and dusty fifteen-acre site would no longer be available for athletic events, political rallies, and concerts. Although the meadow was quickly transformed into a landscape of "incredible softness," similar to the vision of Olmsted and Vaux of more than a hundred years earlier, some recreation enthusiasts contended that New York City's Parks Department was attempting to establish a "grass museum." A 1982 petition signed by some one thousand Central Park bird watchers expressed outrage over "the mass destruction of mature and irreplaceable trees, particularly [in] the Ramble and adjacent areas." When assessing the conflict, Central Park administrator Elizabeth Barlow Rogers pointed to the "philosophical difference" and "violent opposition of attitudes" between bird watchers and those who advocated "the principles of landscape architecture, which hold that a park is a garden—something to be managed and protected and planted."[2]

Today, greater support exists for cultural landscape preservation, restoration, and rehabilitation than was evident even as recently as the mid-1980s;[3]

nevertheless, it is doubtful that these activities are comprehended as readily as the idea and practice of preserving buildings and structures. Indeed, the technical language used in cultural landscape preservation—especially in the documents prepared by governmental agencies and organizations—often poses problems, since many terms and definitions are borrowed directly from architectural preservation. In addition, the very concept of cultural landscape preservation may sound like an oxymoron to some people; because cultural landscapes are composed of natural elements that grow, mature, erode, move, die, and revive once again, how can they possibly be preserved?[4] Since it is not possible to enforce stability in landscapes, "they never arrive at the point of total preservation."[5]

Examples of Cultural Landscapes

What is a cultural landscape, and how do we recognize such places when we see them? Cultural landscapes exist virtually everywhere that human activities have affected the land, although people typically would not specify such a wide range of possibilities. If asked to consider the landscape continuum that extends from wilderness to city, for example, most respondents undoubtedly would associate the cultural landscape with places that lie somewhere between the two poles—environments that clearly display the human organization of natural elements. Examples of such idealized cultural landscapes (sometimes termed *middle landscapes* by scholars) include gardens, parks, and, especially, rural pastoral scenes. One could also argue, however, that cultural landscapes often are part of wilderness areas, whether manifested in faint traces of former trappers and homesteaders, in current policies that protect and preserve wild areas, or in the photographs, postcards, and books that we use to preserve our memories of wilderness. Cultural landscapes are also evident in the city; some advocates of a broad definition even argue that the townscapes and cityscapes that characterize urban areas serve as large-scale examples of the interface between culture and the land.

Topography, vegetation, soil, and water are included as part of cultural landscapes, but these natural elements are transformed by human processes and actions into gardens, parks, cemeteries, subdivisions, lawns, roads, pathways, fields, pastures, hedgerows, orchards, canals, ponds, and so forth; furthermore, objects and site furnishings, which include but are not limited to fences, walls, bridges, dams, signs, lights, benches, fountains, and sculpture, are also part of the cultural landscape. Buildings—especially their siting, arrangement, and organization—are important features of the cultural

Frank Lloyd Wright is primarily identified as an architect of international stature, but many of his projects also serve as important examples of designed landscapes. At Taliesin—the home, studio, and school he initially developed outside of Spring Green, Wisconsin, in 1911—Wright utilized three oak trees as organizational and symbolic elements for the residential portion of the complex; one tree also served as the Tea Circle Oak, where Taliesin's apprentices and staff members gathered daily for tea and conversation. By 1960, one year after Wright's death, only this bur oak remained, but it was toppled by a severe windstorm in June 1998, thereby changing the historic character, context, and appearance of the entire space. Photograph by Alanen, 1989.

landscape, although landscape preservationists typically do not emphasize the structural systems, surface finishes, floor plans, and interior furnishings characteristic of traditional preservation efforts.

Probably the most recognizable and understandable examples of cultural landscapes are those places designed, usually by trained professionals, to satisfy certain aesthetic, ecological, or functional requirements and standards. A listing of such landscapes includes environments laid out by some of America's best-known designers: scores of parks and park systems found throughout the United States, including Prospect Park in Brooklyn, the Emerald Necklace in Boston (both by Frederick Law Olmsted), and the Grand Round in Minneapolis (H. W. S. Cleveland); such scenic roadways as the Blue Ridge Parkway (Stanley Abbott), which stretches from Virginia to North Carolina;

burial grounds like Chicago's Graceland Cemetery (O. C. Simonds); memorials, including recent examples in Washington, D.C., that commemorate the Vietnam War experience (Maya Lin) and the life of President Franklin D. Roosevelt (Lawrence Halprin); and planned cities and communities, ranging from early twentieth-century model industrial villages like Mariemont, Ohio (John Nolen), to such contemporary examples of New Urbanism as Seaside, Florida, and the Kentlands, Maryland (Anders Duany and Elizabeth Plater-Zyrbek). In addition, thousands of designed cultural landscapes, most of which are not as nationally significant as those listed above, serve as locally important environments throughout America.

The vast majority of cultural landscapes, however, have developed without the direct involvement of a professional designer, planner, or engineer. These ordinary, or vernacular, landscapes, which generally evolve unintentionally and represent multiple layers of time and cultural activity, are fundamental to our very existence. The most obvious land-use type within this category of the cultural landscape is agriculture, whether it be expressed in the Amish countryside of Lancaster, Pennsylvania, the dairy farming districts of Wisconsin, or the vast grainfields of the Great Plains. The ordinary landscape also includes areas that have been or are being used (and often abused) for mining, extraction, and production activities. Examples include the tipples, slag heaps, tailings piles, open pits, leaching ponds, headframes, and company housing found in the coal fields of Appalachia and Wyoming, the copper mines of Michigan, Montana, and Arizona, and the iron ore ranges of the Lake Superior region. Other examples are often associated with the field of industrial archeology, primarily the technologically outdated, dilapidated, rust-coated factories and industrial dumps that continue to form the landscape of former manufacturing areas.

Ordinary cultural landscapes characterize not only rural and industrial areas of the country, but also urban and suburban America. The yards, lawns, and gardens that people create to beautify and give order to their own exterior environments are among the most ubiquitous features of the national landscape. Examples include the wide expanses of private open space that define many suburban areas, as well as the small and often makeshift gardens that recent immigrants from Latin America and Asia develop in large cities. And, of course, America's automobile culture also creates its own landscape, whether it be at freeway intersections, the highway-oriented strips that mark the entry to most towns and cities, or the shopping malls (and huge parking lots) that are part of most new subdivision developments on the suburban fringe.

Certain cultural landscapes are also imbued with spiritual values, a phe-

nomenon usually assoc   ples in America.
Most visitors who ven1   1 Alaska, Mount
Shasta in California, C;   lar sites appreciate the aesthetic and w   1st as they might
value them for the clim   ide. To the native
people of these areas, the same landscape features may be filled with sacred and cultural meanings directly linked to the past, present, and future, as well as to the health and well-being of their culture. Some cultural landscapes may also have important ethnographic meaning to nonnative groups, particularly people who are bound together by a common history, identity, or ethos. The house that Martin Luther King Jr. formerly inhabited in Atlanta, as well as the church where he and his family worshiped, are important pilgrimage points for many African Americans. Not to be overlooked, however, are the backyard alleys and the streetscape formed by the trees, vegetation, and row of uniform, closely spaced bungalows that once accommodated workers employed in a nearby factory; all of these elements provide a landscape context for the neighborhood, including the King residence and Ebenezer Baptist Church.

| The Origins of Cultural Landscape Preservation

Countless cultural landscapes, ranging in scale from specific sites to entire regions, exist as possible subjects for preservation activity. Since there are so many cultural landscapes and because they reveal multiple layers of history and meaning, those individuals, institutions, and organizations interested in their protection and preservation must consider several issues: Which cultural landscapes and time periods should be preserved, and why and how should they be preserved?

The early history of preservation activity at Colonial Williamsburg in Virginia is meaningful in this regard. Ever since John D. Rockefeller began to finance the massive restoration of Williamsburg during the 1920s and 1930s, "the world of American historic preservation has not been the same."[6] When considering the landscape, for example, primary attention was initially given to its "correct" treatment, not only from the standpoint of technical and aesthetic considerations, but also from a historical viewpoint. Certain facets of history—especially evidence and interpretations of the oppressive and dehumanizing aspects of slavery—either were not highlighted or were purposefully dismissed and removed; thus, little consideration was given to African American gardens and living quarters. It was not until the 1970s and 1980s that this uncomfortable history received attention at Williamsburg by means of archeological excavations and landscape surveys to document slave conditions and historic plant materials. Despite these recent developments, much of Colonial Williamsburg's identity has been established by presentations of the "historic scene" rather than by portrayals of dynamic landscapes reflective of many histories.

These presentations were reflective of preservation attitudes at the time, when the history of landscape restoration was closely bound up with the desired history of a place. This cleansing of history—actually a form of landscape scrubbing—often has served to deny future generations opportunities for new discoveries and interpretations. Today a much broader view of history is adopted by preservationists; now, for [...]
inated to the National Register of Historic [...]
significance, but also because of their poten[...]
future. Perhaps more than anything else, V[...]
perative it is that we understand the need [...]
our knowledge, not as some might wish t[...]
at Williamsburg "has remained an attempt[...]
Ary J. Lamme III has written. "But definiti[...]
burg's truth and how it should be interpreted have been questioned."7

It is obvious that an open as well as a scholarly approach must be followed when studying, documenting, and interpreting cultural landscapes. Other than a few examples, it was not until the late 1970s and early 1980s that preservationists began to address issues associated with the broader landscape. Leadership was provided by the American Society of Landscape Architects (ASLA), which formed a historic preservation committee during the early 1970s; in 1976, under the direction of editor Grady Clay, several articles that featured landscape preservation and restoration in the United States appeared in the ASLA's professional magazine, *Landscape Architecture*.8 Also of note is the Association for Preservation Technology (APT), which began to address landscape-related issues at this time. In 1978, a small group of APT members formed the nucleus of the new Alliance for Historic Landscape Preservation, an interdisciplinary organization with interests in both designed and vernacular landscapes. It was, however, the National Park Service (NPS), more than any other American organization or agency, that provided the most significant direction to the nascent cultural landscape preservation movement. The NPS first recognized cultural landscapes as a specific resource type in 1981. This was followed, three years later, by the publication of a report, *Cultural Landscapes: Rural Historic Districts in the National Park System,* which spelled out criteria for identifying and defining cultural landscapes. Since then, the NPS has continued to provide both intellectual and practical leadership for cultural landscape preservationist activities throughout America.9

The NPS, which defines the cultural landscape as "a geographic area . . . associated with a historic event, activity, or person or exhibiting other cultural or aesthetic values," also has established definitions for four general types of cultural landscapes that it is responsible for managing:

—*Historic Site:* a landscape significant for its association with a historic event, activity, or person.

—*Historic Designed Landscape:* a landscape that was consciously designed or laid out by a landscape architect, master gardener, architect, or horticulturist according to design principles, or an amateur gardener working in a recognized design style or tradition.

—*Historic Vernacular Landscape:* a landscape that evolved through use by the people whose activities or occupancy shaped that landscape.

—*Ethnographic Landscape:* a landscape containing a variety of natural and cultural resources that associated people define as heritage resources.[10]

Many other nations also have enacted sophisticated cultural landscape preservation programs, several of which preceded activities in the United States. One especially significant action with worldwide implications occurred in 1992, when the United Nations Educational, Scientific and Cultural Organization (UNESCO) established its initial definitions and criteria for three major types of cultural landscapes that can be evaluated as potential World Heritage Sites. The definitions were modified in 1994, as follows:

—*Clearly Defined Landscape:* a landscape designed and created intentionally by man, including garden and parkland landscapes constructed for aesthetic reasons that are often (but not always) associated with religious or other monumental buildings and ensembles.

—*Organically Evolved Landscape:* a landscape that results from an initial social, economic, administrative, or religious imperative and has developed its present form by association with and in response to the natural environment. Such landscapes reflect that process of evolution in their form and component features.

—*Associative Cultural Landscape:* a landscape that reflects powerful religious, artistic, or cultural associations of natural elements rather than material cultural evidence, which may be insignificant or even absent.[11]

Despite certain differences, similarities do exist between the NPS and UNESCO definitions, especially the designed/defined landscapes identified by both organizations. The organically evolved landscapes of UNESCO, which are divided into two subcategories—"relict or fossil landscapes" and "continuing landscapes"—have parallels with both the historic vernacular and ethnographic landscapes of the NPS. The associative cultural landscapes of UNESCO may also be linked to the ethnographic landscapes of the NPS and to some historic sites.[12] The above cultural landscape types are addressed either directly or indirectly in this volume, but the categories are not discrete entities; there is often considerable overlap between and among the types that both agencies have identified.

| About This Book

The chapters in this volume, primarily through examples and case studies, engage many of the questions and challenges now encountered by cultural landscape preservationists. Each author explores ideas and current issues that are both dynamic and provocative in his or her particular area of interest and expertise. As a text of ideas—and this is an educational book rather than a training manual—the book provides a guide to thinking about many of the major issues current in the field of cultural landscape preservation.

The first chapter, by co-editor Robert Melnick, focuses on an essential factor in the preservation of cultural landscapes, the relationship between nature and culture. Citing David Lowenthal, who has noted that historic preservation in the Western world generally seeks to arrest change rather than accommodate transition, Melnick investigates some of the commonalities between language and landscape by exploring three concepts: semantic ecotones, landscape differentials, and landscape as teacher. California's Yosemite Valley, one of the world's foremost landscape icons, is used as an exemplar. Because of Yosemite's outstanding natural features, there has been a tendency to downplay its history and cultural imprints, even though the views and vistas of Albert Bierstadt, Ansel Adams, and countless visitors were and are carefully managed to maintain a recognizable image of the "incomparable valley." Calling for "nonlinear and cyclical modes of thinking about nature, culture, and landscape," the chapter concludes with a discussion of the conundrum: How do we "reconcile the unrelenting need to protect natural systems with the impulse to transform them into human systems?"

Until recently, individuals, groups, and agencies engaged in heritage tourism directed their energies and financial resources to the preservation of buildings and structures. Now, however, landscapes receive considerable attention from the tourism community, a theme that Richard Francaviglia addresses in chapter 2—the "sale" of heritage landscapes. Francaviglia devotes the majority of his discussion to the identification and definition of six different forms of heritage landscape preservation: (1) passively preserved, (2) actively preserved, (3) restored, (4) assembled, (5) imagineered, and (6) imagically preserved. He concludes by noting that heritage landscapes "are important indicators of the restless search for the identity that characterizes Americans as they make the transition from the twentieth to the twenty-first century."

Most cultural landscape preservation activities have occurred in cities. In chapter 3, David Schuyler and Patricia M. O'Donnell give primary attention to the parks and cemeteries that serve as important historic designed landscapes in urban settings. They discuss the factors that require consideration when determining which urban landscapes are historic, as well as the methods that can be used to preserve these environments. Because urban landscapes often serve as contested space—areas that are under constant pressure to accommodate alternative functions and uses—the authors propose that the preservation of these landscapes requires "a stewardship ethic that addresses shared use and reduction of conflict [and] . . . builds consensus among all stakeholders." Such consensus is especially vital in urban areas, for even though all landscapes are multilayered accretions that reflect processes of change occurring over time, nowhere is landscape change more consistently evident than in the city.

A different form of the urban landscape is addressed by Luis Aponte-Parés in his chapter on the Puerto Rican casitas of New York City. The *casitas*—balloon-frame residences constructed on stilts, with metal gable roofs, large verandas, shutters, and vivid colors—reflect a building form that has strong associations with the Puerto Rican homeland of their builders. Aponte-Parés notes that the casitas, as "cogent metaphors of place and culture" and as "metaphors of places past," along with the vegetable gardens that often emerge on vacant land, represent the residents' efforts to reshape "landscapes of despair into landscapes of hope." In New York and elsewhere in the United States, the casitas and gardens provide their builders "the power of place and culture in a city that has yet to offer many of them acceptance and a sense that they belong."

The environments described by Aponte-Parés are examples of the ordinary, or vernacular, landscapes that exist in several of the nation's largest cities. The vernacular landscape, however, is more commonly defined by the rural areas, small towns, and isolated resource extraction sites that are addressed in chapter 5 by co-editor Arnold Alanen. Since the word *vernacular* includes a broad range of ordinary and everyday landscapes within its purview and is probably not familiar to many people, the chapter begins with an overview of the term's origins and evolution and then considers several examples of the methods and tools used to preserve specific vernacular landscapes: local and community efforts, land trusts, National Park Service landscapes (including

A vernacular garden in the predominantly Puerto Rican neighborhood of Holyoke, Massachusetts, managed by a grass-roots organization, Nuestros Raices. Since most of the neighborhood's residents live in rental apartments, the garden serves as their only direct contact with the land. The screens used in the garden have been removed from the apartment windows, thereby allowing more interaction between private (interior) and public (exterior) space. For background on the Puerto Rican casitas of New York City, refer to chapter 4 by Luis Aponte-Parés. Sketch by Thomas Kenly, based upon a photograph by Pat McGirr, 1997.

recent private-public partnerships), and heritage areas and corridors. A review of these examples reveals that vernacular landscape preservation is often difficult to accomplish because of remoteness, a lack of adequate economic support, the size and complexity of the resource, and a shortage of local professional expertise.

The vernacular themes featured by Aponte-Parés and Alanen are carried further by Gail Dubrow, who discusses the cultural resources and landscapes associated with Asian Americans. Dubrow points out that, despite the efforts of preservationists to identify and recognize a greater number of the nation's vernacular landscapes, the majority of landscape preservation activities still feature "mainstream" Americans and their endeavors. Focusing on immigrants from Asia and the Pacific Islands who have settled in California, Idaho, Nevada, Oregon, and Washington, Dubrow notes that these individuals are noticeably under-represented in the National Register of Historic Places and as National Historic Landmarks. She attributes this lack of awareness to two factors: Asian Americans "left remarkably few obvious cultural imprints on the built environment and landscape," and preservation agencies generally have not possessed suitable knowledge and direction to identify, evaluate, and manage the resources that do exist. Dubrow identifies numerous places that reflect the Asian American legacy in the West, including company towns, ranches, farms, truck and flower gardens, railroads, and placer mining sites. Her concluding recommendations, which refer to the recognition and preservation of Asian American landscape features, also have applicability for other minority groups in the United States.

The most complex of the cultural landscape types encountered anywhere in the world are those that have ethnographic overtones, places that have especially significant and even sacred meaning to contemporary peoples. Ethnographic landscapes are truly dynamic, since they represent both past and present to the people who imbue them with meaning. Donald Hardesty, in chapter 7, states that ethnographic landscapes represent the transformation of "nature into culture" and also demonstrate the continuing process of "world-making." In America, ethnographic landscapes have been and are being created by people whose origins are in Europe, Africa, and Asia, although the largest number of places are associated with Native Americans. Hardesty provides examples from several American Indian groups and follows with a discussion of the values collision that can occur when different cultural groups imbue the same landscape with different meanings. He concludes with an overview of methods that might be used to preserve the diversity of America's ethnographic landscapes.

Finally, it is essential to consider the criteria currently employed to evaluate the significance of a cultural landscape. When such landscapes are considered for inclusion in the National Register of Historic Places, for example, determinations of integrity assume considerable importance. Catherine Howett, in chapter 8, notes that, because landscapes "are fundamentally dynamic biotic systems subject to continual change," they seldom are appropriate for analysis that uses "preservation criteria derived largely from architectural models." Tracing the complex evolution of the NPS bulletin *The Secretary of the Interior's Standards for the Treatment of Historic Properties with Guidelines for the Treatment of Cultural Landscapes* (1996), Howett details many of the problems that arise when assessing landscape integrity. Reflecting the observations of David Lowenthal, she then asks how we can preserve the past when we have not experienced it and how we can account for historical bias, which is inevitable whenever we record, describe, and interpret the

A 1975 overview of a portion of the Kickapoo River Valley in southwestern Wisconsin, some years after an anticipated U.S. Army Corps of Engineers flood control project had resulted in the condemnation of 8,570 acres of land and the removal of 140 farms. The flood control project was abandoned in 1976 because of environmental and political concerns, and much of the land intended for a reservoir was reclaimed by vegetation. In 1996, federal legislation led to the transfer of 7,370 acres of land to the State of Wisconsin and 1,200 acres to the Ho-Chunk (Winnebago) Indians. Unlike the cultural clash that can occur when different groups disagree on the meaning of certain landscape features, the two parties now manage the land jointly for conservation and recreational purposes and sites deemed sacred by the Ho-Chunk will be protected. Photograph by Alanen, 1975.

past. To cope with this dilemma, she recommends that integrity be considered when dynamic processes are evaluated, but not necessarily when making static inventories, and that interpretation be given more emphasis than preservation. "The quality and importance of any preservation project is not determined by the integrity of the site," Howett concludes, but "by the quality of what is made of the site through interpretation of its history."

The Cultural Landscape and Cultural Landscape Studies

Although the emphasis of this book is on contemporary issues in cultural landscape preservation, the underpinnings of the current dialogue may be traced back to the 1920s and earlier. In North America, the academic study of cultural landscapes is linked to geographer Carl Sauer. After joining the faculty at the University of California, Berkeley, in 1923, Sauer sought to make

Garden at the Governor's Palace, Colonial Williamsburg, Virginia. The garden restorations at Williamsburg during the 1920s and 1930s, under the direction of Arthur A. Shurcliff and other landscape architects, reflected the design styles and preferences of former British colonists who resided in the American South. It was not until the 1980s that the gardens developed by African American slaves were recognized at Williamsburg, although the reconstructions were not necessarily based upon archeological findings. The issue of landscape integrity at Williamsburg and elsewhere is discussed by Catherine Howett in chapter 8. Photograph by Alanen, 1979.

landscape study the primary research agenda for the entire discipline of geography. In his classic 1925 work, "The Morphology of Landscape," Sauer defined the landscape as an amalgam of physical and cultural forms: "Culture is the agent," he wrote, "the natural area is the medium, the cultural landscape the result."[13]

Since Sauer set forth a very demanding and time-consuming research program that called for the genetic study of landscapes (i.e., beginning with the natural landscape and continuing through all of the subsequent culture groups that inhabited an area or region), the "landscape school" did not develop into an all-encompassing research paradigm for the discipline of geography. In fact, the editors of a major collection of geographical readings, published in 1962, declared that by then cultural landscape study had become a subcategory of cultural geography. Their definition of the cultural landscape, nonetheless, remained very similar to Sauer's: "a concrete and characteristic product of the complicated interplay between a given human community embodying certain cultural preferences and potentials, and a particular set of natural circumstances."[14]

Students of the cultural landscape often found it difficult to have their work published and recognized in mainstream academic journals during the 1950s and 1960s, but John Brinkerhoff Jackson provided an avenue for them to reach a larger audience. From 1951 to 1968, Jackson edited and published *Landscape,* a magazine that also presented his often brilliant, if sometimes idiosyncratic, interpretations of cultural landscapes. Until his death in 1996, Jackson offered a plethora of perceptive ideas and interpretations in numerous books, articles, essays, public presentations, and academic lectureships in the College of Environmental Design at the University of California, Berkeley (1967–78) and the Graduate School of Design at Harvard University (1969–77). Better than anyone else, Jackson succeeded in expanding our awareness and understanding of the cultural landscape. Some of his insights are pragmatic, straightforward, and readily comprehensible, such as the observation that landscape "serves as infrastructure or background for our collective existence." Other comments verge on the poetic, as typified by his description of finding beauty in the ordinary landscape—"the image of our common humanity: hard work, stubborn hope, and mutual forbearance striving to be love."[15]

For about half a century, Jackson and a rather small cadre of individuals in several disciplines have pursued studies of the cultural landscape, although no single paradigm has directed these efforts. The concept of the cultural landscape also remains vague to the vast majority of Americans. Because "most people in the United States do not consciously notice their everyday environments," landscape historian Paul Groth argues in a recent essay, they "are in danger of being poor appreciators and managers of their surroundings."[16]

In addition, relatively few individuals who study the cultural landscape have focused upon preservation issues. Jackson, in fact, adamantly refused to be identified as a preservationist (or an environmentalist) throughout his long career. In a 1976 letter to *Landscape Architecture,* for example, he stated that a "sense of the stream of time" could not be reproduced by "sterile reconstructions."[17] Nevertheless, several individuals affiliated with the American Society of Landscape Architecture's Historic Preservation Professional Interest Group, the Alliance for Historic Landscape Preservation, and the National Park Service have utilized the writings of landscape studies scholars, including Jackson, to assist them in dealing with the world of cultural landscape preservation. Though the number of scholars who study cultural landscapes and also focus upon their preservation is still limited, most of the authors featured in this volume are interested in both.

| *Critical Issues*

The field of cultural landscape preservation has achieved considerable advances in recent years, marked by the efforts of diverse scholars, investigators, and practitioners. Nevertheless, the field still faces critical issues; some are recurring inquiries that confront any scholarly endeavor, others are generic to the overall field of preservation, and some are limited specifically to the practice of cultural landscape preservation itself.

Foremost among the factors that differentiate cultural landscape preservation from its associated fields is the recognition that the landscape is both artifact and system; in other words, it is a product and a process. The essential dynamic qualities of a cultural landscape, regardless of a designer's intention or the use patterns of a cultural group, mark it as separate from other resources we seek to protect through traditional historic preservation.

A second important landscape characteristic is concerned with scale. All physical resources are dynamic, yet the landscape displays that quality within a cycle that is perceptual to us in a day, a week, a season, a year, or a lifetime. The measurement of landscape change, as distinct from archeological or architectural transition, focuses on both shorter and longer periods of time. Likewise, a landscape may be both a system in itself and also part of a larger system. Although we most often think of this as a physical measurement, it can also occur in a temporal sense; the intricate relationship between people and the landscape may be based upon what happened in a day, or it may include years of change and transition.

A historic Civil War battlefield scene at Fredericksburg, Virginia. Battlefield sites generally commemorate events that occurred over a few days only. Preserving such scenes, which represent only a snapshot in time, poses different questions and issues for managers and interpreters than do landscapes characterized by multiple layers of history. The bucolic scene presented today, of course, belies the carnage and landscape damage that occurred at the time of the battle. Photograph by Alanen, 1986.

The field of cultural landscape preservation now faces broader challenges, including the need for a complexity of understanding. In the remarkable surge of federal, state, and local activity since the 1980s, there has developed an inclination to simplify rather than clarify the values inherent in cultural landscapes and, correspondingly, to simplify responses to those values. These efforts, as illustrated by the National Park Service, have understandably been a result of too many years of neglect and inattention. The reliance on codification, as exemplified in *The Secretary of the Interior's Standards for the Treatment of Historic Properties with Guidelines for the Treatment of Cultural Landscapes,*[18] holds the potential to negate the very idiosyncratic landscape qualities that set one place apart from another.

Inherent in the idea of codification is the presumption of equality or equal value that can be quantified. In a social context we obviously strive for the fair and equitable application of law and opportunity. While this is one of the foundations of our democratic society, over the past few decades we have learned that the practice of this value has not always met its aspirations. When rules are applied to historic preservation, for instance, a different situation is

The Boston Common, one of the most venerable cultural landscapes in the United States, was designated a public space when Massachusetts Governor John Winthrop and Boston's citizens purchased the land from William Blackstone in 1684. Except for the Formal Garden (lower area of the photograph), which is on land reclaimed from Back Bay during the early nineteenth century, the configuration of the Common has remained intact for more than three hundred years. Unlike those of many cultural landscapes, the boundaries of the Common are clearly defined and recognizable. (Compare with map, facing page.) Photograph by Alanen, 1989.

presented. Codification, which is necessary within any governmental application of rules and policies, results in a supposedly disinterested application of essentially humane societal values. We must strike a reasonable balance between the "blind" application of regulations and a purely emotional response to historic and cultural landscapes.

Greater understanding might also extend to prescriptive endeavors, such as the interventive actions for preservation so clearly articulated by James Marston Fitch in the 1960s. Fitch's "levels of intervention," spanning a gamut from preservation to reconstruction, established the agenda for a broad philosophical discussion about the reasons and justifications for a range of preservation actions.[19] The implication of this knowledge, however, is a spectrum of values that must be adopted in the process of cultural landscape preservation.

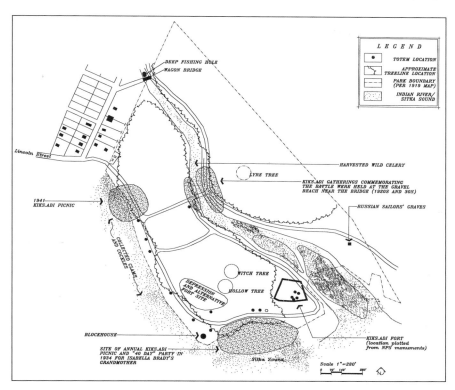

Map depicting activities performed along the nearby Indian River and ocean beach-front by members of the Kiks.ádi Clan of the Tlingit Native American community in Sitka, Alaska, from 1920 to 1940. Based upon interviews conducted with several Kiks.ádis in 1996, the map illustrates the difficulties in establishing exact locations and boundaries for events and activities that shaped the landscape in the past but are no longer evident. The Kiks.ádis also recalled that, during their childhood years, they collected wild celery in sunny areas along the water; gathered clams, cockles, and sea-weed in the tidal flats; gaffed salmon in a deep river pool under an old bridge; chased Mrs. Burkhardt's cows after the animals wandered across the river; played games, which included a broad jump, an obstacle course, and a river crossing; and acquired some money from tourists by making up stories about the totem poles and selling the visitors sea urchins and abalone shells. The outer line noted on the map is the of-ficial boundary of Sitka National Historical Park. Source: Adapted from Smith-Mid-dleton and Alanen (1998), p. 201; cartography by Brenda Wheeler Williams.

In cultural landscape preservation, restoration, and rehabilitation, there is always the challenge to understand the dynamics of natural systems and to in-corporate that understanding into plans, designs, and various degrees of in-tervention. Cultural landscape preservation itself is still a value particular to some cultures and not to others—or at least not in the self-conscious manner practiced in this country, in Canada and Europe, and in a few other areas of the world. After asking why this is so, we need to respond to that knowledge within the context of other societal events, laws, values, and contradictions. Again, J. B. Jackson has taught us that there is a need for ruins and remnants in our culture.[20] Is it possible that in our attempt to preserve cultural landscapes we will forget that some artifacts of the past might best molder and pass on?

Just as there is a creative tension between thinking about and doing cultural landscape preservation, multiple values exist in the cultural landscape, and we address both *culture* and *landscape*. The assumption that one "cultural landscape" exists—including accepted meanings, values, and preservation priorities—is simplistic and faulty. Some cultural landscapes are not visually pleasing by Western standards, and in many cases they may not even be easily recognized or understood.

| *Wilderness and Cultural Landscape Preservation*

It is meaningful to compare the current status of cultural landscape preservation with the development of nature and wilderness protection, a much better organized and longer-lived endeavor in the United States. As Paul Groth notes, more Americans are becoming increasingly sensitized to the needs of animals and ecosystems, but they "rarely have concepts for pondering, discussing, or evaluating their cultural environments."[21] Likewise, proponents of either wilderness or cultural landscape preservation can find themselves at odds when viewing the same site or area. To a wilderness advocate, an abandoned farm field or mine site may appear as a misused or even abused landscape that begs for restoration, if not to its original "pristine" condition, at least to a more natural state. A proponent of cultural landscape preservation, on the other hand, may very well deem the same site worthy of protection and interpretation because of evidence of human forces that have shaped it over time.

While it now appears that both camps are searching for some common themes and approaches—if for no other reason than that both wilderness areas and cultural landscapes are experiencing increasing threats to their existence and integrity—it is critical that the dialogue be continued and expanded. Recently presented definitions and interpretations of wilderness and nature have important implications for the field of cultural landscape preservation. J. B. Jackson, for example, made the following observation in a collection of essays published in 1994: "If the study of nature means anything more than the study of wilderness . . . it also means the study of crops and soils and weather, and the landscapes farmers and ranchers and gardeners create: it always includes the human contribution." Environmental historian William Cronon, citing recent work by several scholars, also notes "that the natural world is far more dynamic, far more changeable, and far more entangled with human history than popular beliefs about the 'balance of nature' have typically acknowledged." Despite our often idealized conceptions of wilderness, the evidence reveals that nature is a "profoundly human construction." Calling on environmentalists to give more attention to the "middle ground" where we live—"the landscape for better or worse that we call home"— Cronon argues that we need an environmental ethic that informs us "as much about *using* nature as about *not* using it."[22]

The cultural landscape provides considerable evidence as to how humans have *used* nature over time. Obviously, however, it is neither feasible nor desirable to preserve all or even most cultural landscapes. How can the protection of even a relatively few cultural landscapes provide something meaningful for society as we enter a new century and millennium? Certainly there are historical, aesthetic, scientific, and educational reasons for protecting these environments, but cultural landscape preservation can also assist us in understanding, appreciating, and valuing an even broader range of landscapes and landscape types, especially those we call "home."

CHAPTER ONE

Considering Nature and Culture in Historic Landscape Preservation

ROBERT Z.
MELNICK

The issues of nature and culture in the American landscape are at once enticing and fleeting. Our fundamental understanding of the ongoing relationship between people and the landscape is complex and intricate, often blurred, and at times contradictory. There are many ways to view this relationship, ranging from an anthropological perspective stressing human culture to an ecological analysis of the preeminence of natural systems. As we consider this relationship, we can recognize how our descriptive and analytical language forms one basis for our understanding of the landscape. We must also consider our actions—intentional and unintentional, considered and ill-considered—which affect both the landscape and our relationship to it. In historical landscapes, the issues of nature and culture can be especially burdensome, loading any discussion of analysis and management with questions of authenticity, originality, appropriateness, and innovation. The discussion, however, may also address understandings of language and landscape, thought and action, intent and result.

While historic preservation has traditionally sought to explain both process and product, the fundamental goal of the preservation impulse has been to recognize and then protect significant and lasting features of our common or idiosyncratic pasts. This attention to stability, as opposed to change, has drawn to a great extent upon the early, and lasting, intentions of the preservation movement in the United States. Historic preservation, as we commonly practice it in Western culture, may be seen as an agent against change, rather than a progressive movement. Although the "heritage crusade" is now very much a part of our common culture, the interest remains one of understanding, explaining, accepting, admiring, and even welcoming the pleasures and burdens of our societal and personal histories.[1]

With landscapes, however, there is an additional set of issues, well known to anyone who has thought at all about this subject. Inherently, landscapes are dynamic in a time frame recognizable within a single human generation. We recognize that all forms of human construction are dynamic, yet we also believe (with a certain hubris) that we can arrest, halt, or limit the extent and rate of change. Landscapes present us with a dramatically different issue; not only are they dynamic, but the robust characteristics of landscape are desirable and essential to their sustainability, whether we consider natural or cultural features.

Any consideration of issues of nature and culture in historical landscapes, therefore, may well take into account a broad range of analytical constructs, extending from ecofeminism to landscape ecology. In this discussion, I address a narrow range of ideas, focusing on three linguistic and landscape frames: semantic ecotones, landscape differentials, and landscape as teacher. The reasons for addressing these three ideas are based upon a desire to recognize the commonalties between language and landscape, not only in the ways we describe places but also in the modes of language that we elect to use in this description.

The idea that landscape is a concept as well as a place is not new.[2] We also must recognize that gender perceptions and experiences play a role in understanding the influence of landscape upon everyday life. To be gender-blind is to deny the historical variants in landscape experience. Certainly, the role of the frontier in American society was not the same for men and women. Rather, the gender-specific experiences fictitiously characterized in 1927 by the Norwegian American author Karl Rolvaag are reinforced by other, more recent scholarly efforts, such as those by the feminist historian Annette Kolodny.[3] This is important because so much of what we understand about our societal relationship has been shaped by literature, which, until relatively recently, neglected the female role in society. It is probably true that, to some extent, landscapes are different places based in part on gender-specific experiences, perceptions, and abilities to change a given landscape. While the characters in Rolvaag's *Giants in the Earth* are equally helpless, regardless of whether they are female or male, their responses to the character and force of the landscape are based in part upon previous gender-based experiences. In this way, culture and nature again intersect, this time through perception and behavior.

In light of these comments, I suggest that additional analytical and explanatory linguistic tools may be considered as we address some challenges of landscape protection and management. These language-based tools are frame, ecotone, and differential.

| *The Frame*

Notions of nature and culture are often situated in our language as opposite ends of a spectrum, much like the proverbial characterizations of black and white.[4] At one end of this dialectic lies wilderness and nature—that which is supposedly free from human intervention and influence. This primeval landscape is often viewed as the embodiment of good and righteous thought and action,[5] a position at times marked by clarity of purpose and the ability to make right that which has been despoiled by civilization.[6] In its most simplistic terms, nature is the unattainable goal, the home from which we have been cast, the Eden of fallen humanity. In language, *nature* (as will be discussed later) is a difficult word, with multiple meanings.[7]

At the other end of this spectrum lies the power and creativity of culture, that which is created purposefully and decidedly by people. It may be material or nonmaterial culture, but it represents the numerous and often uncatalogued actions of individual people. Culture is often and commonly identified as "high culture," such as fine art, the music of symphony orchestras, or the wisdom of the poet laureate. It might also be considered simply as that which is created by the human hand or mind. Culture, in this construct, is the result of the deliberate act of the rational human, set apart from and above the naked wilderness.[8] Culture is much like the valued opposing thumb; without it we would be not human but merely animal.

For the purposes of this discussion, it is instructive to consider a point between these two posited extremes. While we have long familiarity with a dualistic model, we are less comfortable in the middle, with what might be termed the *semantic ecotone.* Much like its counterpart in ecological systems, the semantic ecotone represents a fruitful opportunity for diverse and rich consideration of a variety of landscapes. It provides a model for recognizing that thought, ideas, and actions, much like landscapes, are complex constructions of overlapping layers. These defining world-views of nature and culture are most limited when the vision is too narrowly framed. All too often, landmanaging agencies and those charged with natural and cultural landscape preservation are invested in a construct that emphasizes landscape differentials at the expense of commonalities and potentials and thereby entrenches and polarizes opinion.

The concept of the semantic ecotone is purposefully borrowed from the ecological concept of *ecotone,* the transition zone between two different plant or ecological communities. An ecotone is characterized by vague borders and boundaries and by the potential for both mutual dependence and competition. The purpose of the semantic ecotone concept is to understand that our "zones of thinking," all too often separated by various barriers, may both thrive and seek their strength through competition within another framework. In the world of historic preservation, a robust and dynamic landscape cannot be thought of as simply a historical resource or only a natural system. Thus, a landscape valued for both its natural and cultural intensity can be either a point of contention or an opportunity for collaboration and cooperation. It is the collaboration of ways of thinking about landscapes that may assist us truly to value them in a rich and rewarding way.

| *Semantic Ecotones and Oceanic Tide Pools*

A metaphor for examining these ideas might be taken from coastal waters—the oceanic tide pool. The tide pool contains organisms that not only thrive both in and out of water but also rely upon the cyclical regularity of the varying tides for nourishment and sustenance. In language, as well as in thought, we may learn from this concept. Our understanding of nature and culture in the landscape might benefit from a set of variable conditions rather than a fixed position.[9] We could think metaphorically of a landscape as a tide pool of the mind, ecologically rich and biologically diverse in a variety of settings, rather than limited to solid ground or robust ocean but never the edge between them. The interest here is in not only richness and diversity but also the interplay between nature and culture.

This semantic ecotone is regularly modified through human interaction with the landscape. The notion that some cultures address landscapes with a pure heart while others willingly destroy them is grounded in an overly romantic view of the past.[10] We may consider the past "a foreign country," and past modes of landscape appreciation, perception, and alteration were different from what they are today, but it is the manner of those actions that marks the differences between past and present.[11] The excessively narrow landscape view that institutionalizes the separation of nature and culture stems not so much from the realities of the landscape as from a construct, both common and elite, that seeks to maintain an overly simplistic view of nature and culture. Additionally, the desire to reduce complex history to attractive simplicities is common throughout many avenues of historical re-vision.[12]

In its extreme, this dichotomized construct fails to recognize legitimate management conflicts between natural and cultural resources (such as open stream flow versus historical bridge preservation) while overemphasizing erroneous conflicts (such as meadow protection for drainage and rare species protection). Additionally, through the legitimization of polar opposites, the construct encourages a version of "landscape violence," an extension of the tendency toward violence that pervades American society. The role of violence throughout American history and society has been well documented.[13] A key feature of this concept is the legal recognition, developed over many years, that Americans have "no duty to retreat" in the face of threat or attack. This is a dramatic departure from English common law, which is clear on the requirement to move away or retreat from attack, all the way "to the wall" if necessary, before using force.[14]

Our attitude toward the landscape may be seen, in part, as an acceptance of the attitude toward violence in American society and, subsequently, in the underlying nature/culture conflict that informs our land categorization and management. The idea that these two constructs are in opposition is essentially a violent concept, for it establishes an adversarial relationship between those who give first consideration to either natural systems or cultural systems. Additionally, the ability to strike out at the landscape through ill-considered development and poorly regulated environmental controls results in an inability to gain either time or perspective on circumstances. In turn, this reduces the potential for considerate thought and rational response to difficult situations.

Violence comes in many forms, and it would be ill considered to suggest that all violence toward the landscape is intentional or necessarily malicious. Violence can be premeditated or accidental. It can be the accidental result of a different intentional path. While the actions may be harmful, sadistic, willful, or merely inexcusable errors, the result to the landscape is often the same.

The American acceptance of violence breeds a lack of consideration for the details of a landscape and a belief that power equals right. This can be seen most readily in the ways in which we build and construct on and in such locations as overhanging cliffs, flood plains, steep slopes, and hurricane alleys. The power of technology breeds a hubris of violence toward natural forces and landscape elements. Our myths and stories speak of conquering the landscape and honor those forbears who overcame great odds to establish farms, villages, towns, and cities. This is not a nostalgic view of the past but a recognition that modern technology has enabled us to overcome the limits historically established by the landscape. In this common vision, landscape development is rarely seen as an act of violence, but rather as an act of courage and perseverance.

The adversarial relationship between people and place is implicit in the way we talk and think about the land, the manner in which we continue to refuse to retreat in the face of reasonable odds, and the associated glorification of the violent vigilanteism displayed by continued disregard for natural systems in the American landscape. There are vigilantes on both sides of this argument, and those who spike trees to inhibit logging at any cost are themselves members of what Edward Abbey referred to as the "monkey wrench gang."[15] The issue is not whether one side is right or wrong. The issue is the acceptance of violence as a reasonable means of action and as a way to settle disputes.

The ways in which we think and speak about landscape, therefore, and our understanding of landscapes often reflect the ways in which we have come to revere places as much for what they were as for what they are. These reflections are about what exists today in places of supreme natural splendor and wonder and about the larger and parallel idea that nature, the ideal, often overshadows nature, the real.

| *Landscape Differentials*

Landscape, of course, is both a word and an ideal. While some see landscape as the embodiment of simplified national tendencies, it can conversely be understood as place.[16] We are engaged in a complex relationship with the landscape, which includes the intricacies of nature and culture as they are played out within that relationship and the manner in which we describe these places. While the intent here is to generalize some of these ideas, the primary vehicle for this discussion will be a view of California's Yosemite Valley as a landscape of both nature and culture.

As with the idea of a semantic ecotone, the concept of a landscape differential borrows much from a linguistic model. The research tool of the semantic differential is used to encourage or force research respondents to place their views along a marked continuum from one extreme to another. The most commonly used semantic differential asks whether the respondent strongly agrees, agrees somewhat, is neutral, does not agree, or strongly does not agree with a statement or idea. In landscape terms, the implicit acceptance of a differential model has resulted in an attempt to place any specific landscape at an exact point in a conceptual continuum, resulting in a forced categorization of increasingly integrated landscapes.

Such landscapes as Yosemite Valley are complex systems of both natural and cultural resources. There are ways to manage these places while recognizing not only current societal needs and intent but also the natural and hu-

This classic or "heroic" view of the Yosemite Valley is part of the public image of the great national parks of the American West. Through the broad dissemination of etchings and photographs, the image of big nature has led to a glorification of grand places since the 1850s, often at the expense of detail and depth. Photograph by Melnick, 1992.

man history of the places. Furthermore, these landscapes are inadequately served when we consider them only within one classification of landscape and resource type.

The flawed dichotomy of nature/culture and the landscape violence it breeds inform the framework for land management. Unlike the landscape itself, however, today's management system is not a synthesis of efforts, and integrated resources are therefore treated separately. This, in turn, breeds a competition for scarce resources as well as public favor, a type of nonviolent violence and mistrust of the views of others. Unless we reconsider our attitude toward landscape resources, the way we describe those resources, and our professional and intellectual boundaries, we will continue to be limited in land management and protection potentials.

One of the more puzzling idiosyncrasies of land management in the United States has been the forced and often illogical categorization of land and resource types into rigid pigeonholes of natural, historical, wilderness, and

Yosemite, not far from northern California's population centers, was an early desti-
nation for automobile tourists. Parking—the quintessential sign of urban life in
America—has been an issue in the valley since the earliest days of the automobile.
Source: National Park Service.

recreation. As we have learned more about our environment (physical, social,
and psychological), there has been an increased role for the resource special-
ist (the caretaker) as well as the resource enthusiast (the consumer). We seem
to be mired in a view of isolated resources, not in the sense of ignoring our
fundamental ecological understanding of natural systems, but rather in our
substantial inability to extend that paradigm to a larger world-view, one that
integrates natural and cultural resources. For example, we rely upon legislation to establish wilderness, even if people have lived in an area for generations. We somehow need legislation and codes to inform us that a place is, or
is not, historical.

This dichotomy of land resource management is evident in the history of
Yosemite Valley, a history as much about landscape control (i.e., culture) as
about landscape protection (i.e., nature). This history is as much about landscape abuse and violence as it is about landscape use. Yosemite is one example of the ways in which we think and speak about nature and culture in our
public landscapes. The valley historically has been controlled by planning
based upon a landscape differential but with the potential to be understood
within a richly diverse semantic ecotone.

The Merced River, which winds through the Yosemite Valley, is hugged by a road. The introduction of this road dates back to the management principles enunciated by the Yosemite Valley Commission, which was led by Frederick Law Olmsted during the 1860s. Built in response to both a desire to provide access to the valley and the political necessity to offer public access, this road and others are filled with automobiles throughout the summer months. Photograph by Melnick, 1992.

Yosemite Valley was first set aside and "reserved" by the State of California in 1864. Much has been written about the valley, the Mariposa Big Tree Grove, the battles over Hetch Hetchy, and what has become of this remarkable American wilderness. Scholars and writers, beginning with James M. Hutchings in 1886 and Galen Clark and D. J. Foley in 1910 and 1912, respectively, and followed, from the 1950s to the present, by François Matthes, Carl Russell, Ted Orland, Roderick Nash, Alfred Runte, Stanford Demars, and many others, all have taught us to understand what Yosemite means to us as a people and as a group of peoples.[17] In addition, the photographs of Carleton Watkins, George Fiske, and Ansel Adams, to name a few, have set the landscape of Yosemite concretely in our collective construct of wilderness, westernness, and nature. Along with Yellowstone, that other great icon of the American West, Yosemite has been both revered and criticized, honored and desecrated, attended to and neglected.

Yosemite Valley is not so much the abandoned wilderness as a landscape that has been gradually modified over time until it has reached a point that no longer coincides with its public image. The reality no longer fits the image, but it is a reality that has been changing slowly, not dramatically, over time. The image is based, as Runte points out, on the "art of promotion," ranging from Albert Bierstadt and *Sunset Magazine* to the railroads and the National Park Service itself.[18]

The landscape is also based upon a divergence of thinking about nature and culture. Neil Evernden observes that "what is nature is the not-human"; he argues that we have created nature, and the idea of nature, as a "resource for humans," in great need of management and control.[19] Equally important to this discussion is the understanding of *nature* as a dual term, describing both that which is nonhuman (i.e., the natural world) and that which is the fundamental characteristic of an entity (i.e., the essence of an object or person). We regularly refer to "human nature," never quite realizing that this is a creative juxtaposition of words.

Furthermore, in this line of thinking, "to ask what is the nature of something is to ask about its character or essence," implying that nature is somehow above, beyond, or more supremely delineated than the human characteristics of that same entity. Nature as a place, however, is different. "The domination of nature is not only a right but an obligation," Evernden states. "Nature is to be overcome, not preserved."[20] Nature, however, is also about

The desire to simulate nature, right in nature's own backyard, seems to be an overwhelming human desire. These benches at a concession stand in the Yosemite Valley provide seating in view of some of the world's most spectacular natural scenery. Photograph by Melnick, 1992.

Tent camping on wooden platforms has been a part of the lodging opportunities for Yosemite visitors since the early twentieth century. While the canvas has been replaced many times and new platforms added, the essential qualities of this area in the valley remained unchanged until the floods of 1997. Photograph by Land and Community Associates, 1992.

change and what happens to place. We understand it to imply the dynamic characteristic of a place and those qualities that cause the place to evolve and change. Finally, nature is a thing, an object, a trophy to be displayed in a show-case. We think of preserving nature by inhibiting change in a place, which clearly is a contradiction that is difficult to overcome.

Nature, then, has many forms: characteristic, process, entity, and object. All of these assist in the understanding of Yosemite and of the ways in which, since the early 1860s, nonnative peoples have altered and modified that landscape, sometimes in the name of protection but more often in the name of control, dominance, and exploitation.

Landscape as Teacher

Although we inherently understand that nature is to be dominated and placed in our societal trophy rooms, we also inherently understand that nature is the great educator, the great teacher, a source of knowledge about life and its meaning. While filled with contradictions, this notion allows us to revere what we capture, to venerate what we control, and to worship that which we subjugate. Given the perverse and often contradictory relationship between people and the American landscape, perhaps there is no other way. In geographer Yi-Fu Tuan's terms, we view nature through the dual lens of "dominance and affection," demonstrating a need to both control and love it.[21]

This idea of nature as educator is not recent, of course. One of the most vivid and common examples comes from the writing of James Fenimore Cooper, the first great American novelist, whose writings were popularly published and circulated. In his famous Leatherstocking series, Cooper described his protagonist, Deerslayer, as having the "signs of belonging to those who pass their time between the skirts of civilized society and the boundless forests." Although it is clear that Cooper's gender-focused characterization of this society carries other implications, for this discussion it is the heroic descriptions of the man that are of interest. Deerslayer is a man of the woods and of the edge, the ecotone, the frontier between civilization and savagery, who learns from what is around him. As he and a companion approach an especially beautiful and untouched lake (described by Cooper as having "Rembrandt-looking hemlocks"—America's answer to European culture), Deerslayer exclaims, "This is grand!—tis solemn!—tis an edication of itself, to look upon."[22] This is far more than the noble savage and implicitly better than the book learning of the schoolhouse. The strength of wilderness and nature is clear, not only because it breeds an atavistic nobility but also because there are lessons that only nature can teach.[23]

Yosemite Valley, as both place and teacher, can be read in the same way. In a concise collection of poems, for example, first published in 1897, Yone Noguchi described the valley as "the balance of Glory and Decay."[24] Although we may think of Yosemite as an "embattled wilderness," as Runte terms it, the valley is also a manipulated landscape, molded and shaped as much by human decisions as by natural systems.[25]

Early pamphlets extolling the wonders of Yosemite, however, also reminded potential visitors of the efforts of the federal government to assure that a visit to this wilderness would not be, after all, too wild. In 1919, Secretary of the Interior Franklin Lane prefaced a Yosemite guidebook published by the United States Railroad Administration with the following comments:

To the American People:
Uncle Sam asks you to be his guest. He has prepared for you the choice places of this continent—places of grandeur, beauty and of wonder. He has built roads through the deep-cut canyons and beside happy streams, which will carry you into these places in comfort, and has provided lodgings and food in the most distant and inaccessible places that you might enjoy yourself and realize as little as possible the rigors of the pioneer traveler's life. These are for you. They are the playgrounds of the people. To see them is to make more hearty your affection and admiration for America.[26]

Early examples of rustic design, including this pedestrian bridge spanning the Merced River, reveal the intention, from the earliest days of NPS management, to control or domesticate the Yosemite Valley landscape. In this process, nature becomes a cultural artifact and culture seems to be subservient to nature. Source: National Park Service.

Lane and National Park Service Director Stephen Mather were experts at promotion and public relations, but our interest here is on the understanding that this was (and is) often a landscape to be altered for short-term human enjoyment, satisfaction, and pleasure, without the "rigors of the pioneer traveler's life." While this is not an unknown concept, recent studies of Yosemite Valley reveal a landscape of both nature and culture, one that is popularly revered for its natural splendor to the almost constant exclusion of human history.[27] The idea that one must choose between nature and culture is reinforced in interpretive displays, visitor services, and staff competition for resources and recognition. The organizational and disciplinary structure encourages and fosters this differential approach.

Currently at Yosemite, there is some effort to consider the interrelationship between natural and cultural resources and their interaction in producing this landscape and also to affirm the value of the park's cultural landscape resources while allowing improved visitor services, interpretation, and enjoyment.[28] The essential goals and intentions of the park will not change, and one might anticipate that the conflicts between visitor use, resource protection,

This early tree-planting effort in the Yosemite Valley was indicative of seminal attempts to improve nature through the regularization of this developed landscape. The lessons of the introduction of exotic plants are still being experienced in the valley. Source: National Park Service.

and management intentions will continue. Although there is some hope that the process will seek the ecotone, there is great resistance to this from all quarters.

During the past fifteen years, my colleagues and I have been developing a method for understanding cultural landscapes, especially those in America, and Yosemite in particular. This method is partially based upon the linguistic analogy that, to understand and appreciate cultural landscapes, we must learn to "read" them and to consider the forces that caused them to develop. This process is much like learning to read a language. We recognize patterns, details ("words"), parts that go together, and pieces that "sound" strange next to each other. We must learn the "grammar" of the landscape and allow the landscape to be a teacher. This is, of course, not an easy task. We are accustomed to looking at historical structures and understanding their importance and potential significance. Cultural landscapes, however, are more subtle than structures and require a somewhat different approach. As a visibly dynamic entity, the landscape (natural and cultural) is best understood by an analytical system that responds to the changing details of that landscape.[29]

The sheer rock face of El Capitan has become a mecca for rock climbers, many of whom spend one or more nights hanging on this wall. The management of intrusive sports is a difficult issue, especially when they may or may not be seen by the casual visitor. Not far from this site is an unofficially recognized climber's-only campsite, further institutionalizing the culture of natural sports. Photograph by Melnick, 1992.

| *A View of Yosemite Valley*

Many prominent natural features of Yosemite serve to explain its cultural prominence as a natural landscape, as well as our natural inclination to downplay its history.[30] Formed by alpine glaciers moving through the Merced River Canyon, the horseshoe-shaped Yosemite Valley, sometimes called the "Incomparable Valley," is one of the world's best-known glacier-carved canyons.[31]

The Yosemite Valley's broad, flat floor; steep, sheer granite walls and domes; lush, green meadows; and spectacular waterfalls are familiar scenes well documented in literature, painting, and photography. The Merced and its tributaries wind their way through the valley floor, waterfalls continue to marvel in their power and variety, and wetlands provide wildlife habitat and seasonal wildflower displays. Major geological features, such as El Capitan (3,593 feet),

Half Dome (8,842 feet), and Sentinel Rock (7,038 feet), dominate many valley views and present an imposing facade of natural strength and fortitude. The first Euro-Americans to see this valley were awed by its sheer magnitude, as it was unlike anything they or any of their colleagues had seen before.[32]

Valley vegetation occurs in alternating patterns of open meadowland and dense groves of trees that create a series of landscape spaces. From dark, dense forests to open spaces with long, dramatic views, the character of the valley is heavily influenced by vegetation. The relationship of forest and meadowland is dynamic, however, and subject to changes wrought by seasonal and annual fluctuations in moisture availability, catastrophic weather, pedestrian and vehicular traffic patterns, and National Park Service maintenance programs, such as clearing and planting regimes.[33]

The eleven meadows comprise one of the most sensitive ecosystems in the valley. Over the years, human alterations to the natural channel of the Merced have lowered the water table and changed the composition of the vegetation

The hydrology of the meadows in the Yosemite Valley has been altered and managed since the 1940s, primarily to alleviate flooding of the valley road. This has resulted in unanticipated changes in plant communities and a dramatic modification of the historic dynamic condition of these areas. Photograph by Land and Community Associates, 1992.

in the meadows. Intentional introduction of nonnative species has had an adverse effect on native plant materials. For the protection of human features, the landscape of the meadows, perceived as far less dramatic than that of El Capitan and Half Dome, was readily sacrificed in the name of flood control.[34] The "wilderness" landscape was modified and then modified again to protect previous investments.

Over the years the National Park Service has attempted to control the natural lateral movement of the Merced River channel by deepening, widening, or rechannelizing its flow. These attempts were motivated by the desire to protect investment in bridges and other structures in developed areas. Current degradation of adjacent vegetation has made it abundantly clear that these programs have been detrimental to the environment, and there is now discussion in favor of allowing the Merced to return to its natural configuration. This action, of course, could have profound implications for the landscape, implications that have not yet been adequately addressed. The dramatic floods of 1997 may do more to protect the valley than any management plan could possibly envision. Even though there was remarkable damage, the en-

The conflict between the management of natural resources and the management of cultural resources and recreational activities is sharply illustrated by the erosion of the Merced River's banks. This erosion is caused primarily by the backwash from the restricted flow caused by a historic bridge just downstream. The resolution of the growing conflict between natural and cultural resource management is an increasingly difficult issue for the National Park Service at Yosemite. Photograph by Melnick, 1992.

Parking continues to be a major problem at Yosemite, diminishing the national park experience and the ability to relate to nature apart from urban conditions. The building, which accommodates maintenance facilities, is known locally as Fort Yosemite and includes a small jail. Photograph by Land and Community Associates, 1992.

suing disruption of regular and expected services may argue for changes in visitor access, development plans, and resource protection.[35]

We cling, however, to the understanding that this is a landscape to be used and not always protected for its natural values. The valley is not a landscape of seclusion, nor one of gradual and incremental rejuvenation. Through its multiple uses, inspired by the intense needs of so many visitors so far from other vestiges of Western civilization, the Yosemite Valley has become what in any other setting we would term *urbanized*. Thus, the valley is a landscape of broad differentials.

Controlled views and vistas are critical to the average visitor experience and, as with many other aspects of Yosemite, the experience has been set, programmed, and controlled over many years. At one time the Kodak Company engaged in tree cutting, clearing, and trimming (with the active consent of the National Park Service) to ensure that classic photographic opportunities would always be available.[36] The landscape of Bierstadt and Adams can now be personally reproduced and displayed in photo albums, slide shows, and home videos, along with images of other great California landscape icons.

The notion of interpretation—actively showing and engaging the visitor with what they are seeing so that they may better appreciate it—is funda-

The establishment of set photo opportunities, such as these in the Yosemite Valley, ensure that each visitor will be able to record the same image for his or her personal enjoyment. The development of such "photo ops" has paralleled an increasing desire for equality in the landscape experience. Photograph by Melnick, 1992.

mental to the experience of this landscape. Throughout the valley, views to supreme natural wonders have been carefully framed, described, and made available to the visitor.[37] While nature is something to behold, especially here, it is also a prize to be captured and then revealed again and again as a trophy in the comfort of one's home. More than anything, the idea that we "take" pictures has a special meaning in this landscape. It reflects the profound need to mark ourselves in this space, so that we, and others, may be sure that we were actually here. The marking of oneself in a special place, not through writing or poetry or memories in our minds, but through the taking of photographs, is one of the great sports of our century. It is the fox hunt of civilized America, with a reward that proves to all that we have been "here." Nature becomes culture in this valley.[38]

The landscape of Yosemite, like so many landscapes of the North American continent, is neither the wilderness we seek nor the city we so often fear.[39] For many, it has become the point of quest, the place to meet a personal, societal, and natural history. Although the national parks, both ideal and real, are a major contribution to the democratization of the American landscape, they nonetheless allow us to push aside some broader questions. For example, Yosemite, both ideal and real, absorbs a great many pressures. There are the pressures of the visitor, the pressures of the experts, the pressures of politics, and the pressures of our collective consciousness, which repeatedly says this is a place that must be available to anyone who wants to come to it, but must also be protected for all of those who would come here in the future. In many ways, this is a Herculean task we have set for ourselves. Most importantly, the valley must withstand the pressures of differential extremes imposed upon it in the guise of caring.

Yosemite, and all the other national parks, must respond not only to the immediate pressures and needs of its clients and taskmasters but also to the larger societal realities of population expansion and the increased popularity of nature as an idea. This concept of nature as an artifact to be viewed and extracted sets in motion the perceived imperative to protect Yosemite as an imagined wilderness, forgetting the true reality of the complex past of the American West.[40] If, after all, Yosemite is just another place to spend time in a swimming pool, why come here? If it is, after all, just another place to sit at a picnic table, why spend the time and effort to arrive here? If it is just one more traffic jam, why bother?

Our answers perhaps lie in our need and desire to get close to nature, but only so close; we wish to leave the comforts of our home, but only so far be-

Because of their increasing numbers, visitors to Yosemite are importing urban and nonpark recreational activities. These activities are supported through the development of park infrastructure, such as bike paths, complete with directional arrows and driving lanes. Photograph by Melnick, 1992.

hind.[41] The ongoing dialogue between nature and culture is evident not only in the history of the American landscape, as reflected in Yosemite, but also in its present, a present that raises great concerns for the future of this landscape. The national parks of the nineteenth century were seen by some as lessons for society, and perhaps this is still true today. The confusion, visitor overburden, and intense focus on Yosemite and all of our national parks and public landscapes raise substantial issues about the collective ways in which we treat the places we revere. As Runte reminds us, "Yosemite is too important to be just another place."[42] We may think about it, however, as an indicator species, revealing our past opportunities, our recent foibles, and the future of our mistakes.

| Conclusion

How, then, do we reconcile the unrelenting need to protect natural systems with the impulse to transform them into human systems? How do we "protect" cultural resources that, by nature, are dynamic and always changing? Perhaps we achieve this through an inclusive view that nature and culture are, in fact, not merely "two sides of the same coin." Rather, we need to engage in nonlinear and cyclical modes of thinking about nature, culture, and landscape. This is a complex relationship that is best understood through clarification rather than through simplification.

As with an ecological ecotone, a semantic ecotone (as a model) enables us to look beyond the limited values of a singular view (or landscape type) toward an understanding of temporal- and resource-based changes in both the virtual and the actual landscape. The intensely felt need to stake our landscape views at different ends of the linguistic and managerial spectrum (or even the view that there is a spectrum) is ultimately harmful to the larger goal of landscape sustainability, whether we are grounded in a natural or a cultural perspective. At some level, of course, the concept of the semantic ecotone must address the reality of different "species" competing for the same geography and resources. Diversity can result in its own degree of competition.

Land managers and design professionals, through need, professional impulse, or codified expectations, have come to rely upon narrowly defined understandings of landscape values. There is an opportunity, however, to recognize that a broader and more complex understanding of these values will, in turn, support a richer and more satisfying process for determining and protecting landscape values. At Yosemite Valley this would mean, for example, a policy that allows the inclusive management of its valley meadows. This pol-

In recent years, the Yosemite Valley has experienced an invasion of visitors, primarily during summer months. For many of these people, the moving experience of a visit to the valley lasts less than a few hours, including programmed direction from guides, signs, and interpretive materials. Photograph by Melnick, 1992.

icy might recognize that the meadows are landscapes of both natural (hydro-logic) and cultural (Native American) significance. Unlike the competitive management that now presides, inclusive management could treat this landscape as an integrated and dynamic whole.

In any study of the landscape, we can recognize that the "garden" always has as its subject the relationship between nature and culture.[43] Therefore, if we recognize "landscape" as the integrating force for nature and culture, we present ourselves with the opportunity to move beyond the staked positions at extremes of a landscape differential and toward the inclusive and dynamic ground of the semantic ecotone.

CHAPTER TWO

Selling Heritage Landscapes

RICHARD
FRANCAVIGLIA

Within the past thirty years, a collectively developing appreciation of history has become a major force in shaping the American landscape. Whereas commentators once viewed the American countryside as revealing a people who would tear down anything old in search of progress, America is now dotted with thousands of historic markers, historic sites, and historic districts that enshrine the past. The typical tourist—both American and foreign visitors alike—has developed a strong appreciation for American history and seeks out those places that convey it. Promotional wording for the popular book, *America's Living Past,* informs interested readers that "it is theoretically possible to travel across the length and breadth of America and visit sites that bring to life the entire scope of U.S. history."[1]

Today, in contrast to a brief generation ago, the historic building fabric of America has become a treasured part of our heritage. Historic preservation has a long history in this country but became somewhat popular only after the creation of the National Trust for Historic Preservation in 1949.[2] Following passage of the National Historic Preservation Act in 1966, the pace of historic preservation activities increased, and preservationists who once were satisfied saving individual buildings, and then districts, now speak of preserving entire landscapes. As architects learned lessons from preservationists, many of their practices shifted from new construction to historical rehabilitations. Since the early 1980s, newly constructed buildings have appeared in neotraditional or postmodern designs; their facades, towers, gables, and detailed masonry reflect a stylistic fascination with the pervasive past. Throughout the 1990s, the growth of historically themed construction has kept pace with the booming economy.

The social and economic implications of this change are enormous, for heritage tourism and historic preservation have become big business as well as popular pastimes in America. In many areas of the country, heritage tourism has replaced agriculture and industry as the major source of revenue. In 1990, when the National Trust for Historic Preservation created a Heritage Tourism Program, it estimated that almost half of all tourism—which contributed more than $344 billion to the U.S. economy in 1991—is now heritage based; the trust's Heritage Tourism Program in Denver encourages communities to package and market their built environments as heritage landscapes.[3] Heritage tourism is defined by the trust as "the practice of traveling to experience historic and cultural attractions to learn about a community's, region's, or state's past in an enjoyable and informative way."[4] By the late 1990s, heritage tourism dominated the economy of many areas, including the "New West."

Images of heritage landscapes abound in our popular iconography. In advertising, they serve to set the scene and reaffirm the value of products associated with the past, asserting durability, dependability, and traditional or ethical values. Heritage landscapes are used to reaffirm our connection with the past when we travel. Picture postcard displays on rotating racks, for example, will usually contain several that portray, through rustic images of historical farms and towns, the heritage of the areas we visit. "Kansas . . . as it was" is more or less typical, featuring a caravan of covered wagons crossing a trackless, rolling prairie. The past may be gone, but it still lives, and enterprising individuals and corporations are active in its marketing to the public. Craft and other festivals are often themed with the original historical content of the landscape, and bed-and-breakfast hostelries, historical museums, and guided tours are thriving in historic areas. Historic preservation is supported by a majority of the U.S. population and has been for more than a decade; according to a Gallup Poll conducted in 1986, fully 90 percent of the people interviewed confirmed that "retaining a sense of the past" should be the most important objective in historic preservation activities.[5] Heritage landscapes are a major vehicle by which the past is retained and experienced, and they can take many forms.

Heritage landscapes are defined as those places—and depictions of them—that contain buildings, sites, and other features associated with history. Heritage landscapes possess historical design integrity; ostensibly, they look much as they did during a particular historical period because there are few or no modern intrusions to mar them. This "feel" is an important element in the identification of historic places, though rather difficult to define objectively. Normally the design, massing, and detailing of structures, the positioning of such ancillary features as fences and gardens, and the preservation of open space and rights of way help to define historic landscapes.

Although much preservation is conducted by volunteers with a largely avocational interest in identifying and restoring buildings, professionals are actively involved in preservation efforts. In the 1980s, with efforts to decentralize programs, a partnership was formalized among local, state, and national preservation agencies. The Certified Local Government (CLG) program was one of the legacies of this New Federalism period. As evidence of its power, a minimum of 10 percent of federal (National Park Service–administered) funding to state historic preservation offices (SHPOs) is required to go to local jurisdictions (communities, counties) that have enacted historic preservation legislation and put into place a process to enforce it.

Such legislation affects existing historical structures by providing design guidelines and standards and ensures that new construction takes into account the historical design parameters of areas designated as "historic." It also ensures that sanctions against the demolition of historic buildings are enforced. Because the federal government manages vast areas of the United States, especially in the West, it also has an active interest in heritage landscape preservation of the land it controls. The National Park Service has taken the lead with a landscape initiative aimed at identifying and managing historic landscapes. Working in both the public and private sectors, landscape architects, geographers, and historic preservation consultants have produced an impressive literature since the late 1980s.[6]

Active interpretation and management of culturally or historically significant landscapes have led to a broadening of definitions for heritage landscapes. Whereas most heritage landscapes contain structures, buildings, or other features of the built environment, some that might otherwise be considered "natural" landscapes (e.g., Devils Tower in Wyoming or the Badlands of South Dakota) are now recognized as heritage landscapes because of their association with Native American or pioneer culture. Management practices that keep landscapes in a supposedly pristine condition remind us that *all* conserved or protected landscapes are cultural artifacts. Most heritage landscapes are associated with the material culture of history; that is, they contain features such as buildings, vegetation, and fences that reflect the condition of the place at a particular time. Land ownership, land division, and land use may have changed, but heritage landscapes either preserve the general appearance of the landscape as it would have looked at an earlier time or employ a wide range of techniques, such as reconstructed buildings or the construction of new buildings that are "contemporary but compatible" in design (to use the words of the U.S. Secretary of the Interior's Standards), to do so. An entire community, such as the ghost town of Bodie, California, may be preserved as a heritage landscape by the State Parks Department, or a community with considerable private land ownership, such as Lincoln, New Mexico (home of Billy the Kid), may be preserved as a National Historic Landmark because its entire landscape, including the rangeland surrounding it, conveys a sense of history and isolation in space and time.[7]

Thus, heritage landscapes may be preserved by individuals or groups and by the private or public sector. They may be preserved for what seem to be widely different reasons, such as education or entertainment. The *selling* of heritage landscapes broadly refers to their presentation to the public; they may be marketed for profit or for educational purposes by individuals, agencies, or nonprofit groups. Therefore, heritage landscapes are consumed, in a manner of speaking, and those who experience them are consumers. In this sense, the promotion of heritage landscapes is part of a flourishing and complex service economy. Heritage landscapes, however, may also be considered aesthetic in that their ultimate use is enrichment, which reaffirms the statement by David Lowenthal and Hugh Prince that "landscapes are formed by landscape tastes."[8] Heritage landscapes are a significant aspect of our culture in that they have become a very visible element in the overall landscape signature of America.

Heritage landscapes vary in size from several acres to hundreds, even thousands, of acres. They also vary in shape; some may consist of more or less rectangular property parcels, while others may be linear strips, such as historic railroad or canal corridors or the rights of way of historic roads (e.g., the National Road), in places where sufficient historical integrity has been retained. These are spoken of as heritage corridors, and they remind us of our nearly incessant movement as a people.

The concept of *view* is important in heritage landscapes. Whatever their shape, heritage landscapes possess sufficient design integrity to appear as if they belong to another time. The idea of the view or vista, which the dictionary defines as "a distant view through or along an avenue or opening," is essential to the understanding of heritage landscapes. It assumes that the viewer will experience an image sufficiently large (i.e., a place of sufficient size) to be readily recognized as artifactual evidence of the past.

To be appreciated and marketed, heritage landscapes are associated with recognized patterns of activity in place and time. Themes are required to distinguish one heritage landscape from another. Social or ethnic themes are among the most readily recognized and promoted. The Amish Country of Ohio, Pleasant Hill Shaker Village in Kentucky, or the Amana Colonies in Iowa, all convey a sense of intentionality of utopian sects. Many historic landscapes are regionally identifiable in that their economy and architecture are fixed enough in place and time to signify sectional patterns of culture; the

TABLE 2.1
Classification System of Heritage Landscapes

Type	Description	Examples	Comment
Passively preserved heritage landscapes	Landscapes that are preserved unintentionally through continued traditions of use, ownership, and design	Rural villages of the "Hispano Homeland" (N.M.); Morristown, Ohio; rural Amish farms (Ohio and Pa.); Rice, Tex.	Reflect a renunciation of or inability to change (i.e., the population does not have the desire or ability to modernize)
Actively preserved heritage landscapes	Landscapes that are consciously preserved to retain their historic heritage or charm	Historic districts (e.g., Maysville, Ky.; Bisbee, Ariz.; Granbury, Tex.)	Are often the result of preservation legislation or a preservation ethic based on an appreciation of the past
Restored heritage landscapes	Landscapes in which significant historic features have been reconstructed or replaced (or later intrusions removed) to enable them to regain their original character	Williamsburg, Va.; Mission San Jose (Tex.); Blue Heron Mining Co. (Ky.); Kentucky Bluegrass horse farms; Tombstone, Ariz.	Are often educational but may also serve commercial purposes; shapers of these landscapes seek to regain heritage; usually associated with prestige (reflects high status) or tourism
Assembled heritage landscapes	Landscapes in which historic designs and historical features are constructed to achieve a look of antiquity	Pioneer Arizona Museum; Ohio Village; Greenfield Village, Mich.; Stonefield Village, Wis.	Are often educational and may provide settings in which historic crafts are practiced
Imagineered heritage landscapes	Landscape assemblages designed to appear historic but constructed to convey essence rather than re-create particular locale	Theme parks (Disney's Main Street USA) and historically themed shopping centers (South Coast Village) and residential environments (Seaside, Fla.)	May be instructional (educational) but more often are entertaining, commercial, or residential
Imagically preserved heritage landscapes	Landscape images, models, or dioramas that re-create vanished landscapes for viewing rather than entry	Thurber, Tex. (site marker); Black Top, Ohio (diorama); Washington-on-the-Brazos, Tex. (museum exhibit)	Preserve or re-create the visual image of a lost place, usually for educational or touristic purposes

horse farms of the Kentucky Bluegrass, the historic farmscapes of Virginia's Shenandoah/Blue Ridge, and New England villages have become fashionable remnants of eighteenth- or nineteenth-century regional landscapes. Urban heritage landscapes may consist of entire historic communities (e.g., Harpers Ferry, W.V.) or neighborhoods (the French Quarter of New Orleans) that may also convey a sense of sectional or regional history. Industrial heritage landscapes may be portions of large urban communities (e.g., Lowell, Mass.) or entire towns (Fayette, Mich.; Coketown, Colo.; Eckley [Miner's Village] and Hopewell Furnace, Pa.). Many of these industrial heritage landscapes reflect broad historical themes of investment, capitalization, and resource exploitation. Like all heritage landscapes, however, they are manifestations of human activity in space—the essence of what gives character to and defines place.

Rather than classifying heritage landscapes on the basis of whether they are urban or rural, agrarian or industrial, this chapter employs a classification system based on the *processes* that led to their preservation and that are tied intimately to their marketing. In other words, in addition to the basic issue of historical integrity (i.e., the relationship between their actual content and what originally existed), one can also use the *motivation* behind their preservation to interpret heritage landscapes. Viewed thusly, heritage landscapes occupy a continuum from unintentionally (or passively) preserved to those that are totally contrived. Six main types of heritage landscapes are identified and discussed in this chapter. Like all landscapes, heritage landscapes must be interpreted in the context of the culture that creates them. Like all landscapes, none is more (or less) valid than others, though some certainly reflect history more accurately or authentically than others.

Passively Preserved Heritage Landscapes

Some of America's most interesting heritage landscapes are not deliberately preserved; rather, they represent islands bypassed by progress and change. For example, travelers along Interstate 45 in east Texas may barely notice exit signs for the town of Rice as they mark the miles from Houston to Dallas. If they fail to glimpse a cluster of buildings huddled several hundred yards west of the interstate, they will miss Rice, which has languished for many decades since its halcyon days as a cotton production center at the edge of the great Black Waxie prairie of eastern Texas. Located on the Texas Central (now Union Pacific) rail line from Houston to Dallas, Rice is one of the many towns in the Cotton Belt that have slipped from importance as a result of changes in railroad technology, highway repositionings, and the general decline of agriculture.

Rice looks as if the clock had stopped somewhere back in the 1930s. Its ar-

Passively preserved heritage landscapes such as the Central Business District of Rice, Texas, feature historic structures that have not been restored or renovated. In Rice, the old buildings serve commercial enterprises with little fanfare, and preservation is a result of a direct functional relationship between merchant and consumer. By the 1990s, places of this type were relatively rare as many towns had witnessed aggressive preservation activities. Photograph by Francaviglia, 1994.

chitectural heritage consists of Victorian homes and churches, a forlorn but nearly intact block-long business district of single-story red brick structures facing Main Street, and a seeming outdoor museum of cotton gins, cotton storage buildings, and other artifacts of the cotton economy strewn about. The look of the town reflects the slow economy and Rice's isolated location, despite its proximity to the interstate highway and railroad line. Rice's preservation is, in part, unintentional. Most of the town's residents have little or no awareness of historic preservation, and yet their townscape retains what practitioners call "historic integrity."

The community of Rice is not an exception, for Texas is dotted with hundreds of similar rural towns that no longer function as service centers. Bypassed by change, their townscapes seem to be out of novels or films, such as *The Last Picture Show,* that popularized the image of small historic towns locked in the throes of decay. And one need not be in Texas to find a wealth of passively preserved heritage landscapes. Similar cases are found in Mora County and Cordova, New Mexico, whose townscapes bear the visible imprint of Hispanic cultural traditions.[9] In those towns of the "Hispano homeland" of New Mexico, one may see such new materials as corrugated metal roofs, but their use in the hands of vernacular or folk craftsmen assures that the traditional forms will be preserved. As J. B. Jackson has written, such places are treasure troves of historical information about the traditional relationship between people and the land.[10]

Although the historic preservation movement has swept the country, passively preserved communities still delight the perceptive traveler, for they have not yet been "restored" and much of what one sees there is original historical fabric. In Ohio, New Vienna (Clinton County) possesses a virtually intact downtown commercial district consisting of Victorian Italianate buildings. The community served as a rural agricultural service center and somehow escaped the remodelings and restylings that swept many Ohio downtowns, leaving Victorian trim (including door and window openings) enshrouded in aluminum siding and old signs replaced by more modern signs of the automobile age. In New Vienna, the commercial district is visually integrated; even the signs advertising services seem to be painted by the same sign painter, despite their being of somewhat different styles. Downtown New Vienna represents preservation at its least self-conscious. The building owners maintained the buildings simply by keeping them painted, repairing roofs, caulking windows, and making certain that the gutters and scuppers worked; this is no-frills preservation that reflects a pragmatic sense of merchandising downtown.

This pragmatism is also seen in some of the Mormon communities of the Intermountain West, where old barns, homes, and other buildings—and even fences—remain in the landscape for practical rather than sentimental reasons. These landscapes serve as a badge of identity but have not gone unchallenged. Although many Mormon communities possessed heritage landscapes, including outhouses and typical Mormon fences, by the 1960s criticism mounted by outsiders (Mormon or otherwise) pointed to old barns and granaries as eyesores or, worse, as places where youths might gather to smoke and drink. This pressure resulted in the demolition of many historic but underutilized buildings.[11] By the late 1970s, however, a growing appreciation for the past had begun to filter into the valleys of the mountain West, and old homes began to be deliberately restored for aesthetic and sentimental reasons; they represented a part of the past.

Passively preserved landscapes are found in remote areas or areas of relative economic stagnation. Throughout the United States, passively preserved communities are becoming rare. With the swing of the pendulum, townscapes like those of Rice, Texas; Mora County, New Mexico; certain of the Mormon villages; numerous prairie farming towns of Nebraska; and marginal Ohio hamlets are endangered. To the eyes of an entrepreneur, these passively preserved landscapes are undiscovered, that is, unsold or undersold. A few have been plundered as developers of historic properties elsewhere have acquired elaborate architectural details from vacant homes and left stripped building shells in their wake. Usually, however, such heritage landscapes will either disappear through neglect and attrition if the economy worsens or be transformed by progress if the economy improves and the old structures are either converted to serve new purposes or demolished to make way for new buildings better able to function in the new economy. Only if sentiment or economic incentives are strong enough will they be actively preserved.

| *Actively Preserved Heritage Landscapes*

Few populations actually defy progress; the best-known example is the old order Amish, who live in a somber, nonelectrified and unadorned Plain-Sect cultural landscape traversed by horse and buggy. But many Americans have come to question the indiscriminate acceptance of progress when it means the loss of the historical fabric and the sense of history associated with that fabric. When landscapes reflect a deliberate attempt to save features from the past, they may be said to be actively preserved. Sometimes this preservation is undertaken for sentimental reasons, but it may also make good sense economically. For example, when tax incentives are provided to private developers who actively preserve or restore structures for economic use, preservation becomes very important business that positively affects the commercial scene and visibly affects the landscape.

Today it is becoming difficult to visit a community in the United States that does not have at least one restored building. The influence of the preservation movement can be seen throughout America; perceptive students of the landscape detect it in the maintenance and rehabilitation of buildings. On Main Street, Victorian trim may be painted in tastefully contrasting colors; brick surfaces may have been cleaned or, unfortunately, sandblasted during the early years of preservation activities before its harmful, destructive effects were realized. Restored buildings and signs in old script proclaiming Main Street Cafe or Main Street Hardware (or something similar) imply a generic fascination with the past when, in fact, such enterprises would have borne the name of their owner. Signs with superfluous Old English *e*'s, as in Olde Shoppe, are a dead giveaway that someone is intentionally searching for and capitalizing on the past. To the eye trained in landscape interpretation, such places have the look of preservation written into them. Victorian trim such as corbels, with each individual element painted in two or more complementary colors, is also a legacy of the preservation movement; originally, color schemes

Actively preserved heritage landscapes such as that seen in downtown Bisbee, Arizona, are the result of concerted preservation efforts by groups and individuals. Bisbee, a historic mining town in the Mule Mountains of southeastern Arizona, now has a Main Street Program and is a Certified Local Government (CLG)—two programs ensuring that much of the town's historic fabric will be preserved. Photograph by Francaviglia, 1979.

were somewhat more restrained. These heritage landscapes are more than the past preserved; in fact, they are the artifacts of active preservation efforts.

Bisbee, Arizona, represents the kind of community that has recognized its historical significance and has set out to preserve and market it by using a wide range of private and institutional historic preservation techniques. Residents of Bisbee often compare their community to Sierra Vista, a post–World War II town that developed as the population of nearby Fort Huachuca mushroomed during the Cold War. Whereas Bisbee lost population after the closing of its copper mines in 1974, Sierra Vista had jumped to thirty thousand people by 1985. Sierra Vista's highway strip shopping centers and sprawling suburbs are cited by some Bisbeeites as progress gone awry; they intended to preserve the historical character of their town and, hence, the argument followed, their quality of life.

Bisbee has reversed its population decline while preserving much of its historical character. Driving into Bisbee through the Mule Mountain tunnel is like entering another era, so much so that a wag once spray painted "Time Tunnel" on the concrete portal! Bisbee, nestled in a deep canyon where the colorfully named Tombstone Canyon and Brewery Gulch converge, presents the image of a classic mining town at the turn of the century. Its main commercial street curves along the canyon and is lined with masonry buildings, many of which date from the early twentieth century. Bisbee's hillsides are dotted with miners' cabins and homes dating from the late nineteenth and early twentieth centuries. This Old Bisbee section of town resonates with historical character. A brochure by the Copper Queen Hotel notes that "Bisbee is one of the few towns left today where the streets still echo their colorful past. Unlike 'boom towns,' Bisbee's buildings were made to last, and the town remains architecturally as it stood in its heyday."[12]

Although individual buildings of near-landmark status—such as the fabled Copper Queen Hotel, the Copper Queen Consolidated Mining Company building (now the Mining and Historical Museum), and the Knights of Pythias Hall—served as catalysts for preservation by enterprising entrepreneurs and residents in Old Bisbee in the mid-1970s, it was soon realized that a historic district should be created as a way of focusing attention on the resources and ensuring their preservation. A team of preservationists identified more than 225 historic structures using the major criteria of the National Register, including an association with important people or events, an example of the builder's or designer's art, or the potential to yield information of importance to the history or archeology of the site. After review and approval by the Arizona State Historic Preservation Office Review Board, Bisbee's historic district was entered into the National Register of Historic Places in 1978. This ensured that commercial developers who sensitively rehabilitated the buildings would receive a 20 percent tax write-off, provided that their work met the Secretary of the Interior's Standard for rehabilitating historic structures.

Subsequent preservation efforts led to the expansion of the Bisbee historic district to include many residences. After one unsuccessful attempt in the early 1980s, Bisbee, in 1985, became a Main Street community (one of five in Arizona) under a program originally conceived by the National Trust for Historic Preservation. The Main Street program, as implemented in Bisbee and hundreds of communities in twenty-eight states since its inception in 1978, uses a four-point program of organization, promotion, design, and economic restructuring to coordinate the image of downtown.[13] Using design criteria developed by the National Trust for Historic Preservation and derived in part from the Secretary of the Interior's Standards, the program packages the image and management of downtown. In terms of design, the Main Street program promotes an integrated and historical image; modern signs may be removed and buildings stripped of more recent alterations to regain their earlier appearances. Those buildings that are historic in appearance will remain so by using approved historical methods of maintenance. The Main Street program effectively turns back the clock on the street while ideally keeping the buildings functioning in retail uses.

In 1982, a comprehensive plan called for the redevelopment of Old Bisbee through careful coordination of preservation and tax incentive–driven development projects focusing on the most significant vacant downtown properties.[14] Without question, Bisbee has successfully reversed the depopulation that occurred after the closing of the mines, and preservation efforts played no small part in this turnaround. Like most heritage landscapes, Bisbee has a defined period of historic significance—in this case, a rather wide span of time from the late 1880s to the early 1930s. This period reflects the fifty-year limit normally honored by the National Register Program, with newer structures being considered intrusions or exempt unless they possess *exceptional* historical significance. Architecturally, Bisbee's commercial buildings range from late Victorian to early Art Deco in style, and the town possesses a wealth of vernacular miners' housing typical of mining towns in the region. As in most mining towns, Bisbee's preservation efforts focus on commercial and residential properties, though the Copper Queen Mine Building now serves as an important tourist destination and the huge open pit copper mine, now defunct, is also a scenic attraction.

| *Restored Heritage Landscapes*

Whereas residents and developers in Bisbee started with a significant critical mass of historic fabric, some heritage landscapes have been resurrected from near oblivion through actual reconstruction. Consider, for example, the Mission San José, one of five historic Spanish missions in the vicinity of San Antonio, Texas. (The others include La Espada, San Juan Capistrano, and Concepción, all administered by the National Park Service, and San Antonio de Valero, also known as the Alamo, located in what is today downtown San Antonio and administered by the Daughters of the Republic of Texas.)

Mission San José is well marked on the San Antonio missions heritage tourism trail, which showcases missions as part of the region's early Hispanic heritage. To find the San José site, the traveler follows distinctive blue and

Restored heritage landscapes involve a recapturing or restoration of badly damaged or lost historic fabric. The Mission San José near San Antonio, Texas, is a good example of a restored heritage landscape: The church building itself, as well as many of the buildings surrounding the mission's courtyard, have been rebuilt and otherwise restored using historic guidelines. Photograph by Francaviglia, 1992.

white mission signs and arrives at the destination after driving through neighborhoods in the city's Hispanic south side. Significantly, it is necessary to park one's car outside the mission grounds; in other words, one must become a pedestrian to experience the mission. After passing through a doorway in the massive stone wall surrounding the mission complex, visitors find themselves in a huge courtyard facing a building that was originally constructed 180 years ago. Safely within the walled enclosure, the San José mission presents the classic picture of Hispanic art and architecture: thick stone walls, heavy wooden doors, ornate statuary, and a bell tower. The mission is surrounded by one-story buildings that form the outer wall of the courtyard.

Once within the walls of the courtyard, the present is temporarily forgotten as the sights of contemporary San Antonio are blocked from view. This, it would seem, is a true historic landscape, untouched by time. However, guides and brochures hint that San José may not have always been in this pristine condition. In fact, many of the buildings had fallen into near ruin and have been actively restored by the Conservation Society, the National Park Service, and the Compadres of San Antonio Missions, the latter a private group created to assist the efforts of the National Park Service. A part of the mission itself still remains to be reconstructed. Preservation at San Antonio missions has been under way since the 1920s, and Mission San José was opened to the public as a restored historic site in 1937. Thus, for more than three generations, the goal of restoring and interpreting the historic fabric has been steadily pursued.

How are decisions made to restore lost or nearly lost buildings and other features such as gardens, wells, walls, and fences? In San José, research was conducted into early records, and extensive archeological survey work was done to determine the locations of features such as old *acequias* (irrigation ditches), the quarters of Indian converts (neophytes), grain threshing areas, and gardens. Some of these features have been reconstructed; others are implied by a series of signs or markers. Mission San José presents a picture of solitude today, but a diorama at the visitor's interpretive center illustrates life as it appeared when the church brought local American Indians to the site for conversion. Considering the human drama that occurred here, including a regimented work force engaged in numerous frontier industries under the supervision of the church, San José seems haunted, a peaceful site that once buzzed with human activity.

A similar situation exists at the Hagley Museum's industrial village near Wilmington, Delaware, where the impressive Du Pont Mills features reconstructed buildings associated with the early nineteenth-century production of gunpowder. Among the more interesting sites in this interpretive heritage landscape are a stone quarry, a rail line, a power plant, and other mill buildings situated along the beautiful and historic Brandywine River. Through interpretation, the visitor realizes that the availability of water power was a deciding factor in the location of this once-thriving community. Almost everything in this bucolic setting was affected by industry, and yet the scene is one of serenity today.

The interpreters of this site have attempted to depict the drama and even the danger of everyday life in such an industrial community. As in most heritage landscapes, not everything in Du Pont Mills is preserved. None of the workers' homes, for example, remained, nor have they been reconstructed. Nevertheless, the workers' lifestyle is depicted creatively through marked interpretive signposts and family gardens. Although the laborers are recognized as having made a contribution to the community and enterprise, the best-preserved feature at this location is the home of the du Pont family foreman who oversaw the site. This situation, the preservation of the best feature in a landscape that once possessed hundreds of more mundane or plebeian features, is typical of many preservation efforts in which only the lifestyle of the prominent entrepreneurial family is interpreted.

The serenity of this industrial landscape helps distance it from the present, and yet the entire area was filled with strife, difficulties, and even industrial explosions during its halcyon days. Among the most poignant of such formerly industrial settings is Hopewell Furnace, Pennsylvania. The visitor to-day experiences a bucolic, villagelike setting complete with the home of the entrepreneur, the homes and gardens of the workers, and even the iron furnaces. But all of this appears more like a still life than a bustling industrial workplace. At the point of highest production, the sun over Hopewell Furnace was blotted out by clouds of smoke from the furnaces, and the din of industry overwhelmed the most prominent sound in today's landscape, birdsong. Today their singing is punctuated by the town bell that summoned workers to the mines and mills; of course, the bell has a different meaning for today's visitors as they tour the site at their leisure.

| Assembled Heritage Landscapes

By definition, heritage landscapes are different from their surroundings; that is, they are isolated in space and time from those landscapes where progress is evident. Although we tend to think of preserved heritage landscapes as *real* historic places (such as the Mission San José or Hopewell Furnace), the term may be loosely used to refer to *any* landscape that conveys a sense of heritage through its design. Some heritage landscapes are actually carefully assembled for the purpose of depicting history or historical events where none actually occurred. These assembled heritage landscapes are nevertheless among the most important places for selling a sense of history because they must be carefully engineered to be convincing.

Consider, for example, the traveler's experience in Phoenix, Arizona: After traversing about a dozen miles of Interstate 17 (the Black Canyon Freeway) through the sprawling suburbs north of downtown, the traveler sees a brown and white highway sign at the Pioneer Road exit, indicating the Pioneer Arizona Museum's historic village. There, at what was once the far northern edge of the Phoenix metropolitan area, one can "step back in time" to experience an Arizona community during the territorial period. The 300-acre pioneer village is laid out in a grid pattern and has dirt streets, wooden sidewalks, and two dozen buildings that one might otherwise see only in historical photographs of small-town Arizona at the turn of the century. One may be aware of a background hum of highway noise and the overhead passage of jet aircraft bound for Phoenix, but the Pioneer Arizona Museum village seems otherwise unaffected by progress. Its brick, adobe, and wooden buildings appear well maintained. The museum's village includes commercial buildings, houses, and a school. Many are built in the territorial style typical of the 1880–1910 period, that is, before Arizona entered the Union in 1912. On this spacious site one also finds a simulated mine and a ranch at the edge of the village.

Assembled heritage landscapes involve the placement of buildings and the selection of historical architectural styles to re-create seemingly authentic scenes in new locations. In the Pioneer Arizona Museum village north of Phoenix, historic and historically themed buildings have been moved to the site from elsewhere to re-create the landscape of an Arizona frontier town. Photograph by Francaviglia, 1990.

The visitor to Pioneer Arizona may ask several questions. Presumably, the first might relate to the site itself: Why does this place appear to be so historic? Did someone discover a community that had been bypassed by progress and open the buildings to the public? More sophisticated visitors might also ask other questions. Why do these buildings, which are obviously historic because of their style or design, look so new or so well maintained despite their age? This leads to other questions: Were these buildings restored? If so, do they look the way they did in the past? The next set of questions might relate to the buildings' significance or importance: What do these buildings, and this town, mean? What am I supposed to do here?

These questions are answered by the printed literature and the staff of the village. A synopsis of the Pioneer Arizona Living History Museum informs the visitor that the village was begun in the late 1950s to represent a typical Arizona frontier town during the territorial period and that more than ten thousand schoolchildren visit the village annually.[15] Some of the buildings in this outdoor "museum" are authentic, having been moved to the site; others, however, are re-creations. As one experiences the village, it soon becomes apparent that the buildings are actually a *setting* in which the lifestyle of the period is to be depicted through "living history" scenarios. In other words, the design of the village is intended to set the scene for human activities, such as blacksmithing and merchandising, that were typical of the period. A similar situation is found at Stonefield Village in southwestern Wisconsin. "Although the re-created village never existed as such," John Bowen informs readers of his popular *America's Living Past*, "it combines historic and reconstructed buildings and relics to form a community typical of the hundreds that catered to farmers in southern Wisconsin in the 1890s."[16]

In re-created historic villages or open-air museums like Pioneer Arizona, Stonefield Village, and the Ohio Village complex built by the Ohio Historical Society in Columbus in 1971, visitors experience heritage landscapes by observing craftspeople actively performing now obsolete trades. Ironically, Ohio Village was intended only to be a modest setting in which the public could experience the crafts of the mid–nineteenth century as an adjunct to the museum at the adjacent Ohio Historical Center. In the years since it first opened, however, Ohio Village has become an immensely popular historic site in its own right; the Halloween and Christmas programs are sold out weeks in advance. In Ohio Village, the era is set in the 1850s, before the Civil War and the sectional strife it represented.

Although many re-created villages may seem typical of the period and the region, on closer examination they may be seen to be the result of a careful selection of elements (such as buildings, fences, and vegetation) that "belong." In Ohio Village, all buildings are re-creations, and the staff of the Ohio Historic Preservation Office conducts occasional tours to inform visitors about the architectural styles represented. Despite the staff's reminder to visitors that they are experiencing reproductions, not the genuine product, the average visitor thinks of Ohio Village as a historic place, even though it is more recent than the interstate highway alongside it!

Assembled heritage landscapes are very powerful visual icons. They may become, in effect, historic places in the popular mind. Ironically, this may be especially true if the goal of such places is educational, for they become convincing when their activities are endorsed or authenticated by professionals or volunteers enacting living history. Daniel Porter of the New York State Historical Association has noted that critics have called open-air museums "peaceable kingdoms" but goes on to state that "these tidy, three-dimensional recreations of past ages have enjoyed enormous public popularity since World War II and have grown in numbers, especially since 1960."[17] Assembled historic places such as Old World Wisconsin, a multiethnic outdoor museum, are designed to capture the architectural elements and the flavor of the past but are always subjective; the motive behind their creation is the generation of a sense of community that may or may not have existed in the past.

Professional preservationists know that all assembled and otherwise re-created places are abstractions of reality. Even if based on prototypes or historical photographs, re-created villages, farms, seaports, and the like portray very selective images of the landscape: images that the photographer originally chose to record (as opposed to the scenes that were ignored), images that escaped oblivion through preservation (as opposed to the many images that were deliberately or accidentally discarded), or images that were later selected by someone searching for history as having significance or meaning (as opposed to the other images of places that were disregarded). In other words, the images that were preserved and reassembled were selected through a rather complicated, if subconscious, process of inclusion and exclusion. This process is not unlike that which surrounds the preservation of all material culture, including landscape preservation.

Like all heritage landscapes, an assembled or re-created landscape "survives" as an icon by being validated in the present. Our culture filters or screens out those elements that should not be preserved, and they are, in effect, discarded. The factors that influence inclusion or exclusion may be economic, social, or cultural. Just as preserved mining towns rarely feature the former "cribs," or brothels, of the red light districts for social reasons, they may neglect other elements, such as the homes of minorities or the gritty waste dumps that typify such "hard places."[18] In looking at such re-created places, one is struck by how fresh and new everything appears; the landscape does not often reflect the poverty and economic hardship that may have prevailed during the place's period of significance.

| *Imagineered Heritage Landscapes*

If, as we have seen, heritage landscapes can be *created* in the present, then using the most liberal of definitions, Main Street USA in Disneyland (and its counterpart in Florida's Disney World) may also be considered heritage landscapes in that they are based, or themed, on real main streets in the American Middle West and other locations. Like its prototypes, Disney's Main Street USA serves both commercial and social functions. Unlike their prototypes or other types of heritage landscapes, however, places like Main Street USA have been "imagineered," as Disney designers call the process, to reflect *essence* rather than *reality*. Purists may object to both real Main Streets and those of popular culture being considered heritage landscapes, but we should remem-

Imagineered heritage landscapes involve considerable imagination and elements of fantasy in recapturing the essence of symbolic historic places. The public square in Disneyland's Main Street USA features slightly miniaturized Victorian-style buildings, elaborate street furniture, and carefully contrived plantings to convey a dreamlike image of small-town America at the turn of the twentieth century. Photograph by Francaviglia, 1995.

ber that such landscapes occupy a complete continuum from authentic to contrived. The merchants who created real towns in the nineteenth and early twentieth centuries often used fanciful styles imported or derived from elsewhere (such as Greek Revival, Victorian Italianate, or Mission Style), dictated by the latest fads. The real American landscape is eclectic, ever in search of historical identity, and so are many heritage landscapes. That Disney and others successfully created the essence rather than substance of reality helps explain why such landscapes have become icons of Americana.

Let us look more closely at Main Street USA in Disneyland, a masterfully engineered heritage landscape designed to funnel all visitors to the theme park through a streetscape that reflects the heyday of the American small town at the turn of the century. Here, buildings are stylized versions of their Victorian prototypes, some three-quarters lifesize and all carefully coordinated as to color, design, and setback. As the centerpiece for Main Street USA, the public square has become the most memorable heritage landscape in America, surrounded as it is by commercial and institutional buildings, including the town hall, fire department, and emporium. A close investigation reveals that the design of Main Street USA was inspired by real features in the American town-scape but was romanticized, abstracted, and sanitized.[19] In Main Street USA, significantly, there is no "other side of the tracks"; the Santa Fe and Disney-land Railroad encircles the park.

A similar situation exists in Old Tucson, a movie set constructed near Tucson, Arizona, in 1939 for the filming of the movie *Arizona*. Stylized and carefully designed to convey an image of the typical southwestern town in the late nineteenth century, Old Tucson has become an icon after appearing in more than eighty films. It is a very popular tourist destination, visited by almost half a million people per year.[20] The type of overt manipulation of the past seen in Main Street USA or Old Tucson may seem objectionable, but most heritage landscapes are, in a sense, contrived, some more so than others. The numerous interpretive rural or agricultural villages (e.g., Sturbridge Village, Mass., or the Georgia Agrirama) often feature structures that have been moved to the site and placed in conjectural locations; the factor that enables us to think of such "interpreted" places as more "real" than commercial theme parks is the motivation of the creator (academicians naturally suspect the educational value of something that entertains or makes a profit) and the accuracy of the research involved in their reconstruction. Whereas most heritage landscapes are ultimately educational, few critics will deny that they also serve aesthetic purposes.

We receive enlightenment *and* pleasure in beholding a pristine scene with no modern intrusions to distract the eye. Consider, for example, Seaside, the popular seaside residential environment in Florida, designed by Andrew Duany and Elizabeth Plater-Zyberk during the 1980s. Seaside is much like a new town in concept but features historically styled residences and commercial buildings that, as many observers have noted, have a decidedly Victorian ambience. In England, the new town of Poundbury was designed to look and feel like a community built several hundred years ago. Its popularity confirms that American heritage landscape sentiments are deeply rooted in Western culture. Such heritage landscapes appeal to our sense of visual integrity; architecture and its surroundings combine to set the scene for us to better understand historical events and vanished lifestyles.

In this regard, it is not coincidental that the popular appreciation of heritage landscapes coincides with the rise of film and television as popular media. Ironically, heritage landscapes like Seaside, which may arise from the romanticism of historic places in film, feature porches and small-town intimacy to rekindle social interaction between people, that is, to encourage residents to turn off their television sets and socialize with neighbors. In describing the peculiar relationship between film and reality, one is reminded that actor

Henry Fonda's small 1883 frame bungalow in Grand Island, Nebraska, was moved to the Stuhr Museum's Prairie Pioneer Village site at the request of Fonda, who recorded a commentary of his family history for the museum.[21]

Life can, and does, imitate art. Thus, the downtown section of a real town (Medina, Ohio) has been enhanced to possess a turn-of-the-century image. What began with restorations has concluded with the construction of historic-appearing new structures, including a modern three-story Victorian style building that replaced a 1950s era service station. Medina's public square features a gazebo, or bandstand, that never existed there in the past but was styled after one in a historic town (Belleville) nearly a hundred miles distant. This beautification and improvement occurred after merchants in Medina visited Disneyland and concluded that their real town could be improved to attract trade and commerce.[22] They were correct, and their townscape today is a composite image, partially restored and partially imagineered. Paradoxically, Medina today looks more Victorian than it did during the Victorian era. Such is the power of image building.

| *Imagically Preserved Landscapes*

This fascination with the power of imagery, as expressed in imagineering, leads to the last type of heritage landscape, that which does not exist as a real place or location at all but rather as a miniature or an *image* only. For decades museums have used images and dioramas of places to reconstruct the past imagically. In re-creating the historic mining community of Black Top, which had vanished by the 1940s, members of the Guernsey Valley Model Railroad Club in Cambridge, Ohio, created a diorama in HO scale (1:87 ratio). Their results are stunning, for the model community features several dozen grimy company houses lining the road (and railroad) to the Black Top mine. The entire scene is illuminated, and the railroad activity is very realistic. Ironically, the buildings are also more realistic in appearance—gritty and showing signs of wear and tear—than they might have been if they had been part of a heritage landscape run by a historical agency. The model version of Black Top reminds the viewer that real buildings of this type are normally used and worn out, rather than preserved, as they simply served the economic interests of the mining company. Although preservation ultimately attempts to stop or reverse the inevitable, imagic re-creation can capture the essence of decline and deferred maintenance that would lead to ruin in real life.

These miniaturized heritage landscapes present us with a dilemma; in some ways they can be made very nearly as realistic as—and perhaps visually more realistic than—their real but preserved counterparts. Given that heritage landscapes are comprehensible as scenery, these miniaturized heritage landscapes can be more effective precisely because they *distance* the viewer rather than relying upon actual entry into the scene by an observer. In other words, dioramas permit overall comprehension of a scene that normally would have to be viewed in separate glimpses. That perspective makes it easier to appreciate, by proxy, the overall feel of the community's design.

In some ways, then, the most effective landscape preservation efforts are, paradoxically, simulations. Even "real" heritage landscapes, such as Fayette Historic Park in Michigan—the partially reconstructed site of an iron company town on the Garden Peninsula near Escanaba—feature historical photographic images on marker posts to help the visitor envision how the town looked during its heyday. When used effectively, images can actually be superimposed onto the real scene, thus increasing the sense of drama about the passage of time. This means, somewhat startlingly, that a historical photographic image of a real landscape in the past is actually as authentic as the deliberately preserved landscape today. Although an intentionally preserved landscape is validated by its survival, one might argue that it is falsified by that very survival because measures have been taken to stop the passage of time. Image is actually as important as substance, at least in the perception of heritage landscapes.

This brings us to a dichotomy or conundrum: Is preservation experiential or visual? What significance does the "real" object have outside of its association with the past? In reality, of course, preserved landscapes contain actual remnants from the past, but they often feature enough new "old" material to be synthetic; thus, image and substance are inseparable, in that heritage landscapes consist of both conserved images and actual fabric that convey mythic or shared cultural interpretations of significance. Preserved places and contrived images of them are ultimately related; they both are interpreted as iconic evidence of the past. Imagic preservations, in other words, are every bit as "real" as preserved features.

In an economic sense, the concept of imagic preservation is plausible where complete reconstruction of a landscape is not feasible. Thurber, Texas, a long-vanished coal mining ghost town with a rich ethnic heritage, provides a case in point. When the Texas and Pacific Coal and Oil Company abandoned the site in the early 1930s, the firm tore down virtually every building. Today only five of the more than three hundred buildings that once existed remain. Even the town's dirt streets were obliterated by chains dragged across the landscape. How can such a vanished landscape be comprehended? The Thurber Historical Association has mounted an active preservation movement and has reconstructed a few features—including one company house, Saint Barbara's

Church, and a miners' railroad car—at its New York Hill site. The actual interpretation of the site, however, is approached through a forty-five-minute videocassette production; this presentation is supplemented by a metal historic marker placed on New York Hill, overlooking the ruins of Thurber in 1995. The marker features a drawing of the town's major buildings keyed to those remaining features in the landscape, such as the power plant smokestack and the dry-goods commercial store. The visitor views the plaque and reads a brief text about the community during its heyday, and thus the past (and the place) comes alive. Among the most interesting techniques used to interpret historic landscapes are ghost structures (simple frameworks outlining the building shape), such as those at the Blue Heron Mining Company site in Kentucky. Ultimately, we may expect to see hologram images serving the same purpose, conveying a feeling of how the community looked by becoming images that, in effect, fill psychological space.

Someday, we can probably expect to experience historic landscapes vicariously, through virtual reality featuring images of the place being transmitted to individual headsets. In this way, historical photographic images of places, as well as computer simulations, could reconstruct three-dimensional versions of vanished landscapes in the mind of the observer. Given their positive experiences with themed and imagically preserved heritage landscapes, one

Imagically preserved heritage landscapes are depictions of places as images: The now nearly vanished coal mining town of Thurber, in north-central Texas, is depicted on a metal plaque overlooking the abandoned townsite. Erected by local historians, these imagically preserved scenes, which were based on historic photographs, help the public better visualize what Thurber looked like in the early twentieth century. Photograph by Francaviglia, 1995.

can expect interesting and innovative treatments of heritage landscapes from the Disney studios working in concert with other filmmakers.

Although these engineered landscapes can be distributed through computer hardware/software, they are likely to be pioneered at theme parks like the controversial Disney's America, which had been planned for Manassas, Virginia. Conceptual designs of Disney's America called for "a unique and historically detailed environment" that was to feature representations of Native America (1600–1810), Crossroads USA (1800–1850), Civil War Fort (1850–70), We The People (Ellis Island 1870–1930), Enterprise (1870–1930), State Fair (1930–45), Victory Field (1930–45), and Family Farm (1930–45); all were to celebrate "a diverse and unlikely society, made up of every culture and race on earth."[23] Although the specific project was abandoned because of efforts by influential local residents, who opposed the development of the land, and by many eminent historians, who were opposed to such popularized history, a new site undoubtedly will be developed in the future. In addition to three-dimensional buildings, the park will probably present virtual heritage landscapes for the education and entertainment of visitors.

| Conclusion

This chapter provides an introduction to heritage landscapes that are "sold" and the processes by which their preservation and interpretation are effected, but also encourages the reader to ask questions about the heritage landscapes that he or she encounters. Are some of these landscapes more liable than others to become, and to be sold as, heritage landscapes? How accurately do the heritage landscapes we encounter reflect their originals—that is, how accurate is the landscape image that is marketed as historic? What types of compromises must be made for heritage landscapes to meet current expectations? And what purpose, ultimately, do heritage landscapes serve?

If all landscapes are selective images and all preserved heritage landscapes are further filtered through selective lenses, then their cultural content is particularly revealing. Generally, heritage landscapes preserve those systems or images that are most acceptable to our culture, which explains why saccharine examples of rural prosperity, virtuous small-town life, and harmonious urban neighborhoods are preserved, marketed, and consumed rather than images of countryside poverty and slums. Even the Disney imagineers, who courageously offered a graffiti-emblazoned subway car as representative of New York City life in Walt Disney World, were chastised by officials from the metropolis, who noted that the subway car sent the wrong message about their city.

In truth, heritage landscapes also reveal a darker side of the past; economic failure, social problems, and obsolescence are messages waiting to be interpreted. That Mormon villages can be viewed as failed vestiges of nineteenth-century utopian socialism may explain why the church was slow to endorse their preservation;[24] similarly, that the small-town Main Street has been translated as the successful roots of American marketing and social life may explain why it has been so revered as an icon by developers. Former mining communities that now serve tourists instead of producing metals vaguely remind us of the rewards of risks taken on the frontier while, at the same time, their revitalization distances us from the consequences of that risk. Heritage landscapes are sold, but the price is often a complete reinterpretation of the past.

Why are heritage landscapes so popular and so successfully marketed? Preservation is such a successful movement, we are told, because good preservation makes good economic sense and is ultimately better for the environment. That is true, but the ultimate goal of preservation is didactic—to convey messages about the meaning of the past. Our preserved heritage landscapes are reminders of what we cherish—and have lost—in our transition from an agricultural and industrial country to a service economy. Heritage landscapes are easy to sell; they enable us to reconstruct, or reinterpret, the past, sometimes as it should have been rather than as it was. In actively preserving and creating heritage landscapes, the underlying assumption, always operative, is that the past is *worth* preserving; when places are preserved to a certain time period, that preservation validates the premise, often unspoken, that certain periods in time are more significant than others. That has led to the creation and selling of themed heritage landscapes by both the private and public sectors. These heritage landscapes have been sold for educational as well as commercial reasons or motives. That sobering realization might make some observers less critical of commercial ventures, for both commercial and educational efforts at preservation ultimately sell—that is, *persuade* us to both consume and perpetuate—heritage landscapes.

There is some evidence that professional preservationists are becoming disenchanted with ensembles of buildings frozen in time. Rather than creating set pieces of the past by restoring historic landscapes to a certain period, many now applaud and encourage efforts directed toward recognizing that landscapes are dynamic, evolving entities. According to Charles A. Birnbaum of the National Park Service Historic Landscape Initiative, efforts should be directed toward preserving those *dynamic* qualities (including change), rather than restoring or reconstructing landscapes as we think they may have appeared during a particular period.[25] Thus, heritage landscapes are not as important in themselves as for what they can tell us about *processes,* many of which still operate. In this sense, all of the nation's heritage landscapes are important indicators of the restless search for the identity that characterizes Americans as they make the transition from the twentieth to the twenty-first century.

CHAPTER THREE

The History and Preservation
of Urban Parks and Cemeteries

DAVID
SCHUYLER
AND
PATRICIA M.
O'DONNELL

Historic landscapes abound in America's cities. These spaces vary in scale from less than one acre to more than one thousand acres. They are also diverse in history and purpose. The best-known historic urban landscapes are the great nineteenth-century parks, but other historically significant open spaces include cemeteries designed by engineers and horticulturists; subdivisions platted by architects, landscape architects, and speculative builders; the grounds of public, institutional, and private buildings; remnants of orchards or farms; and the streetscapes of historic neighborhoods. Important, too, are city plans and the complex patterns of streets and rights of way that have structured urban growth and residential life. Collectively, these elements of the city's fabric represent attempts to order the urban environment and to define the public and private spheres of human interaction.

Urban landscape preservation began, appropriately, in the nation's great public parks during the 1960s and has matured over the last three decades. A critically important step was the designation of Central Park, in New York City, as a National Historic Landmark. At a luncheon at the Tavern on the Green on 7 June 1965, Secretary of the Interior Stewart L. Udall presented Mayor Robert Wagner with a plaque denoting the park's historic status, which Wagner handed to Parks Commissioner Newbold Morris. The plaque, Morris promised, would remain in his office, "because so many others in the park have been stolen in the past."[1]

The *Times* article announcing Central Park's historic status was a sidebar to a larger story about a new federal initiative, the Land and Water Conservation Act, which Udall envisioned as a means of acquiring much-needed park space in the metropolitan area, particularly vest-pocket and smaller neighborhood parks. But in its recitation of the facts, the *Times* missed the significance of Udall's remarks: Central Park was the first landscape included in the National Register of Historic Places. Two other aspects of the occasion were perhaps more ironic than historic. First, the announcement took place in the posh restaurant located in the Sheepfold, a structure designed by architect Jacob Wrey, which the park's creators, Frederick Law Olmsted and Calvert Vaux, considered an awkwardly sited intrusion upon the landscape. Second, the public's use of the park, which Olmsted considered the most critical and fragile component of its success or failure, had deteriorated to the extent that its bureaucratic steward refused to place a plaque outside for fear that it would be stolen.

In still another respect, the June 1965 acknowledgment of Central Park's historic status was an unintentional testament to the general neglect of the history and preservation of urban landscapes. The National Register designation honored Central Park as a consciously designed, nineteenth-century work of landscape art and as the progenitor of similar parks in most other American cities. In recognizing Central Park, Udall (and preservationists in general in the mid-1960s) projected a narrow definition of both *historic* and *landscape*. Indeed, the initial stage in the preservation of historic landscapes was similar to early efforts in architectural preservation, which addressed individual buildings, often those structures associated with great people and great deeds. Only gradually did preservation embrace architecture in many forms—as individual masterworks, to be sure, but also as vernacular structures and whole neighborhoods as elements of larger historic districts.

The Beginnings of Landscape Preservation

The emergence of historic landscape preservation in urban areas can be traced to three significant sources. First was the evolution of architectural preservation. Until the 1960s, urban landscape preservation was mistakenly called *restoration;* it usually involved the creation of period settings around historic houses and public buildings, not the retention and repair of original circulation, plantings, and spatial characteristics. In these projects, often prompted by well-meaning local citizens, landscapes were decorative adjuncts to the more important architecture. Only with the establishment of historic districts did preservation thinking begin to extend to the streetscape and public parks within the area, but even in this later stage architecture usually remained the dominant factor. For example, the National Register of Historic Places designation of the Washington Park Historic District, in Albany, New York, presented historic data and detail on the structures framing the park, including

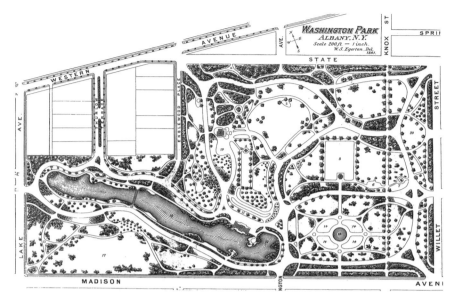

The 1891 plan for Washington Park in Albany, New York, implemented by William Egerton and originally designed by John Bogart and John Y. Culyer. The National Register documentation for the Washington Park Historic District, prepared during the 1970s, is typical of other nominations from the period in that nearby buildings and structures were given much attention but little note was made of the historical and cultural significance of the park landscape. Source: Office of the Mayor, City of Albany, New York.

a building designed by Henry Hobson Richardson; however, Washington Park, the centerpiece of the district, received scant attention as a culturally and historically significant landscape. Park designers John Bogart and John Y. Culyer, who worked with Frederick Law Olmsted Sr. on Prospect Park in Brooklyn, were not mentioned. Neither was William Egerton, the superintendent who implemented the early plan and added to it over thirty-eight years. This lack of attention to the landscape is especially ironic because it was the park that attracted the graceful homes that surrounded it. Unfortunately, other early National Register nominations that include historic landscapes as elements of larger districts contain the same cursory treatment of the landscape. As a result, one aspect of future landscape preservation activity will be the upgrading of these early nominations to address, more adequately, the history, integrity, and significance of the historic landscape as a distinct cultural resource.

When Central Park was honored in 1965, the historic landscape—its structures, bridges, paths, watercourses, lawns, shrubs, and trees—was seriously deteriorated. In the 1970s Mayor John V. Lindsay testified to the value of Central Park as a historic and artistic ensemble when he appointed architectural historian Henry Hope Reed as the first Central Park curator, followed by the employment of two preservation students at Columbia University, Joseph and Adrienne Bresnan, to develop the first preservation plan for the park. These efforts paralleled widespread recognition of park deterioration in many cities. The initial attempts to redress decades of neglect were not always grounded in history, however, and sometimes resulted in further harm to the landscape. One such misguided project placed modern benches and lighting in the small Olmsted-designed parks in Rochester, New York; another brought about the removal of the woodland understory and the addition of lighting in Prospect Park's Ravine. Much of the activity in the 1960s and 1970s brought incompatible encroachment on these historic landscapes. The formation of friends groups and citizen commissions served as a counterpart to poorly planned improvement projects. In Buffalo, New York, during the late 1970s, mayoral-appointed citizen groups brought a somewhat unsophisticated rehabilitation and improvement voice to the city on behalf of Delaware Park and the Parade, later named in honor of Martin Luther King Jr.

A second contribution to urban landscape preservation was the environmental movement that rose to prominence in the late 1960s and early 1970s. The celebration of the first Earth Day in 1970, followed two years later by the 150th anniversary of Frederick Law Olmsted's birth, was more than coincidence. Olmsted became a well-known figure from the past precisely because he created cherished open spaces within cities and anticipated many of the ecological concerns of the late twentieth century. One result of environmentalism was renewed concern for safeguarding urban open spaces. As the focus of the environmental movement evolved from the conservation of ecologically or aesthetically distinctive places, especially the distant wilderness, to neighborhood open spaces as natural resources, activists rediscovered nineteenth-century parks and cemeteries, waterfronts, and other open spaces, many of them neglected for a generation or more, which once again became cherished places. Mount Auburn Cemetery, in Cambridge, Massachusetts, for example, is a haven for bird watchers, while Prospect Park, in Brooklyn, New York, is a major stop for birds migrating along the Eastern seaboard flyway. Current projects in several urban historic landscapes that focus on improved ecological health and sustainability include the renewal of woodlands in Central and Prospect Parks and the restoration of the Picnic Grove and Trout Pond in Rochester's Seneca Park.[2] One welcome result of the environmental movement has been the rediscovery of local parks as historical and cultural as well as ecological treasures.

A third source of historic landscape preservation has been an interest in the associative values or special qualities of urban landscapes cherished by neighbors and frequent users. Just as architectural preservation traces its origins to a handful of activists, landscape preservation, both urban and rural, has frequently resulted from the efforts of a single person or a small group organized to save or improve a degraded resource. Often these individuals have been motivated by intensely personal concerns for quality of life rather than by a more general understanding of or commitment to historic preservation. Sometimes these groups have incorporated as effective nonprofit friends organizations and have supported preservation through volunteer cleanups, research, and fund-raising.

The Downing Park Planning Committee, in Newburgh, New York, received funding for preservation planning from the New York State Council for the Arts between 1987 and 1991. These grants enabled historic landscape architects and historians to refine and focus the efforts of numerous volunteers on short- and long-range initiatives. Both this citizen nonprofit and the City of Newburgh gained a detailed agenda for park preservation, rehabilitation, maintenance, and management. Supported by this comprehensive plan and guidelines, the Downing Park Planning Committee has worked with the city and obtained funding from private and public sources to complete two important projects, the dredging and repair of the lake and the rehabilitation of the lake shelter. They have also organized volunteers for seasonal cleanups, obtained in-kind services, hosted special events in the park, and used low-security prison labor for maintenance and repair.[3] Larger, more established groups, such as the widely known Central Park Conservancy, and lesser-known organizations, such as the Buffalo Friends of Olmsted Parks, the Massachusetts Association for Olmsted Parks, and the Louisville Olmsted Parks Conservancy, have played significant roles in advocacy, documentation, and preservation of historic urban parks and parkways.

During the 1980s landscape preservation became widely accepted as a discipline in its own right and cities began planning efforts on behalf of their historic parks. The New York City Department of Parks and Recreation commenced a comprehensive set of historic landscape and structures reports for Prospect Park, Seattle planned for the preservation of Interlaken and Lake Washington Boulevards, and the Commonwealth of Massachusetts began its statewide Historic Olmsted Landscape Preservation Program. The Historic Preservation Open Committee of the American Society of Landscape Architects and the Alliance for Historic Landscape Preservation sponsored professional development seminars, while the National Park Service published National Register Bulletin 18: *How to Evaluate and Nominate Designed Historic*

Landscapes. During the 1980s thematic and multiple resource nominations brought groups of historic parks and parkways into the National Register system, including the DeBoer-designed Denver system, the Olmsted system in Buffalo, and the Chicago park system that incorporated important designs by Olmsted, William LeBaron Jenney, and Jens Jensen. The creation of a Historic Landscape Initiative within the National Park Service in 1989 and the publication in 1996 of *The Secretary of the Interior's Standards for the Treatment of Historic Properties with Guidelines for the Treatment of Cultural Landscapes* are still other measures of the professionalization of landscape preservation.[4]

| *Landscape Preservation Planning*

Determining which urban landscapes are historic and how best to preserve them is a complex process. Once the culturally valuable landscape has been identified, its integrity must be understood. *Integrity* is the degree to which the landscape continues to portray its historic identity and character (see chap. 8). The character-defining components of a historic landscape are tools that reveal integrity through a comparison of historic and current conditions. These character-defining components are topography, circulation, vegetation, natural systems, water features, structures, site furnishings and objects, spatial and visual relationships, and surroundings. By thinking about landscapes as a compilation of inseparable but distinct components, we can understand, evaluate, and analyze their character and condition as a basis for professional preservation planning.

The National Park Service recommended a comprehensive strategy for landscape preservation planning in *Preservation Brief 36: Protecting Cultural Landscapes* (1994) and in the more complete *Guidelines for the Treatment of Cultural Landscapes* (1996):

1. Historical research, both to determine the history of the site and to establish a context by comparison with other landscapes created either at the same time or by the same designer;

2. Detailed inventory of existing conditions;

3. Site analysis of the character-defining features of the landscape as they have changed over time to determine integrity and significance;

4. Development of a preservation treatment approach and selection of preservation, restoration, reconstruction, or rehabilitation strategies;

5. Development of a cultural landscape management plan and philosophy;

6. Development of a strategy for ongoing maintenance;

7. Documentation of the preservation action undertaken and recommendations for future research.[5]

The first three steps are essential in the preparation of National Register nominations and form the basis for preservation planning. The fourth—preservation treatment selection and implementation—is perhaps more challenging. The period of significance for a given historic landscape may be one or several days, as is often the case in historic battlefields; it may involve the years of association with a prominent individual, as with the grounds of a historic house, estate, or farm; or it may embrace centuries, as is often the case with a town common, when the landscape has evolved over time and become an aggregate of culturally valuable elements. The proper preservation strategy obviously will vary based on the period of significance determined, the landscape's integrity, the completeness of the historic record, the intended uses, management and maintenance capabilities, financial realities, and other relevant factors.

The final three steps are critical to the ongoing preservation and stewardship of cultural landscapes. The development of a landscape management plan and a staff able to undertake both short- and long-term maintenance and preservation projects is essential. In the absence of such a plan and a competent staff, the spaces and structures that were restored in Prospect Park during the 1970s quickly deteriorated. Moreover, to a greater extent than with buildings, the preservation of landscapes requires systematic attention—the cyclic care, management, repair, and replacement of vegetation, drives, paths, infrastructure, furnishings, and all other components of a landscape that a management plan must address.

Experience has demonstrated that two additional steps are essential to the preservation process and to the long-term viability of preservation efforts. One is the need for the appropriate interpretation of a historic landscape to its visitors. This is important not simply to increase the public's awareness of historic values but also to promote respect for and proper use of the landscape. Innovative public education offerings are part of the activities of historic site staff and volunteers functioning as docents in some historic landscapes.

The other step, which is becoming increasingly important as an ingredient in landscape preservation, is the building of collaborations and the use of volunteers. Partnerships between the public and private sectors have taken various forms in recent years, such as fund-raising for capital projects or equipment, organizing volunteer labor, supporting planning efforts, establishing tree trusts for tree care and plantings, and leading landscape tours. A good example of such a partnership is the current master planning and first phase project work in the Olmsted parks and parkways of Louisville, Kentucky. The Louisville Olmsted Parks Conservancy was established in 1989 as a planning and funding partnership between the City of Louisville and the private sector. The conservancy has secured a multidisciplinary team of consultants to develop master plans for the preservation and renewal of Shawnee, Iroquois, and Cherokee Parks and the fourteen-mile-long Olmsted Parkway system. The planning process has been a consensus-building collaboration with Metro Parks, citizen stewardship councils, Louisville Friends of Olmsted Parks, and the general public. This integrated planning process takes a rehabilitation approach that balances historic preservation, ecological sustainability, diverse contemporary use needs, and maintenance resources while building community commitment to a long-term renewal process involving capital projects, staff skill and equipment upgrades, and private sector support.

Preservation planning is a linear, cumulative process often undertaken in separate steps by various persons or groups with different levels of skill and experience. Bridging urban and rural boundaries, several states have commenced the identification and inventory of public and private historic landscapes, the essential beginning for any future preservation action. The Historic Olmsted Landscape Preservation Program in Massachusetts is one well-known endeavor; Maine has undertaken a three-phase program of assessment of historic landscapes, beginning with public parks, proceeding next to private designed landscapes, and culminating with city and town planning initiatives. Georgia has studied common residential landscapes, Connecticut has inventoried town commons and greens, and Rhode Island has examined its heritage of public landscapes. These statewide initiatives require the effective collaboration of several groups, including state historic preservation offices, statewide and local nonprofits, and Olmsted parks and other historic landscape organizations.

Maintenance Issues in Preservation Planning

Recent preservation efforts have attempted to redress decades of neglect in the nation's historic urban parks. Despite the significance of parks—the largest open spaces within densely built cities and the playgrounds of the urban population, as well as historic landscapes—adequate levels of funding have never been assured. As important as they are to the overall health and well-being of the urban population, over the last 150 years parks have been subject to periodic and often dramatic cuts in funding for maintenance. Land set aside for park use included terminal moraines and other areas too rocky or hilly for more intensive urban development; the cost of grading and filling to construct streets and lots was simply prohibitively high.

Most historic landscapes, whether urban or rural, date from times when labor was inexpensive, and both the economics of maintenance and prevailing horticultural tastes were reflected in their design. Olmsted's parks, for example, necessitated the expenditure of substantial sums for construction to achieve the intended scenic effects. Surviving planting plans and other documents indicate that park designs were also predicated upon regular maintenance by large work crews, especially for horticultural compositions that were not self-sustaining. In many parks, massive multiple-species shrub beds were planted with large numbers of small plants. These plants required care to become established and in pruning and selective removal, only achieving their intended form after a decade or more, and they then required care to maintain the proper balance. Olmsted's plans also required the ongoing care and periodic replacement of trees. Many structures, particularly the rustic bridges, arbors, and seats that contribute to the parks' ambience, needed regular repair and periodic replacement. As park use soared, the various shelters and public bathrooms required increased maintenance.

The lack of adequate funds and skilled labor for maintenance has plagued virtually every historic urban landscape and not just in modern periods of fiscal austerity. In the second half of the nineteenth century, skilled estate gardeners, masons, and engineers participated in the building of these landscapes, but through a series of cycles, skilled construction and maintenance staff have been lost and regained over the decades. Central Park, for example, began to experience inadequate maintenance shortly after its opening, when staffs were cut and political patronage brought unskilled workers to the force, a pattern that has continued intermittently ever since. In the mid-1870s, after the collapse of the Tweed Ring, Olmsted confronted straitened budgets even as he attempted to repair what he considered the neglect and misuse of the park.[6]

The sequence of economic recessions and shifts of political fortune has affected public landscapes throughout America's cities. During the 1873 depression, day laborers were used in Buffalo's park and parkway construction as a work relief program, and the same was true in other communities. In the aftermath of the Panic of 1893, Newburgh, New York, finally commenced construction of Downing Park as a means of providing work to the unemployed.[7] Following the outbreak of World War I, European banks called in their loans to New York City, which, faced with the inability to borrow money, slashed spending on parks in half. A professional park manager who examined Central Park in 1927 found that several areas of the park had deteriorated, that other parts had "a neglected and unkempt appearance," and that there was an "appalling number of wholly or partially dead trees."[8] During the Great Depression of the 1930s, Robert Moses used armies of relief workers to repair and restore New York City's parks; at the same time he added modern features, such as the perimeter playgrounds, that were encroachments on the historic designs. In many cities the last major work efforts in urban parks along riverfronts and parkways were undertaken using federal dollars during Franklin Roosevelt's New Deal era. Surveys conducted under the aegis of the Works Progress Administration (WPA) and other New Deal agencies continue to serve as critical records, infrastructure was cleaned and repaired, and new bridges, buildings, and plantings were added to the nation's parks. Unfortunately, the pattern of neglect resumed in the post–World War II period. New York City's fiscal crisis of the 1970s forced a 60 percent reduction in appropriations for the parks department, which resulted in another period of deferred maintenance that took a dramatic toll on the city's historic landscapes.[9] At the same time, Newburgh's Parks and Recreation Department was disbanded, leaving an understaffed Public Works Department to fill the gap.

The oft-repeated saying that parks and other "amenities" will always be slashed before "essential" public services rings true because it has been true. Participants at the 1993 annual meeting of the National Recreation and Park Association argued, however, that parks are indeed essential. Linking current societal issues of drug abuse and crime, especially among the nation's youth, to the lack of care we are bringing to our shared public spaces and their youth and family programs, recreation professionals launched a public education program with three ambitious goals: to promote a greater appreciation of the importance of parks, to persuade civic leaders that the overall well-being of their communities is directly linked to the health of their open spaces, and to gain support for investment in the public realm. Better recreational opportunities of all kinds, they asserted, will more directly address these problems than will additional police, judges, and jails.[10] Parks and recreation are anything but unnecessary amenities to be slashed from the budget in times of economic distress: They are essential to the renewal of the fabric of our nation's communities.

| Conflicts over Use in Preservation Planning

In addition to the lack of adequate maintenance over time, most historic urban landscapes have been subjected to exogenous forces that have altered and in some cases radically transformed their appearance and function. As is true of other significant landscapes, historic urban spaces represent specific responses to social, economic, cultural, and ecological conditions. The great nineteenth-century parks, for example, were attempts to shape large expanses of pastoral and picturesque beauty—the kinds of settings urban growth was destroying—within the confines of burgeoning cities. The earliest parks, particularly those associated with public buildings, were settings for public ritual, affirmations of social order, and pleasing contrasts to the relentless rectangularity of the cityscape. "Rural" cemeteries, parkways, and leafy subdivisions were likewise cultural statements that employed landscape art to project a particular aesthetic or to order the domestic environment. As has been true of all types of historic landscapes, these have been subjected to changing definitions of taste and the emergence of alternative uses that have resulted in modifications to the original design. If historic landscapes are "among our nation's most threatened and vulnerable historic properties," as Genevieve P. Keller has argued, those located in cities are especially at risk.[11]

The changing nature of park usage is one such threat to the historic landscape. Olmsted and other nineteenth-century park makers thought of the park in terms of specific patterns of use and behavior. A visit to a park was an opportunity to experience an alternative to the crowding, the bustle, and the density of building that characterized the rest of the nineteenth-century city. Leisure was largely passive—walking or promenading, riding on horseback or in carriages, listening to concerts—though the parks also made provisions for a few more rigorous activities, such as ice skating. These activities, Olmsted remarked, provided opportunities for the "*unbending* of the faculties," a process of recuperation from the strains of urban life. Olmsted was aware of the threat of alternative uses of the park as early as January 1859, when he explained that "no kind of sport can be permitted that would be inconsistent" with the goal of providing healthful recreation, nor any "species of exercise which must be enjoyed only by a single class in the community to the diminution of the enjoyment of others."[12]

The demands of active recreation have affected the nation's historic parks, just as Olmsted feared. As the most accessible open spaces for millions of city dwellers in the United States, parks have long been focal points in the contestation of public space. Anticipating that diverse groups would compete for the use of parks, Olmsted resisted active recreation when it would intrude upon other uses of the parks he considered more important. Precisely because of their open condition and gently rolling topography, however, these spaces have proven especially attractive for modern recreational uses. In the late nineteenth century, park recreation included organized play for schoolchildren as well as lawn tennis, golf, and croquet. The pattern of competing uses increased during the twentieth century. Robert Moses, for example, energetically transformed many of New York City's historic parks to provide facilities for modern sport. Moses had little use for the more passive recreational uses of the parks, and he filled the landscape with playgrounds (twenty-two in Central Park alone), skating rinks, and tennis courts, as well as ballfields. Moses's attitudes toward parks emphasized active uses as the principal reason for their existence. According to his biographer, Moses often referred to natural woodlands in newly created parks—areas not yet provided with facilities for active recreation—as "undeveloped for park use."[13]

Recent user studies of Lincoln Park in Chicago and Central Park in New York City demonstrate that active users accounted for less than 12 percent of the populace, yet they are often organized into such groups as little league and youth soccer, which bring a strong voice to elected officials. Passive users rarely appear at public meetings or give comment on potential park improvements. Athletes and spectators are not the only users of historic parks; walking, cycling, relaxing, reading, and countless other activities take place there, as well. Indeed, the most common use for public landscape is passive recreation by individuals and groups. The 1991 user survey of Lincoln Park found that 62 percent of people were exclusively passive users, while 30 percent used the park both actively and passively, and only 8 percent indicated exclusively active park use.[14] In a use study for Central Park conducted in 1982, some 80 percent of people used the facility passively, including 58 percent who cited "relaxation" as their primary park use; in this study 9 percent were involved in sports and just over 3 percent were playground users.[15]

What Olmsted termed gregarious recreation, involving groups of people, is another form of park use that should not be overlooked. Members of an extended family, as well as gatherings of friends or neighborhood groups, may all wish to use parks. These friendly encounters in well-appointed public spaces would, Olmsted believed, have a civilizing influence on the people of a city. Such positive encounters with persons of other ages, races, and ethnic backgrounds were essential foundations for a greater harmony among the ethnically and racially diverse people of the modern city. Passive users also defend their interest in the park. Bird watchers, for example, vigorously protested "the mass destruction of mature and irreplaceable trees" in Central Park's Ramble, a measure intended to restore the historic sight line from Bethesda Terrace to Vista Rock, because they feared that the action would destroy the habitats of certain species.[16]

In attempting to balance habitats and sight lines, historic and contemporary uses, Elizabeth Barlow Rogers, the former Central Park administrator, was criticized on one hand for fealty to Olmsted and Vaux in attempting to re-

Historic aerial view of the Benjamin Franklin Parkway in Philadelphia (c. 1940s), showing red oak allées as originally proposed in the Jacques Gréber plan of 1917. Source: This image, acquired in 1993 by LANDSCAPES of Charlotte, Vermont, from the Fairmount Park Commission of Philadelphia, is no longer available in the commission's files.

store the park and on the other for her accommodations to modern recreation or the restoration of buildings at the expense of necessary improvements to infrastructure and the landscape. Across the East River, in Brooklyn's Prospect Park, Park Administrator Tupper Thomas struck a compromise with contemporary uses of the southern end of the Long Meadow, the largest and most distinctive space within the park: She moved the infields of baseball diamonds to the periphery of the meadow, where they would be screened from view from the north, and removed all fences and other structures that intruded upon the lawn.[17] To a remarkable extent the result respects the striking visual character of the Long Meadow and also accommodates modern recreation.

The intensity of some uses has had a detrimental effect on historic urban landscapes. The Benjamin Franklin Parkway is a broad urban boulevard connecting City Hall and the Philadelphia Museum of Art at the gateway to Fairmount Park. The Trumbauer, Zantinger, and Cret plan, commissioned by the Fairmount Park Art Association in 1907, envisioned a parkway that would extend diagonally northwest from the downtown civic and business area through a grouping of institutions devoted to educational pursuits at Logan Square to an artistic center at Fairmount Plaza and the entrance to Fairmount Park. This parkway was to be the American equivalent of the Parisian Champs Élysées, lined with grand civic buildings. This early plan was not implemented, but by 1917 the Fairmount Park commissioners had adopted a highly articulated, formal plan by Jacques Gréber. Unfortunately, annual festivals drawing over a half million people to the Benjamin Franklin Parkway had struck a death knell to its double rows of red oak trees by 1987. Soil compaction, electrical wiring, basal damage from automobiles, and the attendant weakening of the trees brought disease and death.

The details of the rehabilitation approach included the choice of three species (red oak, red maple, and sweet gum) to replace the red oak monocul-

By 1987, after the death and decay of the red oak monoculture along the Benjamin Franklin Parkway, new red maple, sweet gum, and red oak trees were planted in continuous trenches rather than in pits. Photograph by LANDSCAPES, Charlotte, Vermont.

UNCOMPACTED PLANTING SOIL

COMPACTED PLANTING SOIL

As the soil compacts, the large stones will keep the matrix of soil loose preventing soil fines from packing together and therefore allowing gas exchange and drainage to occur.

Benjamin Franklin Parkway
Fairmount Park Commission
South Street Design Company

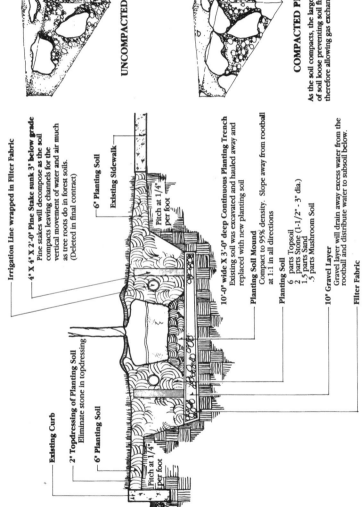

Irrigation Line wrapped in Filter Fabric

4' X 4' X 2'-0" Pine Stake sunk 3" below grade
Pine stakes will decompose as the soil compacts leaving channels for the vertical movement of water and air much as tree roots do in forest soils.
(Deleted in final contract)

6" Planting Soil

Existing Sidewalk

Pitch at 1/4"
per foot

10'-0" wide X 3'-0" deep Continuous Planting Trench
Existing soil was excavated and hauled away and replaced with new planting soil

Planting Soil Mound
Compact to 95% density. Slope away from rootball at 1:1 in all directions

Planting Soil
6   parts Topsoil
2   parts Stone (1-1/2" - 3" dia.)
1.5 parts Sand
.5 parts Mushroom Soil

10" Gravel Layer
Gravel layer will drain away excess water from the rootball and distribute water to subsoil below.

Filter Fabric

Existing Curb

2" Topdressing of Planting Soil
Eliminate stone in topdressing

6" Planting Soil

Pitch at 1/4"
per foot

CONTINUOUS TRENCH PLANTING

1/2" = 1'-0"

Detail of the trench planting used along the Benjamin Franklin Parkway to provide as much room as possible for tree root growth.
Source: South Street Design Company, Philadelphia.

ture. The selection of these mixed plantings resulted from the need to diversify to avoid blights and diseases that had, in the past, destroyed entire formal, urban tree features. The trees chosen had comparable upright forms with straight trunks, medium foliage, and branch texture, so that species diversity would not compromise the intended formality of the avenue. The environment for the trees was designed to improve tree health with continuous trenches rather than pits. Trenches six feet in width were excavated three and a half feet deep and backfilled with a compaction-resistant soil mix to provide for the health of the tree roots while allowing intense use.[18]

Another example of innovative planning to bridge historic and modern uses occurred in Baltimore's Druid Hill Park. Originally designed by Howard Daniels in 1860 and altered under plans prepared by Olmsted Brothers in the twentieth century, for most of its history Druid Hill Park was segregated. African American residents have vivid memories of the swimming pool, tennis courts, playgrounds, and picnic areas, all of which were part of the fabric of neighborhood life. The preservation planning process, completed in 1995, included a broad cross section of community members, many of whom were African Americans. The first project to commence construction will be the "Negro Pool" area. Today the pool is deteriorated and unused. The plan for the area calls for filling the pool space with a grass panel, repairing or replacing the concrete pool deck and the grand entry stairway, and creating a seating area and perhaps a shelter as part of an interpretive program on Baltimore's African American community and the city's segregationist era. When completed, the project will preserve in tangible form the heritage of twentieth-century race relations. Projects in other cities that focus on issues of ethnic, racial, and gender histories contribute to the significance of our urban landscapes.[19]

Still other uses compete for park space because it is publicly owned and accessible. Museums, historical societies, zoos, and other cultural institutions have been located in parks since the nineteenth century, but as they have grown in size the demand for additional park space and the degree to which their buildings intrude upon the landscape have provoked controversy. So has the location of statues, memorials, and other works of public art within historic parks and the construction of massive gateways on their perimeter. Whether perceived as valuable additions to or detractions from the landscape, these represent a different conception of the park as civic space and usually incorporate an aesthetic different from that of the historic landscape.

If parks have always been contested space, the intensity of competition for use has increased in recent years. Perhaps the best example of the recurring debate over appropriate use of park space is Tompkins Square in lower Man-

The segregation-era "Negro Pool" in Baltimore's Druid Hill Park is currently deteriorated and unused. Future plans project that it will be redeveloped as a memorial landscape commemorating the history of the local African American community. Source: L A N D S C A P E S, Charlotte, Vermont.

hattan. Bounded by Avenues A and B and Seventh and Tenth Streets, the site of Tompkins Square was designated for a public market in the Commissioners Plan of 1811. The square was dedicated for park use in 1834, and some time thereafter the city erected a fountain in the square and planted trees and grass. In 1866, however, the state legislature enacted a law making Tompkins Square a parade ground, as the area designated for parades in Central Park had never been used by militia, even during the Civil War. At that time the fountain and all trees except those on the periphery were removed from the square. Military use of the park quickly destroyed the grass, and in 1868 the parade was paved with a composition of pitch and sand, which quickly proved disastrous. Neighbors objected to the parade ground and wanted the park returned to its former function as a pleasure ground. In 1873, when "working-boys" petitioned the park commission for permission to play baseball on the square, mothers of small children protested that such use would render the park unsuitable for their needs. The following year, in the midst of an economic panic, unemployed workingmen seeking jobs from the city organized a demonstration in the square and battled police in what labor organizer Samuel Gompers described as an "orgy of brutality." In 1875 Olmsted prepared a design for Tompkins Square that attempted to reconcile military and different types of recreational uses, but that plan could not possibly provide adequate space for the many different kinds of activities desired by residents.[20]

Thus the competition for park use continued in succeeding years. Given its proximity to the tenements of the Lower East Side and the scarcity of open space at the southern end of Manhattan Island, Tompkins Square became a vibrant center of community life for East European immigrants. In the 1930s, when Robert Moses attempted to place baseball diamonds in the park, residents succeeded in reducing the scale and impact of those facilities for active recreation on other park uses. More recently, with the depopulation of the Lower East Side, Tompkins Square has become the focal point of city efforts to rout the homeless who had erected tents and shanties there and more broadly of many residents' resistance to the gentrification of the neighborhood.[21]

What is striking is the degree to which the battle between police and the array of homeless and other defenders of contemporary uses of Tompkins Square continues a longstanding pattern of conflict over appropriate use of the space. The meaning and purpose of the space has varied over time and among different groups competing for its use. Central Park, Elizabeth Hawes has observed, "is and has always been sacred ground, and New Yorkers feel personal, possessive and protective" about it.[22] In varying degrees, the same is true for all historic parks.

One person's historic preservation is, to another, the loss of a precious natural environment or a favorite recreational facility, but a common ground that honors both is being found. Clearly, over the years historic parks have developed many constituencies, each of which has come to consider its use paramount to other considerations. A stewardship ethic that addresses shared use and reduction of conflict, that builds consensus among all stakeholders, is critical to historic landscape preservation.

| *The Influence of the Automobile*

Still another change affecting historic landscapes has been the rise of the automobile. The great nineteenth- and early twentieth-century parks, as well as many other historic urban landscapes, were designed before widespread ownership of the automobile. Olmsted and Vaux included carriage drives and equestrian paths in Central and Prospect Parks and placed a pleasure drive in Riverside Park, to be sure, but they anticipated that driving in the parks would be a leisurely pursuit. As traffic congestion increased with automobile registrations, park drives were opened to cars, which introduced new levels of noise, pollution, and speed into what had been a serene landscape. The first automobile fatalities in Central Park occurred in 1906, when three people died in a crash.[23] As the number of motorized vehicles using park drives increased, road surfaces were widened and paved with asphalt, traffic lights installed, and speed limits established. In Central Park, the widening of drives necessitated the destruction of the Marble Arch, which had led pedestrians entering the park from the southeast under the drive to the Mall and the interior. Ironically, to accommodate the automobile, park administrators eliminated important elements of separation of ways at the very time when the increasing volume and speed of traffic made the park more dangerous to pedestrians.

Efforts to accommodate the automobile have devastated some historic parks. The 200-foot-wide Humboldt Parkway in Buffalo became a sunken inner-city expressway in the 1960s; Riverside Park in Hartford, Connecticut, was severed from its community by a raised embankment for Interstate 91; and Genesee Valley Park in Rochester, New York, was bisected by Interstate 390 and its associated concrete sound walls. High-speed, limited access roadways in Manhattan's Riverside Park and Philadelphia's Fairmount Park effectively severed pedestrians from one of the most precious assets of each city, a waterfront of incalculable recreational value. New Yorker Peter Black has bitterly observed, "In place of great parks and terraces and promenades, we have built, along almost every single foot of the coastline of this city, gigantic viaducts of steel and concrete that carry streams of automobiles and effectively block our view of the water, a passing steamer, a seagull or, possibly, a sunrise."[24]

The threat presented by the automobile has not been limited to historic parks. A ten-year citizen-based struggle succeeded in defeating the proposed highway to the Jimmy Carter Presidential Library that would have enlarged and altered the Olmsted drives through the Druid Hills subdivision of Atlanta, Georgia. Still another effect of the automobile on historic landscapes has been the degrading effect of poor air quality and acid rains on park plantings and monuments. The roads encircling the Lincoln Memorial in Washington, D.C., have been closed periodically to reduce the effects of pollution on the marble. A recent study of the Lancaster Cemetery in Pennsylvania by geology students at Franklin & Marshall College demonstrated that older tombstones located close to adjacent roads are deteriorating at a more rapid rate than elsewhere in the burial ground.

In some public spaces today, such as Piedmont Park in Atlanta and Iroquois Park in Louisville, much of the former drive system is closed to private vehicles and the space is shared by pedestrians, joggers, bicyclists, and in-line skaters. In other cities, wide park roadways have become shared routes for multimodal movement patterns. The emphasis on integrated transportation systems, rather than still more highway building, required by the Intermodal Surface Transit Efficiency Act (ISTEA) and its successor, the Transportation Equity Act for the Twenty-first Century (TEA 21), presents an opportunity to develop bicycle and pedestrian routes and linkages to historic urban landscapes.

Public Safety and Vandalism

Questions of public safety and vandalism are also critical for urban landscapes of all kinds. Unfortunately, the measures taken to prevent the occurrence of crime can be antithetical to the historic character of a place. The problem of crime in parks is not new. In February 1858, when Olmsted received authorization to organize a force of Central Park keepers, he knew that public safety was "the most vulnerable point" in the development of the park. Because of its irregular terrain, dense plantings, and "sylvan seclusion," Olmsted recognized the "danger of the misuse of the park for criminal ends."[25] Thus, his and Vaux's design was predicated on three principles: that the majority of park users would be law-abiding citizens; that the park would be closed at night, when it was most dangerous; and that, during the hours it was open to the public, the park would be patrolled by an energetic, disciplined force of park keepers. These were not police in the strict sense of the term, because their most important purpose was to instruct the public in the proper use of the park. In the early years of Central Park, the keepers' maintenance of order resulted in a small number of arrests, but by the early 1870s public safety had become a concern, particularly after October 1872, when the first murder occurred in the park.[26]

As park users have come to resemble the demographic complexion of the city and as society itself has become more violent, public safety has become a major concern. Fully one-fourth of all employees working in Central Park in April 1984 were responsible for safety and security, at a cost ten times greater than the total capital expenditures for a normal year. Clearly, the fear of crime has redirected resources away from essential maintenance and renewal projects and toward safety. Because of the topography and design of most historic parks and cemeteries, as well as increasing levels of violence throughout society, the perception of personal danger will continue to be a problem. The actual number of criminal occurrences within parks is generally lower than that in surrounding urban neighborhoods, but sometimes, as in the highly publicized rape and disfigurement of a Central Park jogger in 1989, the actual events attract media attention and perpetuate a sense of fear. Experience has demonstrated the importance of strategies for increasing safety and the public's perception of safety. The following principles have proven effective in eliminating or alleviating the fear of crime in public spaces:

—Public landscapes must be better maintained and appear well cared for, as dereliction and litter encourage fear rather than comfort.
—Public landscapes must be protected more effectively with security patrols.
—Furnishings can be made more durable through vandal-resistant detailing.
—Repairs must be made in a timely manner when damage occurs.
—Park users must be educated about the value of historic, public open spaces to gain a sense of respect and stewardship for shared resources.

In some cities interdepartmental task forces are learning from each other and amplifying their staffing resources, undertaking public education campaigns, and enhancing repair techniques to combat repeated vandalism.

| *Urban Cemeteries*

A somewhat different pattern of use and preservation issues affects many historic cemeteries. The nineteenth-century "rural cemeteries" were created in response to a variety of factors, including dramatic urban growth, the closing of older churchyard cemeteries because of the lack of space and concern for the public health, and new attitudes toward death. Incorporating many of the same aesthetic characteristics later adopted by park designers, "rural cemeteries" quickly became favorite resorts for residents. Andrew Jackson Downing praised Laurel Hill Cemetery, outside Philadelphia, as a "charming *pleasure-ground*" and described Green-Wood Cemetery, in Brooklyn, as "grand, dignified, and park-like." Rural cemeteries, Downing wrote, were "the first really elegant public gardens or promenades formed in this country," and so people used them. In the absence of public recreational areas in the neighborhoods of cities, many visitors frequented rural cemeteries to escape the confines of the urban environment.[27] Despite what a writer in *Scribner's Monthly* termed a "certain incongruity between a graveyard and a place of recreation," many residents of cities went to rural cemeteries "to get fresh air, and a sight of grass and trees and flowers."[28]

In the twentieth century, however, as passive recreation gave way to more active leisure, visits to cemeteries became rare events. The breadth of landscape appreciated by nineteenth-century visitors has been replaced by acres and acres of tombstones even as the neighborhoods surrounding many once-

Since many urban cemeteries, as illustrated by this example from Boston, no longer have social ties to their neighborhoods, they often are neglected and vandalized. Source: LANDSCAPES, Charlotte, Vermont.

rural cemeteries became more urban. Woodward Hill Cemetery in Lancaster, Pennsylvania, for example, was established in 1851. At that time located at a distance from the densely built part of the community, today it is surrounded by row houses and the seemingly obligatory florist's shop. The population, now principally African American and Hispanic, feels little attachment to the history the cemetery commemorates, which includes the graves of James Buchanan, fifteenth president of the United States, and generations of Lancaster families. Vandalism in the cemetery has reached crisis proportions as the plague of drugs and crime has affected the surrounding neighborhood. Despite the efforts of a concerned board of directors and a small group of volunteers, what in the nineteenth century was a sacred space and an emblem of civic pride has become a place to be avoided.[29] The same is true of numerous other historic urban cemeteries.

In Boston, however, a comprehensive program to address its historic urban burying grounds and cemeteries has led to their rehabilitation. Since several cemeteries are on the Boston Freedom Trail, these tourist attractions have received interpretive signage and new pathways. The Burying Grounds Initiative has also garnered some project funding to address tomb and marker deterioration. Larger neighborhood cemeteries have been rehabilitated effectively with neighborhood involvement and have become more vital local open spaces. At Dorchester Heights Cemetery, for example, deteriorated stone walls were partially removed and replaced with more open iron fencing to provide views into the cemetery. As a result, criminal uses decreased and neighborhood uses increased. The entire system of burying grounds and cemeteries has become a destination for visitors, the subject of special tours and training programs, and a source of community pride.

| *Preserving Urban Public Landscapes for Today and Tomorrow*

The fate of historic urban parks and cemeteries is inextricably linked to the communities of which they are a part. Together, the changing demographic complexion of cities, the increasing nuisances of urban life, and the fear of crime have contributed to the flight to suburbia and the erosion of public culture. In 1870 Olmsted asserted that public parks were the most democratic social spaces in the United States. Central and Prospect Parks were the only places in their respective cities, he informed a Boston audience, where "all classes [are] largely represented, with a common purpose, not at all intellectual, competitive with none, disposing to jealousy and spiritual or intellectual pride toward none, each individual adding by his mere presence to the pleasure of all others, all helping to the greater happiness of each."[30] The park, he believed, had become the place of resort for all classes, and as population growth brought millions of residents to within walking distance, Central and Prospect Parks did indeed function much as he had anticipated.

Olmsted envisioned the park as the centerpiece of a vigorous public culture. One of the most striking changes to affect America's cities since World War II has been the retreat to the private sphere, the withdrawal from urban life, and with it the erosion of public culture. According to sociologist Richard Sennett, "two consequences of the search for refuge" have been "an increase in isolation and in inequality."[31] Another casualty has been the widely shared agreement that public open spaces are important. While efforts in some cities have raised awareness and resulted in broad recognition of value, many historic landscapes are without a strong constituency and continue to be seen as dangerous places to be avoided or as blank spaces waiting for development. Critically important components of the nation's landscape heritage, spaces that are essential to the quality of urban life, remain at risk.

Historic urban parks and cemeteries are a precious legacy belonging to all Americans. As is true of the vast majority of cultural landscapes, these open spaces within cities are often the result not simply of a single design but of generations of adaptations. To paraphrase Colin Rowe and Fred Koetter, they are multilayered accretions that have evolved over time.[32] Indeed, if anything has

CITY OF BOSTON
Boston Parks & Recreation Dept.

Raymond L. Flynn
Mayor

Lawrence A. Dwyer
Commissioner

Invite you to attend a

COMMUNITY MEETING

To discuss clean up and preservation activities at

Dorchester North Burial Ground

Thurs., September 7, 1989

7:00 pm

The meeting will be held at
Dorchester Historical Society
195 Boston St.
Dorchester

All are welcome to attend
For more information call 725-4505

This 1989 flyer put out by the Boston Burying Grounds Initiative demonstrates that community participation is solicited as a crucial part of urban landscape preservation. Source: Boston Parks & Recreation Department.

been constant in the history of urban landscapes, it is change. Thus, the most basic problem in the preservation of historic urban landscapes is determining what history should be preserved. The cornerstone of historic preservation is the recognition, in detail, of what remains that is truly historic. We can only preserve what remains—repairing, stabilizing, restoring, or reconstructing these features and components of the past. In urban public landscapes the approach must be determined in a consensus-building planning process that goes beyond simple consent to active participation in renewal. Physical planning that lacks broad support will remain a report rather than a renewed historic landscape. As change continues to accrete new layers, the historic character of our urban landscape must be thoroughly researched, clearly recognized, eloquently articulated, and embraced by the landscape's owners, stewards, and users. Only then can the whole cloth or remaining fragments of our shared cultural history in the land be safeguarded, while necessary resources are committed and current and future needs are served.

Appropriating Place in Puerto Rican Barrios

Preserving Contemporary Urban Landscapes

> The power of place—the power of ordinary urban landscapes to nurture citizens' public memory, to encompass shared time in the form of shared territory—remains untapped for most working people's neighborhoods in most American cities, and for most ethnic history and most women's history. The sense of civic identity that shared history can convey is missing. —Hayden, *The Power of Place*

LUIS
APONTE-PARÉS

We live "where space and time cross to produce complex figures of difference and identity, past and present, inside and outside, inclusion and exclusion."[1] One important example of this phenomenon is our failure to recognize and examine the Latino contribution to the urban cultural landscape of the United States. Indeed, the long history of people of Hispanic descent in North America remains a puzzle to most people. Awareness is lacking despite the fact that people of Hispanic descent, before the arrival of the Mayflower in Massachusetts in 1620, had already shaped cultural landscapes in the Caribbean, in Central and South America, and in North America, where their influence was evident west of the Mississippi, extending as far as Oregon, and also in Florida in the south. Their concealed voices have now come forward to claim spaces and a place in the urban narratives of cities in the United States.

Latino urban history, notably the history of Puerto Ricans in New York City, has been poorly documented. Puerto Ricans and other Latinos are absent from most accounts of the history of the city and remain generally invisible. The spaces and places created by the settlement of Puerto Ricans over the past century have been all but destroyed, with an attendant loss of memory: they represent a "deterritorialized" community.[2] This loss compounds the common view that all Latinos are immigrants, that they have not contributed to the development of the city, and that somehow Latinos do not have a place in the city's history.[3] Nevertheless, the demographic explosion of Latinos in the city and elsewhere and their increased political activism have made it all but impossible to keep them invisible. The increased Latino presence now intersects with profound changes in the cultural landscapes of American cities. Latinos continue to contribute to the development of cultural landscapes in these cities by appropriating neighborhoods and producing environments that narrate their history.

This is the case of Villa Puerto Rico, a *casita*, or little house, in the South Bronx built by Jaran Manzanet. When I last talked to Jaran, in 1996, his face filled with joyful pride as he showed photographs of the latest party held at his casita. He recalled building it with his family and neighbors at 142nd Street and Saint Ann in the South Bronx some years back and christening it, evocatively, Villa Puerto Rico.[4] Looking through those recent images, Jaran told us of the many times that Villa Puerto Rico had served the neighborhood as a place for celebrations and get-togethers of all kinds: birthday parties, Puerto Rican Day Parade ceremonies, Thanksgiving dinners, block association meetings, political rallies, and so forth. Like the many memorable events, the casita itself is a source of pride and memory—it articulates and validates the community's Puerto Rican identity in space.

Villa Puerto Rico embodies, in emblematic ways, the endurance of Puerto Rican culture in New York and the strength of Jaran and his neighbors in appropriating the environment and conferring meaning on it by building alternative landscapes throughout the devastated urban milieu. On 142nd Street and throughout the South Bronx, East Harlem (el Barrio), the Lower East Side (Loisaida), and Brooklyn, casitas stand as cogent metaphors of place and culture.

Casitas belong to a family of balloon-frame wooden structures (shacks, bungalows, or cottages) generally associated with Third World vernacular architecture.[5] Built on stilts and often surrounded by a vegetable garden, they can be identified by their corrugated metal gable roofs, shuttered windows, bright colors, and ample verandas, so favored in the Caribbean. This architecture took shape during the nineteenth century, when increased trade between the Caribbean and the United States led to exchanges of people and culture, bringing about the transformation and modernization of the islands' traditional, or vernacular, architecture.[6]

Casitas built in New York have specific roots in Puerto Rico and are generally located in neighborhoods that witnessed massive population displacement over the past three decades and now suffer from extreme poverty. In these neighborhoods, large tracts of empty land are surrounded by abandoned tenements and the ubiquitous "tower-in-the-park" enclaves, legacies of government housing paradigms that were envisioned, perhaps, as instruments that helped "eradicate the most vocal and visible pockets of non-white inner-city life" and were so successful in fracturing the city.[7]

Two casitas on 119th Street in el Barrio, Manhattan, which formerly were part of a group of eight units very heavily utilized by residents during the spring and summer months. The casita shown close up was painted bright red and provided a small social space for one family. In 1996 the entire group of casitas was demolished by New York City officials who feared that some people would utilize them as permanent homes and thus generate a squatters' settlement. Photograph by Aponte-Parés, c. 1992.

| *Displacement and Replacement and the Architecture of Resistance*

Jaran's smile betrays the deeper role and complex meaning assumed by these humble structures in the lives of his fellow Puerto Ricans in New York City. As industrial jobs relocated from New York to other parts of the world, significant numbers of the displaced industrial workers and their families, many of them Puerto Ricans and African Americans, were not integrated into the new economy, leading to sharp increases in their poverty rate, decreased labor participation, increased dependence on transfer payments, and an overall decline in their standard of living.[8] The inability of the new economy to incorporate fully these displaced workers and the added pressures exerted by the influx of new immigrants have led to growing numbers of New Yorkers being connected with the "informal," "floating," illegal, or underground/street economy—a language closely associated with Third World countries rather than with the metropolis.[9] This is reflected in changes in the landscape; there is an increased presence of street vendors, illegal sweatshops, and an assortment of unregulated jobs accompanied by squatters, cardboard condos or "Bushvilles," and casitas—all of which make up the new alternative, informal urban landscapes of the postindustrial city.

At the same time, massive dislocations impacted many neighborhoods throughout New York, with the loss of hundreds of thousands of homes. Declining numbers of ethnic minorities and poor and working-class households in some Manhattan districts,[10] furthermore, is evidence of their displacement from select neighborhoods that now enjoy renewed investment value under the emerging economic logic of New York as a "control center(s) of the global economy," a World City, with Manhattan as its center.[11] Not all neighborhoods fared equally. Some became surplus with diminished value to the financial hub; el Barrio, for example, lost close to one-third of its structures. Others, like Loisaida, experienced gentrification. Still others in the outer boroughs became new or reconfigured "borderlands." These high-density ethnic enclaves burst with the dynamism and energy of a Third World metropolis like New Delhi, Mexico City, or Sao Paulo.

The losses, of course, were not only of buildings and people but also of primary "life spaces," places in which people's "dreams were made, and their lives unfolded."[12] This signaled the detachment of a people from their most recent history, their memories (*sus memorias*), rendering them invisible and making them guests, visitors in the very neighborhoods to which they were forcibly relocated. The dislocation also represented a loss of place. The decline and loss of institutions, bodegas, churches, social centers, schools, friends, and neighbors led to a collective need to play an active role in rearranging the environ-ment and thereby restore the community's sense of well-being.

These transformations have led to sharper contrasts in the everyday spaces of New York, a divergence in the quality of life among various neighborhoods, perhaps greater than ever before, and the rise of a unique form of American urban apartheid—"fortress cities" brutally divided into "fortified cells of af-fluence" and "places of terror" where police battle the criminalized poor.[13] As class polarization increases, there is an increasing inequality in the ability of different populations to choose where to build and appropriate place and to establish a foundation for their identity as people in a neighborhood.

Thus, casitas are built by the disenfranchised urban poor who live in land-scapes of pollution, joblessness, and violence, who are increasingly invisible to the rest of society, and who represent the underside of the "triad imagery of post-industrial landscapes like Silicon Valley, i.e. ecology, leisure, and liv-ability."[14] Predictably, these are the same people who are unable to "buy" man-ufactured landscapes or are left out of information circuits/highways; they represent "lag-times—temporary breaks in the imaginary matrix"—of the new city.[15] Paradoxically, in cybercity—the city with no ostensible material spatial needs, the virtual electronic city of computers, modems, and electronic highways that link virtually every place on the globe—the need for meaning-ful and precious places that validate cultural identities in space may have in-creased.

It was to address these needs that Jaran and others like him and their fam-ilies chose to take an active role in reshaping landscapes of despair into land-scapes of hope. By transforming fragmented and discontinuous urban land-scapes into "cultural forms with continuity" that are rich in values and that bring forth a sense of "attachment"—a feeling of "congruence of culture and landscape"—they are, perhaps, provided with a sense of regional identity.[16] The key to this attachment is the ability to take possession of the environment through simultaneous physical orientation and a more profound identifica-tion.

But Jaran and other builders of casitas can hardly boast the means to build any model communities; their will to reshape is tempered by meager resources and their recent history. Their language is thus limited to one of circumscribed impact, where holding ground, turf, *rescatar,* takes on the primary role, a true architecture of resistance that subverts the traditional city. The casita, like the ubiquitous Puerto Rican flag, becomes a vehicle through which its builders articulate and defend their national identity and their *imagined community,*[17] their innate essence determining who they are.

| *The Puerto Rican Experience: From Bodegas to Casitas*

Since arriving in New York City in the early decades of the twentieth century, Puerto Ricans have defied severe housing problems, involuntary resettlement, or displacement—with the last being the most disruptive. After a half-century of slowly giving shape, character, and meaning to many "life spaces" in places like East Harlem, the Lower East Side, Bellevue, Chelsea, Lincoln Square, or Hells Kitchen, Puerto Ricans began to lose even this weak control over their environment.

From the 1950s through the mid-1970s, urban renewal and the private market intersected to accelerate displacement, inducing a "process of loss, rupture, and deterritorialization" within an entire community.[18] Building community was less an act of settling and shaping neighborhoods into ethnic enclaves and more a resettlement process of a people being expelled repeatedly by the relocation officers of city agencies, unscrupulous landlords, or the heat of the last fire. This removal of buildings and people resulted in the "erasure" of images that recorded Latino presence in New York, including the destruction of contributions they had made to the built environment, the replacement of historical and environmental narratives, and the loss of memory.[19]

By choosing names like *Villa Puerto Rico, El Jaragual, Añoranzas de mi Patria,* and *Rincón Criollo,* casita builders introduce and defend the possibility of place, both physical and metaphorical. In addition to reoccupying abandoned and misused territory, the practice of building casitas imparts identity to the urban landscape by rescuing images (*rescatándo imágenes*) and by alluding to the power of other places that are recognized by everyone, that generate good will among everyone, and that provide a source of identity for everyone.

Building casitas is an act of reterritorialization that both affirms the power of culture in space and offers resistance to further deterritorialization. Casitas become place to displaced people, new "urban bedouins" who are removed from other places.[20] Perhaps they also become new *invented traditions,*[21] new segregated "public arenas" in which "the other" can congregate and celebrate their self-identity in a city where their invisibility in the public discourse renders many of them non-*personae,* at best, or *personae non gratae,* at worst, and where unifying and inclusive images of the urban narrative seem to be fading daily.

Puerto Rican migration patterns have been fundamental to the development of casitas. As colonial citizens of the United States, Puerto Ricans circu-

Los Vecinos (*top*), a casita on 119th Street in el Barrio, Manhattan, has evolved through many reconstructions. It was originally "owned" by a large family living on the same block, but the City of New York demolished the structure in 1997 and forced the owners to rebuild a facade that looks like a casita. The photograph reveals the juxtaposition of Caribbean vernacular and a major low-income housing project called Taíno Towers. The Villa Puerto Rico in the South Bronx (*bottom*), which provides a major social space for the block, is surrounded by abandoned tenements and a new middle-income housing enclave. The view also depicts the juxtaposition of a Caribbean vernacular form with leftovers of the industrial city. Photograph by Aponte-Parés, c. 1992.

late freely between two spaces, colony and metropolis, thus circumventing or destroying traditional barriers associated with borders, or *fronteras.* This condition has provided several generations ongoing contact with "fresh" images of the *otra Patria,* the "other country or homeland," which allows a fluid exchange of people, culture, and images. Luis Rafael Sánchez has articulated these sentiments: "On the airbus . . . Puerto Ricans who are there but dream of being here . . . Puerto Ricans who are permanently installed in the wander-go round between here and there and who must therefore informalize the trip, making it no more than a hop on a bus, though airborne, that floats over the creek to which the Atlantic Ocean has been reduced by the Puerto Ricans."[22]

La Guagua Aérea, the "airbus," permits boundaries to be continuously crossed and transformed, created, and erased. Time is disordered—the before and after confuse their sequential logic—a "journey [that] goes not only from South to North, [but] from Spanish to English,"[23] and becomes an agent linking contiguous social realities: Puerto Rico and Nueva York. East Harlem and La Perla, a shanty area in San Juan, become adjacent and culturally closer than East Harlem and Battery Park City. Hence, casita builders, when introducing the casita language to Nueva York, do more than just provide places for the local neighborhood; they also release a new urban language, a Caribbean vernacular, the language of Third World *favelas,* squatters, shanties, *arrabales,* or *villas miserias.*

There is something ominous about the presence of casitas on the streets of New York, something that is threatening to many people who may otherwise live in relative security. The abiding message of the casita is one of shelter, a squatter's metaphor that many find disturbing, particularly in the increasing presence of the wandering homeless in the most advanced and richest urban center in the world. Casitas signal that the visual discourse of *favelas, arrabales, comunidades marginadas*—the destitute slums ringing the periphery of Third World cities—has its place in the urban vocabulary of the developed world, alongside concocted theme parks and the places for the rich, all of which form "dreamscapes of visual consumption."[24] Casitas become "conquered space," where the "separation of the Puerto Rican Diaspora is defeated."[25]

Whether they instill fear or joyful pride, casitas add fascination to the visual texture of the New York landscape. They break with traditional cultural models usually associated with European-derived architectural and urban forms, reweaving the otherwise ordinary modern industrial city with what many would consider traditional or premodern cultural images. These images are made possible by the spaces created in the emerging "borderlands" of the postmodern city.

| *Popular Dwellings and Changing Urban Landscapes*

Casitas represent the amalgamation of architectural styles and building techniques from Europe and North America with those of two other cultures—
the Amerindians, who contributed the hut (*bohío*), and the Africans, who gave
the *bohío* its final configuration in the plantation hut. Casitas evoke a pan-
Caribbean language, shared among all the islands (although manifested
somewhat differently in each) and regions that were in close trading contact
with them in the late nineteenth and early twentieth centuries.[26]

Before Columbus arrived in the Caribbean, Puerto Rico was called
Borikén; it was home to the Taíno, descendants of Arawak cultures. The Taíno
lived in *yucayeques,* nucleations whose principal structures were the *caney,* the
cacique's home, and the *bohío,* the common hut; *yucayeques* were organized
around a central open plaza, the *batey.*

Between 1509, with the founding of Caparra, the first European settlement
in Puerto Rico, and 1535, when the conquest of the continent began, somewhere between five thousand and fifty thousand people were conquered and
permanently displaced. In their initial effort to control the conquered, the
Spanish destroyed all *yucayeques,* resettling the people of Puerto Rico into *encomiendas* (medieval institutions transformed into compounds for the purpose of colonization), where they were enslaved to mine for gold. The attendant loss of place and identity contributed to the eventual eradication of the
Taíno.

The invaders soon abandoned the island and their *encomiendas,* but only
after having demolished the territorial systems of the indigenous people. *Bohíos* and a reconstituted *batey* endured, nonetheless, as the common dwelling
and the fundamental cultural space, albeit at a personal, family scale, particularly in the countryside. In time, this became associated with the yard adjacent to the peasant's home. The *bohío* and *batey* became the foundations of a
Puerto Rican vernacular that expressed its dual parentage: the Taíno and the
African.

Between 1535 and 1830 the *mestizaje,* or crossbreeding, of the Taíno, African,
and Spanish cultures occurred as the island slowly repopulated. In these years,
the two major spatiocultural arenas were the farm and town. The farm (homestead) was isolated and severely limited by the island's mountainous topography. *Bohíos* and, later on, *casas de hacendados* were the principal structures
in the self-contained social and economic compounds of haciendas throughout the centuries.

Towns had a major public place, usually an unadorned plaza, often not
more than a clearing at the center. The plaza was surrounded by the symbols

of European power—church and *cabildo*—the religious and civil governmental buildings that formed the core of the meager new civic life. The plaza was also where informal markets and religious festivities occurred. It mediated between the town and its hinterland, while attesting to the hegemony of European culture over the island's landscapes, demonstrating the relationship between the "landscapes of the powerful and the subordinate." [27] The presence of the church and *cabildo* was always a counterforce to an island whose economic isolation had forced most of its people into a subsistence agriculture that retained many characteristics of the indigenous Taínos, that is, the culture of yucca and casaba.

This territorial differentiation made for sharper class demarcation in housing structures, particularly between the *bohíos* of the *jíbaros,* or rural peasants, and the casas of the townspeople, usually clergy, artisans, merchants, and military. Casas were made of wood or masonry, emulating Spanish or other European architectural styles, with those owned by merchants being the most elaborate. *Bohíos* were the pre-Columbian huts that the peasant-slaves had appropriated; their building characteristics, which retained an organic relationship to the local ecology, changed very slowly, with their builders adhering to traditional building methods. [28] The quality of *bohíos* varied in relation to their owner's social position; those of slaves and the landless, *agregados,* were possibly the most rustic and least evolved from the original Taíno dwelling.

One pictorial record of this differentiation is found in *El Velorio,* a painting made in 1893 by the Puerto Rican artist Francisco Oller. *El Velorio* depicts a peasant child's wake, a *jíbaro* celebration emulating a *Baquiné,* an African traditional ritual. [29] The site of the celebration is not a large public place, like a church building or a plaza, but a *jíbaro's* home, which comprises a *bohío* (a small, rustic, single-room hut) and possibly an outside room, the *batey.* The *bohío* depicted in the painting has a wooden floor isolating the structure from the terrain and thereby protecting it from the elements, a significant improvement over early Taíno huts built on compacted dirt. Doors and windows have double shutters, a clear reference to Spanish architecture. The walls, although framed by tree trunks, are covered by a skin of commercial-grade wood on the outside. It appears that the house has a balcony or veranda on one side. The hut is covered by tree trunks that support a more humble thatch roof. Apparently the *bohío* is still a one-room configuration. Although sparse, the furniture depicted in the painting—a comfortable chair and a wooden table covered with lace—suggests that the family either has some economic means or borrowed these pieces for the occasion.

The bohío in *El Velorio* had become a new structure, an emerging vernacular combining cultural elements from three sources: from the Taíno, the hut; from Africans, the ritual and the building hands; and from the Spanish, the furnishings and the structure with the added veranda. It coincided with the birth of a national identity that evolved throughout the nineteenth century. It codified a rural emblem—a narrative of the transition from folk to popular culture, from a precapitalist to a capitalist society—an emblem that survived throughout the twentieth century.

The *jíbaro's* home had become the center of his life, an integral part of the declining subsistence existence that had been the dominant economic mode of the island for over three hundred years of Spanish colonial rule. To people who are deeply rural like the *jíbaros,* their isolation on farms was a centripetal force bonding them to their land and neighbors. Events like that depicted in *El Velorio* provided social and cultural bonding in the most important of the ordinary landscapes of the period: the rural *bohío* and the *batey,* which suggest poverty as well as independence.[30]

| *Urban and Rural Casitas*

In the nineteenth century the spectacular growth of commercial agriculture brought unequaled wealth to the poor island, incorporated Puerto Rico into world markets, and brought it into ever closer interaction with other cultures, particularly the United States. The island's territorial systems were reshaped to facilitate the production of commodities for export. In the early port cities, Europeans and Creole elites managed trade and gained power and prestige over the rest of the island. By the early twentieth century, the collapsing coffee economy resulted in massive migration from the *altura,* or highlands. Meanwhile, in the *bajura,* or lowlands, the expanding sugar economy resulted in the construction of sugar factories, *centrales.* These compounds, at times even larger than the built-up core of many towns, enabled the production of sugar at a greater scale. Neither rural or urban, their massive industrial aesthetic altered the traditional landscape of the island, "irreversibly re-shaping socio-spatial production to reflect market norms."[31]

Balloon-frame construction, the underlying building technique of casitas, was introduced in the large compounds of worker housing built around the *centrales.* The generalized adoption of this imported technology signaled the commodification of the popular dwelling, thereby accelerating the loss of traditional building techniques, an essential part of the collective narrative of rural society. The popular dwelling was now linked more strongly to the economic forces of the marketplace, signaling its transformation from vernacular architecture to an architecture of the poor, both urban and rural. In the *bajura,* before long, many new arrivals became surplus labor as the new economic order could not absorb them. By the 1940s, most were compelled to migrate once again. This time workers moved to the island's principal nucleations. The built-up areas in the center of these urban complexes served as residential quarters for the elites and for a small middle class (mostly professionals), as well as the location of major civic, cultural, and economic institutions. The new arrivals were driven to marginal or peripheral lands of lesser value, usually around rivers or swampland. Casitas became the principal form of shelter in these new communities.

Urban casitas were called upon to serve added functions, particularly for the new arrivals whose skills were not needed in the city. Unable to own farmland, a necessity for survival, most casita dwellers created small subsistence urban farms—small plots of land surrounding the shanties—where they could raise their chickens and a pig or two and grow a few staples. In this way they brought the farm or country to the city. Thus, the garden became an integral element in the urban casita.

By the 1950s, a second wave of industrialization had transformed the island's economy. The introduction of *urbanizaciones,* tract suburban housing, made older working-class neighborhoods obsolete and exploded residential districts into class-specific, segregated segments. The generalized adoption of concrete construction technology and tract housing produced further differentiation in popular dwellings. Wooden architecture (in casitas) was further reduced to housing the truly urban poor, the shanty dweller, the working poor in the outlying towns, and people in rural communities attempting to survive as farmers. As Puerto Rico continued to transform into an industrial society, from traditional to modern, casitas acquired a new status in the island's lore. They became part of the narrative that recalled the destruction of a peasant agricultural society, one that seemed less threatening when looked at from a distant time.[32]

Puerto Rican migration to New York City and elsewhere peaked during the same period. In the collective memory of those who left, casitas were implanted as emblems of the old world, of a lost "fantasized paradise" they had left behind.[33] These images collapsed ecological, social, and built landscapes into a new symbolic architectural language. To those who remained on the island, casitas became deposits of tradition that modulated change while assuring permanence and the transmission of a legacy.[34]

| Casitas and the Puerto Rican Diaspora

The accelerated migration of people of Hispanic origins to the United States and their current cultural influence represent opportunities to be explored.

Top, a balcony view of the Rincón Criollo in the South Bronx. By the late 1990s this casita had been in existence for over a decade, but it has avoided demolition by the City of New York because of the efforts of local community organizations. The casita is also home to "Los Pleneros de la 21," a *plena* music group that provides neighborhood residents, particularly children, with music lessons in *plena,* a music genre that emerged during the first decades of the twentieth century in Ponce, Puerto Rico. *Bottom,* middle-class houses on a main street in Ponce, Puerto Rico. These urban casitas were built during the 1920s as the city was being transformed by an emerging group of middle-class residents. The casitas were restored recently and represent some of the best examples of urban vernacular architecture in Puerto Rico. Photographs by Aponte-Parés, c. 1992.

The diaspora of millions of Puerto Ricans, Cubans, Mexicans, Dominicans, and others presents challenges that must be addressed. Studying how and where these diaspora are constructed and interconnect, most likely in the many urban centers of the nation like New York, Los Angeles, Miami, and Chicago, will be a difficult and arduous process.

In an island nation like Puerto Rico, which just "celebrated" five hundred years of colonialism, the new millennium brings the identity issue to a higher level of complexity. More than one-third of all Puerto Ricans live outside Puerto Rico. New York is home to the largest urban concentration of Puerto Ricans anywhere, followed by San Juan, Chicago, and possibly Ponce. Increasingly, Puerto Rican immigrants return to the island to retire.

Circular migration continually exchanges people and refreshes cultural images; thus, casitas continue to be summoned by Puerto Ricans, both on the island and in New York, as metaphors of places past. On the island, their rebirth may have been ignited by economic and cultural forces. Lumber companies, for example, have promoted new uses for balloon-frame construction. Economically strapped urban dwellers can build wooden additions to their homes. The small group who can afford to build leisure homes can construct second homes, *casas de campo,* nostalgic references to yesterday's *quintas.* This has resulted in peculiar typologies being built across the island, in *urbanizaciones* as well as in poor rural areas, where casitas are built atop flat-roofed concrete tract housing. For those who can afford an exurban microfarm as a second home, the casita brings them closer to their identity as Puertorriqueños. To those who recall them in New York, casitas grant their builders, like Jaran, the power of place and culture in a city that has yet to offer many of them acceptance and a sense that they belong.

| *Preserving Casitas as Cultural Landscapes*

In 1992, New York City's governmental officials acquiesced to the power and prestige of Columbia Presbyterian Hospital by demolishing all but a small portion of the building and the facade of the Audubon ballroom and theater complex in the Washington Heights area of upper Manhattan. The hospital wanted to build an office and laboratory complex on the site.[35] The Audubon was a major example of theater/ballroom complexes designed earlier in the twentieth century by Charles Lamb, known for the terra cotta details on the facades of his buildings.

The Audubon Ballroom was where Malcolm X was assassinated decades ago. In the original architectural proposal, the only mention of the assassination was to be a small wall plaque commemorating the event. After pressure

Top, a casita on Eighth Street in Loisaida, Manhattan, is currently "owned" by an elderly couple who chose not to retire in Puerto Rico. One could argue that the casita serves as the couple's country house in the middle of Manhattan. *Bottom,* a casita in Trujillo Alto, Puerto Rico, a town located just outside the San Juan metropolitan area. On concrete columns on an island that is almost entirely urban, these casitas are built by the working-class poor in what would be termed "exurbia" in the United States. Photographs by Aponte-Parés, c. 1992.

from many sides, the city agreed to preserve only a small portion of the room where the assassination occurred. The ballroom had recorded the history of many ethnic groups in the city, including Jews, the Irish, and, beginning in the 1930s, Hispanics and African Americans. With such multiple layers of history, as well as the building's architectural value and association with the assassination of Malcolm X, it should have been important enough to the history of New York City to merit preservation.

The disregard of the city's administrators for the history of people of color in general, the weakness of the African American community's preservation efforts, and the building's location in upper Manhattan were made painfully evident in the process. Upper Manhattan, particularly Washington Heights, had been transformed decades earlier and was home to African Americans and Latinos, two groups with little or no voice in the city's preservation policies.

The Audubon also was home to the San Juan Theater, a major *place* that had recorded the cultural history of Puerto Ricans and other Latinos in New York since the early thirties. The absence of Latino preservation groups with adequate monetary and political means to stop this demolition gave city government free reign to ignore Latino history. The theater had been a landmark in the history of Puerto Ricans in the city, a place used by major political figures, artists from Puerto Rico and Latin America, and others for both political rallies and artistic presentations. By the 1960s and 1970s, the San Juan showed the latest movies produced in Mexico and Latin America, but by the 1980s the theater was dark and in disrepair, considered an eyesore by many.

Scores of other important places in East Harlem and elsewhere that recorded the social and cultural history of Puerto Ricans and other Latinos had been ravished in earlier decades. The demolition of these buildings all but obliterated the century-long cultural history of Puerto Ricans and other Latinos. During the late nineteenth century, for example, New York was home to Cuban and Puerto Rican radicals struggling for the independence of their islands from Spain. José Martí, the Cuban patriot, lived in the city for close to two decades while working for the independence of Cuba, and he wrote some of his major political and sociological works during his time in New York. The Puerto Rican flag was designed in New York City in 1895 by Puerto Rican patriots as part of this liberation movement. Later, during the 1920s and 1930s, scores of tobacco workers migrated to the city and toiled in tobacco factories, sites of important cultural events for them. A myriad of early cultural, political, and social institutions was established in many sites in Manhattan and wider New York City. These sites are remembered only in books, and to this day no one has attempted to identify them for preservation.[36]

Throughout the 1940s and 1950s, a new migration of Puerto Ricans and other Latinos took place. This migration brought the working poor, mostly factory workers, who moved to the traditional slums of the city, particularly East Harlem and the Lower East Side in Manhattan, the South Bronx, and Red Hook in Brooklyn. In these neighborhoods Puerto Ricans and other Latinos engaged in the process of community building. Theaters, restaurants, bodegas, bookstores, and social and cultural clubs, for example, were embedded with signs and symbols depicting Puerto Rican culture and provided the community with places for cultural bonding and support.

With the demolition of most of these institutions and life spaces during the 1960s and 1970s, many Latino neighborhoods became wastelands with no history apparent to those who were left behind. During the late 1970s and early 1980s, casitas emerged. For over two decades now, casitas have been admired, scorned, celebrated, ignored, destroyed, or seen as representations of the "other" by anthropologists and other students of urban lore. No one has considered that casitas may have value beyond the gaze of the curious. An argument can be made to preservationists to consider casitas in their agenda as part of the cultural landscapes of New York City during its postwar period.

First, the presence of casitas attests to the willingness and strength of Puerto Ricans and other Latinos to continue recording their cultural lives on city landscapes. As cultural objects, casitas are embedded with history at both personal and collective levels. This history is both painful and celebratory. It is painful in that casitas reveal the erasure of a people's contribution to the well-being of their communities; celebratory, in that casitas provide their users with hope for a better future. A casita represents a deep civic motivation by its builders to improve the quality of life of its neighbors.

Another important role casitas may play in the collective memory of all city residents is that they record the deep transformations of cities in the United States during the postwar period, a period that led to the wholesale demolition of so many buildings, tenements, and factories that carried the histories of twentieth-century immigrants. The wastelands produced by these transformations, the countless vacant blocks that marred communities of color, became symbols of urban decay during the 1980s. If preservationists want to reclaim the significant places that recorded the history of so many of the city's residents, they should begin by "claiming the entire urban cultural landscape as an important part of American history, not just its architectural monuments."[37] Indeed, current preservation efforts look like a "near equivalent to stage designing or an emotional remembrance of a nostalgic past."[38] But, which group's past?

Perhaps casitas also carry the message of the power relationships between those who were able to control the images that symbolize the city (the elites) and those whose imagery was lost (the powerless). These images are sources of memory and tell the story of "who belongs" and whose "heritage" is to be preserved.[39] Also missing from preservation efforts is an acknowledgment that the loss of public space through privatization in many cities of the United States adds another pressure point to the use and definition of what actually are public spaces in these urban areas. Sharon Zukin, for example, has argued that current efforts to preserve and reclaim public spaces induce a "loss of authenticity, that is compensated for by a re-created historical narrative and a commodification of images." Too many men and women, particularly people of color, are displaced from these public spaces they once considered theirs.[40] As more and more traditional public arenas in the city, such as Central Park, Bryant Park, and other major places, are privatized, the need for casitas increases, for they are claimed by communities that have been excluded from these reconstituted cultural landscapes.

Finally, the power of casitas stems from the remembrance of an earlier period in the nineteenth-century history of the United States, when the emerging industrial giant began searching for commercial markets. The linkages created during this period led to exchanges of goods and culture between the United States and the Caribbean. It is ironic that the casita's underlying building technique, the balloon frame, was invented in Chicago in the nineteenth century and that what appear to be alien structures (i.e., Caribbean vernacular architecture juxtaposed over the traditional industrial landscape) are, indeed, a collision of the islands' vernaculars with the North. Thus, the casita's historical value lies beyond its present configuration: its value is primarily derived from a long historical lineage.

CHAPTER FIVE

Considering the Ordinary
Vernacular Landscapes in Small Towns and Rural Areas

ARNOLD R.
ALANEN

If landscape is, as John Stilgoe has claimed, a "slippery" word, then anyone who seeks to describe and decipher the term *vernacular landscape* must cope with an even more difficult semantic concept. The word *vernacular* is still quite unfamiliar to many people, although terms such as *ordinary, common, typical,* and *everyday* are often used as more understandable descriptors. Vernacular is often contrasted with academic, high style, and formal expressions, leading some scholars to lament over the "unfortunate divisions" between vernacular and stylistic terminology; the lack of a common vocabulary, geographer Michael Conzen noted in 1978, was a hindrance to researchers who sought to study and assess the built environment of North America.[1] Likewise, during the 1980s a group of Midwestern vernacular architecture specialists prepared a draft of a National Park Service bulletin for use by individuals and organizations seeking to identify and survey ordinary buildings, but they saw their efforts end in futility when reviewers could not agree upon a terminology for describing and classifying vernacular architecture, let alone definitions, criteria, and identification standards for nominating properties to the National Register of Historic Places.[2]

Many approaches are now used to preserve vernacular landscapes in small towns and rural and less settled areas of the United States: local organizational efforts; land trusts; National Park Service landscapes, including national reserves and units managed by public-private partnerships; and heritage areas and corridors. These examples do not, however, cover the full array of available methods.[3]

| *The Term and Its Usage*

J. B. Jackson, the seminal player in the development of a contemporary landscape studies movement in America, has traced the roots of *vernacular* to its Latin origins in the word *verna,* which referred to a slave born in the home of his or her master. In classical times, it meant the place of one's birth or a native of a village or place who engaged in routine labor. When considering the English language, the term initially was employed during the late Middle Ages to identify the language or dialect of a country or district. The syntax of such a vernacular language was confused, Jackson has stated, "its vocabulary, spelling, and pronunciation were capricious, and it was less a work of art than a tool, a rough-and-ready instrument for workaday relationships and communication."[4] Vernacular languages, in other words, were vital, functional, and flexible.

Scholars of British rural culture began to define the architecture of the countryside as vernacular by the 1830s. To them, Jackson has noted, the word was "appropriate to describe the vestiges of a culture which was rural, traditional, and on the verge of extinction." The evolution of scholarship devoted to vernacular architecture since that time has been highlighted recently with publication of the *Encyclopedia of Vernacular Architecture of the World* (1997), a massive, three-volume work that opens with a discussion of different research approaches employed to study ordinary buildings: aesthetic, anthropological, archeological, architectural, behavioral, cognitive, conservationist, developmental, diffusionist, ecological, ethnographical, evolutionary, folkloristic, geographical, historical museological, phenomenological, recording and documentation, spatial, and structuralist.[5] To recognize the estimated 800 million dwellings and countless numbers of other structures that may be considered examples of the vernacular, the *Encyclopedia*'s editor defines them as follows: "Vernacular architecture comprises the dwellings and all other buildings of the people. Related to their environmental contexts and available resources, they are customarily owner- or community-built, utilizing traditional technologies. All forms of vernacular architecture are built to meet specific needs, accommodating the values, economies and ways of living of the cultures that produce them."[6]

Also of note is the Vernacular Architecture Forum (VAF), a North American organization formed in 1980. The forum conducts an annual conference, provides a quarterly newsletter for a membership that now approaches nine hundred individuals and institutions, and publishes a collection of scholarly essays in its biannual *Perspectives in Vernacular Architecture.*

Since the 1960s, assessments of the vernacular and of vernacular culture have become a hallmark of several other disciplines. Authorities in American studies, art history, folklore, history, literature, material culture studies, music, womens' studies, and related fields now devote considerable time to the study of the writings, records, thoughts, observations, and artifacts of people who traditionally have remained outside the mainstream of academic discourse: minority groups, women, laborers, farmers, children, immigrants, untrained artists, and so forth. A notable example is provided by academic history, where social history quickly emerged as a force that shaped the direction of the entire discipline.[7]

Some forms of vernacular culture are defined as folk, although *folk* usually refers to traditional facets of culture that do not change in light of popular taste or practice. The assessment offered by folklorist Henry Glassie, who divided culture into three categories—folk, popular, and academic—is useful in making such distinctions. "Folk material," Glassie noted in 1968, "exhibits major variation over space and minor variation through time, while the products of popular or academic culture exhibit minor variation over space and major variation through time."[8]

Several art scholars devote considerable attention to the study of folk art, although they often use terms such as *Art Brut* (raw art), visionary art, naive art, marginal art, intuitive art, grass-roots art, and outsider art to describe the work of untrained artists. Michael Kimmelman, however, finds the term *vernacular art* more useful, especially when comparing it to the the majority of contemporary artistic expressions. The term is also used by some behavioral scientists who seek to discover "vernacular grammars" that define local and regional environments and thereby determine whether the vernacular "is meaningful to its inhabitants beyond appearances as a medium reflecting cultural thought and everyday experiences." In the biological sciences, a few restoration ecologists are even exploring the usefulness of "the vernacular approach to environmental repair" in describing their work.[9]

| *Vernacular Landscapes*

When considering vernacular landscapes, Robert Riley, in a remarkably wide-ranging and thorough survey of literature published before the mid-1980s, offered a straightforward definition for such environments: "a human-made outdoor setting not of a type usually attributed to design professionals." In one of his perceptive discussions of vernacular landscapes, J. B. Jackson noted that many examples exist in places where the formal organization of space is barely evident. Such landscapes, according to Jackson, display a degree of mobility and flexibility that reflects adjustments to changing situations; they offer, Jackson wrote in 1984, "an impressive display of devotion to common customs and . . . an inexhaustible ingenuity in finding short-term solutions."[10]

While vernacular landscapes include a broad range of examples and generally embrace large land areas, smaller sites such as lawns and gardens are also included within the purview of the vernacular. These versions of the vernacular are, as John Dixon Hunt and Joachim Wolschke-Bulmahn note, "gardens which did not come into being as a result of the powerful intervention on a site of some wealthy patron or of some 'name' designer." These gardens are small scale rather than monumental, reflect the products of new technologies like the lawn mower, emphasize maintenance and management over creation, and seldom consider aesthetics as a primary concern. Since vernacular gardens embody many of the societal changes that affect their creators, Hunt and Wolschke-Bulmahn conclude that they should not necessarily be interpreted as products, but rather as expressions of a process.[11]

Although vernacular landscapes are virtually ubiquitous throughout America, only a relatively small number have received attention from organizations and individuals concerned with their preservation. The ensuing discussion provides examples of several approaches, methods, and techniques that have been employed by governments, organizations, and individuals seeking to preserve vernacular environments. Many of the landscapes described in this chapter are also listed in the National Register of Historic Places, where they generally are referred to as *rural historic landscapes.* Such landscapes are defined in National Register Bulletin 30 as "a geographical area that historically has been used by people, or shaped or modified by human activity, occupancy, or intervention, and that possesses a significant concentration, linkage, or continuity of areas of land use, vegetation, buildings and structures, roads and waterways, and natural features."[12] Bulletin 30 also states that such landscapes mirror the endeavors of people who pursued everyday work in farming, fishing, mining, or related activities. Rural historic landscapes that include large land areas and several buildings, structures, and sites are generally classified as historic districts; small landscapes that have no buildings or structures are typically referred to as historic sites. The examples in this chapter include both historic districts and sites.

| *Local Level Preservation: Communitarian and Ethnic Examples*

The United States has served as home for numerous communitarian and utopian ventures, the majority of which emerged on the nation's frontier from the 1660s to the 1860s.[13] These settlements often included landscapes held in common by an entire group or community. Today, only traces remain of many communities, others display historic remnants or serve as museums, but some continue to function as active and viable settlements. Among the latter are farms and communities operated by the old order Amish of Pennsylvania, Ohio, Indiana, Wisconsin, and elsewhere, as well as Hutterite ranches that dot the landscape of the northern Great Plains states and Canada's Prairie Provinces. Many of these communitarian landscapes reveal a strong ethnic identity; likewise, the uniqueness of several other landscapes is tied directly to their ethnic origins and characteristics or to the commonly held religious beliefs and practices of their settlers, even though the land is not owned or held in common by a single group. The landscapes discussed in this section include one of the largest areas of nonpublic, singular land ownership in the United States, a former utopia, and two ethnic enclaves.

The Amanas

Travelers who visit east-central Iowa encounter a striking organization of land, buildings, and villages: the Amana Colonies. Without a doubt, the Amanas comprise one of the most visually distinctive rural landscapes in the entire nation; in fact, the 26,000-acre property actually appears more European than American. The origins of the Amanas are found in the Society of True Inspirationists, a pietistic German religious sect that emerged in Europe during the 1700s. After a large group of its members immigrated to New York state in the 1850s, plans were made to acquire enough land in Iowa to accommodate twelve hundred people; by the late 1860s, the Inspirationists were well established in this area of the Hawkeye State.[14]

The majority of soils included within the newly acquired property proved ideal for agricultural purposes, and the Inspirationists situated their farm-villages—Amana, West Amana, South Amana, High Amana, East Amana, Middle Amana, and Homestead—on the highest, least fertile land that also was flood-free. (Six of the villages were established between 1855 and 1861; Homestead was an existing village when purchased in 1861.) From a land-use planning standpoint, the "superb" placement of the seven villages may very well have been linked to "common sense and divine inspiration." For almost one hundred years, the pietistic, communitarian life that the Inspirationists pursued was directly reflected in the architecture and landscapes of the Amanas. Each village cluster—including its small business district, a church, a school, and a store, all of which were bordered by farm buildings—was virtually uniform in function and appearance. Given the materials employed in construction (stone, brick, and wood), along with the "textures, scales, similar forms,

The central area of an Amana, Iowa, village. Most of Amana's seven villages include inward-directed blocks that feature a church surrounded by six or seven residences and their attached kitchen houses. A system of "foot streets" provides the only access to the central district of the village. Despite many changes in Amana since 1932, these exterior spaces, developed almost 150 years ago, continue to function as safe, communal areas for residents. Photograph by Alanen, 1980.

and siting of their buildings," the Inspirationists "unconsciously created the art of townscape." Virtually every available area of ground within the villages was planted to kitchen gardens and orchards; very little area existed for grass and shade trees, and only a few flower beds existed.[15]

In 1932, the members made a "pragmatic business decision" when they voted to modify their communitarian way of life and enter into the secular world to a greater extent. Termed the Great Change, the transition also led to modifications in the appearance of the Amanas. Many communal woodsheds and washhouses were demolished, neglected, or converted into garages; community gardens were replaced by small private gardens; the use of herbicides killed the majority of grapes that grew on trellises fastened to the houses; and fences situated along walkways were removed. When viewed individually, these changes may appear rather small and seemingly insignificant, but when considered in their entirety, they represented "a major alteration and destruction within the historic and visual environment of the Amana Colonies."[16]

The Great Change resulted in the bifurcation of Amana into two organizations: the Amana Church Society, which deals with religious, charitable, and benevolent activities, and the Amana Society, a stock company that focuses upon profit-making endeavors. Amana's unique culture and landscape received recognition in 1966 when the entire holding was designated a National Historic Landmark (NHL); this was followed, two years later, by the development of a museum by the Amana Heritage Society. Once the society realized that its obligations went beyond the preservation of artifacts to include architecture and landscapes, a Historic Landmark Committee was formed in 1974, followed three years later by the hiring of a consultant to help with the preparation of a master plan.[17]

During the planning process, residents and tourists alike made many suggestions for the management of Amana's future. These included proposals to establish historic districts, to plant historical crops in some fields, to reintroduce livestock types common before 1932, and even to construct an eighth village. None of the ideas was implemented to any extent. Several elders opposed the development of another village because to them the idea of seven was sacred, and the recommendation to designate historic districts was opposed by residents who expressed concern about any controls that might limit individual decisions. According to urban historian and architect Dolores Hayden, the lack of controls contributed to such extensive "crass remodeling" of the original architecture that demolition would have been a "kinder" alternative.[18]

Since the 1980s, increasing numbers of permanent residents from outside the Amanas have been attracted to the colonies' small villages and bucolic countryside. A land-use plan was adopted in 1986, but its conventional provisions failed to address directly the unique character and resources of the Amanas. Some new ranch and split-level houses in Main Amana, Middle Amana, High Amana, and Homestead are fairly attractive and well sited, but the majority reveal little awareness of the original townsite arrangement and architectural ambiance. Rather than clustering into sequestered enclaves, many residences are strung out along the roadways, thereby compromising the open landscape character that traditionally separated one village from the other. The overall affect, according to one in-depth assessment, has resulted in the development of a "visually jarring" environment that is "destroying the coherent village landscape." Similarly, a major rezoning in the 1980s permitted a 200-acre golf course and several high-priced residences just outside Main Amana.[19] The contrast between the traditional Amana housing units, including their associated landscapes, and the new, suburban-like subdivision—complete with its two- and three-car garages and well-manicured lawns—is jarring at times. A 1995 assessment of Amana by a consultant hired to update the 1977 master plan summarized the immediate and long-term needs of the settlement:

Largely unrestricted modifications in the physical environment since the Great Change of 1932 make it time for [the] Amana people—as a community—to decide to manage and conserve wisely their physical environment as a vital part of their heritage. The outcome of the struggle to balance demands of industrialization, modern agriculture, heritage tourism, suburbanization, and the entrepreneurial spirit of local businesses with rural life and the distinct cultural heritage of the Amana people may well determine whether the community enters the new century as uniquely Amana or as a community found anywhere in the United States.[20]

Utopia in the Tennessee Cumberlands

Most communitarian undertakings in America were much smaller than the Amana Colonies. One such example in the southeastern area of the nation, Rugby, Tennessee, is relatively similar to many of the utopian experiments once found throughout several areas of the country. In this case, however, the original architecture and landscape of Rugby provide the nucleus and inspiration for current restoration and preservation efforts and serve to guide the direction of new development.

Rugby's genesis may be traced to Thomas Hughes, a nineteenth-century English author and social reformer. Hughes wished to provide opportunities for the younger sons of English upper-class families who were unable to inherit land or wealth because of the laws of primogeniture. After visiting the United States in 1870, Hughes dreamed of establishing a colony "where England's 'second sons' could engage in farming and the trades free of the suffocating stigma of caste and class." Joining with a group of Boston capitalists, Hughes created the colony of Rugby in eastern Tennessee in 1880.[21]

Rugby's population quickly peaked at 400 to 450 residents, but after 1887 a series of misfortunes led to the gradual decline of the community. Over subsequent decades, buildings were destroyed or removed, and much of the land was subdivided and sold. In the 1960s, a historically conscious sixteen-year-old youth from the nearby community of Deer Lodge helped to organize Historic Rugby, a local restoration association; soon, the group was rehabilitating and preserving a few buildings in the village and protecting about one thousand acres of land at the core of the original settlement. Public buildings restored by the association are now open for tourists, and several residences have been rehabilitated by private parties. When the adjacent Big South Fork National River and Recreation Area was designated during the early 1980s, a master plan to guide restoration and development activities began to be prepared for Rugby.[22]

The master plan, completed in 1988, has also been used to guide the contemporary development of Beacon Hill, a forty-acre tract of land originally designated for residential purposes in the 1880 town plan. The self-management planning process and historical understanding displayed at Rugby had already been recognized in 1986 when the community received a national award from *Progressive Architecture* magazine: "This plan reaches into the history of the community and really tries to understand it," one impressed juror commented, "drawing the design solutions out of that as opposed to superimposing an idea." Since 1993, new "colonists" have been able to purchase lots in Beacon Hill and construct residences that are compatible with the original landscape and architectural features of Rugby. Throughout both historic Rugby and the new Beacon Hill tract, flowers and plant materials continue to reflect the practices and appearance of the original community. Overall, from 1974 to 1997, Historic Rugby secured $1.4 million in grants from various organizations to support its preservation activities, although some 65 percent of the association's operating budget comes from tourism.[23]

Ethnic Expressions in the Upper Midwest

Minnesota and Wisconsin were settled by waves of European immigrants who flocked to the two states during the nineteenth and early twentieth centuries. When describing Wisconsin, one historian has noted that for many years the state "was something of a living ethnological museum . . . the natural result of immigration from a variety of countries, settlement largely in homogeneous groups, and attachment to inherited ways of doing things."[24] Though time and development have contributed to a steady decline in the region's inventory of ethnic landscapes, a few that remain have been recognized, documented, and even preserved to a certain extent. In most cases, preservation activities are only beginning.

In Wisconsin, the Namur area of Door County once embraced the largest concentration of rural Belgians in the United States. Today, the material and nonmaterial cultural expressions of the original Belgian American immigrants continue to be displayed in the area: the French language, inflected by the Walloon dialect, is still spoken by some residents; numerous Catholic churches continue to provide for the spiritual and social needs of local parishioners; traditional Belgian foods are served in homes and restaurants; religious and ethnic festivals mark the annual calendar of the area; and a significant concentration of buildings reflect the Belgians' integration of frontier building materials with traditional methods, plans, and motifs. In addition to their distinctive red brick houses and large wooden barns, many Belgian American farmsteads contain a variety of smaller outbuildings, including examples of two especially distinctive cultural forms: (1) summer kitchens with attached outdoor bake ovens and (2) wayside or votive chapels. As stated in the documentation that initially led to the nomination of Namur as a Rural Historic District and later to its designation as a National Historic Landmark, the area reveals "an ethnic architectural expression that is unique in the rural American landscape." In addition to its display of Old World culture, the Namur district received NHL recognition because of the strong support for the nomination from local individuals and organizations. Overall, the district embraces forty farmsteads, a church, two cemeteries, a hamlet, and expanses of agricultural and natural landscapes. It is the first NHL to represent European migration to America.[25]

The Namur district is also situated along a major gateway to the attractions of northern Door County, a leading tourist destination in the Midwest. During the early 1990s a proposal called for improved access to the northern part of the county by expanding and upgrading the existing highway passing through the Namur settlement. The proposal triggered the Section 106 review and mitigation process—established as part of the National Historic Preservation Act of 1966—that must be followed when a federally funded project affects a designated or potentially eligible National Register property.[26] In this case, interested individuals and representatives from the Wisconsin Department of Transportation, the Historic Preservation Division of the State Historical Society of Wisconsin, and local public and fraternal organizations formed a Historical Focus Group in 1994 to propose and evaluate highway expansion alternatives. The group offered a recommendation calling for the construction of a bypass highway to skirt the Namur district, along with the development of a scenic wayside or overlook to provide visitors with views of the historic buildings and landscape.[27] In 1995, the major recommendations made by the Historical Focus Group were approved, thereby maintaining the integrity of the NHL district, at least for the near future.

Farther to the north of the Namur district is the Lake Superior region of upper Michigan, Minnesota, and Wisconsin, which includes numerous enclaves developed by Finnish immigrants during the late nineteenth and early twentieth centuries. One of the largest of these settlements comprises three townships in Minnesota that focus upon the small settlement of Embarrass. The hundreds of Finns who established themselves in the area constructed scores of farmsteads that typically included several log buildings that satisfied a variety of functions. By expending prodigious amounts of labor, the Finns also cleared small fields from the stump- and boulder-strewn land.[28] Farming began to experience a sharp decline during the 1950s; today, few active farms remain in the area, and many have been abandoned.

When a school in the Embarrass area was threatened with demolition during the mid-1980s, local officials sought assistance from the National Trust for Historic Preservation. Trust representatives who visited the site saw little merit in preserving the school, but after being exposed to the greater Embarrass area, they admonished local residents to "start saving those log buildings," especially since the local fire department was engaged in burning the structures for practice. In 1987, the school preservation group reorganized and formed Sisu Heritage to identify, interpret, and preserve the community's ethnic legacy. (*Sisu* is a Finnish word referring to intestinal fortitude, or "guts"; one older resident of the area defined *sisu* as "stubbornness beyond reason.")[29]

Also in 1987, the National Trust, along with the Society for Photographic Education, selected the Embarrass area as one of sixteen sites nationwide to celebrate the bicentennial of the U.S. Constitution; these places were chosen because they represent several of the historical events and civil liberties engendered by the Constitution over a time span of two hundred years. Such obvious sites as James Madison's home at Montpelier, Virginia, and Independence Hall in Philadelphia were selected, but Embarrass was recognized as an "uncommon place" that displays the historical significance of America's immigrant diversity, including one of the nation's "most conspicuous collections of log buildings associated with a single ethnic group."[30] Almost simultaneously, the Minnesota State Historic Preservation Office and Sisu Heritage sponsored a study to determine whether various properties in the area were eligible for nomination to the National Register of Historic Places. Overall, close to two hundred log buildings in various states of repair were found; within a year a Multiple Property Nomination form had been prepared that ultimately led to the inclusion of some forty buildings (including six entire farmsteads) in the National Register.[31]

The nomination noted that the structures, built in the traditional Finnish manner with tightly fitted, horizontally stacked logs locked together at the corners by notches, exhibit "an aesthetic component and quality of log construction which is unsurpassed in this country." Furthermore, the ethnic building heritage and traditions were seen as blending "the experience and memory of centuries-old technologies within an entirely new setting to create a distinctive cultural landscape."[32] Sisu Heritage then proceeded to develop a visitors' center and sponsored the construction of Timber Hall, a large log structure now used for community events throughout the year. The organization also conducts guided tours of several historic properties during the summer, sponsors workshops on log building restoration, organizes a traditional Finnish midsummer celebration each June, and is seeking to preserve two farmsteads and several individual buildings within the district. A grassroots preservation effort of the purest form, the enthusiasm and dedication

A Finnish American meadow hay barn (*lato*) in the northern Minnesota community of Embarrass, a settlement that includes one of the nation's largest concentrations of log buildings constructed by a single ethnic group. In addition to saunas, the rural Finnish American landscape of the Lake Superior region was once distinguished by numerous field and meadow hay barns of this type. This *lato* burned to the ground in May 1995. Photograph by Michael Koop, 1991.

of the Embarrass volunteers is limited only by their limited numbers, increasing ages, and lack of monetary resources.

| Land Trusts

Land trusts have been used to protect selected landscapes in the United States ever since 1891, when Massachusetts landscape architect Charles Eliot founded the Trustees of Reservations (TTOR). This organization, the first of its kind in the world, continues to preserve, for public use and enjoyment, Massachusetts land that has outstanding historic, scenic, and ecological value. Initially, TTOR focused upon the preservation of beaches, river and stream banks, waterfalls, and mountains, but later, historic buildings, formal gardens, and farm fields were included. One hundred years after its founding, TTOR had protected more than eighteen thousand acres of land on eighty-three separate properties.[33]

As of 1998, more than twelve hundred land trusts were situated throughout the United States; the New England states supported the largest number of trusts (417), while the Plains (23), Southwest (37), and Rocky Mountain (52) states had the smallest numbers. These trusts, which include local, regional, and statewide nonprofit organizations that protect important land resources for the public good, are funded through membership dues, donations, and taxes.[34] Two major organizations formed during the 1980s—the Land Trust Alliance and the American Farmland Trust—offer expertise and support to indivdual trusts throughout the United States.

In 1988, land trusts protected 2 million acres of land in the United States; by 1998, the figure had grown to 4.7 million acres. About 70 percent of all land trusts include the protection of forests and timberlands, wetlands, and scenic areas; farm and ranch lands are protected by 50 percent; historic landscapes by 33 percent; and cultural sites by 16 percent. Many trusts purchase land outright and often transfer ownership of the properties they acquire to governmental agencies. By the 1990s, however, the most commonly employed measure was the conservation easement, a legal mechanism that typically involves two different approaches to land protection: the purchase of development rights (PDR) and the transfer of development rights (TDR). PDRs are often used in agricultural areas experiencing growth pressures; the trusts typically purchase conservation easements from local farmers by paying them "the difference between the value of the land for agriculture and the value of the land for its 'highest and best use,' which is generally residential or commercial development." TDRs, which involve the transfer of building rights from land requiring protection to areas more suited for development, often are utilized when the latter can be supplied more readily with public services than the former. These programs are unique because they often involve transactions between developers and private landowners, but they have been termed "notoriously difficult to administer" and generally are pursued only by "the most sophisticated local governments."[35]

Suffolk County, New York, initiated the nation's first farmland PDR program in 1976. One year later, Maryland enacted PDR legislation, the earliest effort at a statewide level; within the first fourteen years of the program, Maryland protected more than 100,000 acres of farmland. Overall, PDR programs in fifteen states protected some 400,000 acres of farmland by 1997. Among local land trusts, one of the best known is the Marin Agricultural Land Trust (MALT) in California. Founded in 1980, MALT has waged a successful program to preserve large areas of agricultural land in Marin County (north of the Golden Gate Bridge) from the relentless forces of urbanization and suburbanization that typify the San Francisco metropolitan area. By selling the development rights to their properties, farmers in Marin County have used the proceeds "to stabilize an operation in trouble; to expand a thriving one; to buy land or stock or equipment; to pay off a mortgage; to build a retirement fund; to assist a land transfer between generations; or perhaps to buy out a co-owner who isn't interested in agriculture."[36]

In the Midwest, Michigan has emerged as a regional leader in organizing land trusts to protect agricultural areas threatened by urban or seasonal home development. These activities were initiated after a 1993 study revealed that Michigan's rate of farmland loss was greater than that of any other Great Lakes state. Another survey, one year later, determined that residents believed landscape deterioration was the state's most pressing environmental issue. To date, the single program that has received the most attention is the Mission Peninsula Land Trust, located in the northwestern section of lower Michigan. The project, which includes the first tax-funded PDR in the Midwest, was termed "extraordinary" by the *New York Times*.[37]

The peninsula extends sixteen miles into the northern section of Lake Michigan, is nowhere more than three miles wide, and includes forty-eight miles of shoreline. Its sandy loam soils and long growing season (the latter due to the ameliorative effect of the lake) have been responsible for the evolution of a thriving fruit-growing enterprise that is now more than a century old. (Some 70 percent of the nation's red cherries are grown on the peninsula and nearby areas.) In recent years the peninsula has proved especially attractive to prospective residents who are drawn to its scenic views and rural countryside. Between 1990 and 1995, the population of the peninsula increased from 4,800 to 6,000 people, with new subdivisions accommodating most of the growth. If these rates of expansion were to continue, it is estimated that no agricultural land would remain on the peninsula by the year 2025.[38]

A 1990 survey revealed that over 85 percent of Peninsula Township's voters believed the protection of scenic views and the preservation of farmland from residential development were important. Four years later, after a campaign to educate landowners and residents about the possibilities of PDRs, 53 percent of the voters approved a referendum authorizing the township to implement a fifteen-year, $2.6 million land trust program to be financed by tax rate increases.[39]

The overall plan received mixed reviews from the 137 farm operators who resided on the peninsula in 1995. Owners seeking to garner the highest price for land they have or plan to put up for sale reportedly claimed that preservation efforts were "a day late and a dollar short." They predicted that the PDR program would not control growth because agricultural land on the peninsula had become such a valuable commodity. Other farmers, however, favored the plan because it both protected scenic and productive land that, in many cases, had remained with some families for several generations and provided income without requiring operators to sell their holdings or give up farming.

A soon-to-be-abandoned barn at the edge of a new subdivision located about twenty-five miles west of Madison, Wisconsin. The American Farmland Trust (1997) has identified the Southern Wisconsin and Northern Illinois Drift Plain as the third most threatened Major Land Resource Area (MLRA) in the nation. Of the 136,000 acres of land that were developed in the Drift Plain MLRA between 1982 and 1992, almost 60 percent was identifed as "prime or unique" for agricultural purposes. When considering the entire United States from 1982 to 1992, the most productive agricultural counties experienced population growth rates of twice the national average. Photograph by Alanen, 1998.

By 1998, the program had achieved wider acceptance: 3,770 acres were protected, and plans were being made to secure conservation easements on an additional 5,430 acres over ensuing years.[40]

Even in the American West, where land trusts are much less common and a more recent activity than in other regions of the nation, new alliances are being forged among unlikely participants who seek to protect prime ranch land from prospective purchasers who reportedly want to find "five acres five miles from town." These trusts, such as one formed by the venerable Colorado Cattlemen's Association, assist ranchers in protecting their land for agricultural purposes, not open space. Even The Nature Conservancy (TNC), primarily known for its programs to protect natural areas, has come to accept the realities of the situation in the American West. "Cows, not Condos," and "Herefords, not Highways," are used as slogans by ranchers, TNC, and state tourism officials alike. In Routt County, Colorado, for example, voters in 1996 approved a real estate tax to purchase development rights from ranchers when they recognized that "vacationers would not fly from Chicago to see condominiums." However, some environmentalists advocate a much less conciliatory approach to collaboration with groups such as cattle-production organizations. "How can they [The Nature Conservancy] call themselves green?" asks Peter Galvin, a founder of the Southwest Center for Biological Diversity in Tucson, who has been an especially vocal critic of the organization.[41]

Since agricultural holdings comprise the largest areas of vernacular landscape in the United States, the protection offered by land trusts will only continue to grow into the future. To achieve their desired outcomes, however, land trusts that focus upon agricultural land will succeed only if farming and ranching remain economically viable activities. It is essential that land trust advocates coordinate their efforts with zoning, growth management, and economic development programs. Without farmers, knowledgeable observers note, there obviously can be no farmland.

| The National Park Service

For almost a century after Yellowstone was protected in 1874, the vast majority of national parks designated in the United States were selected because of their spectacular and sublime natural landscape features. Now, however, the National Park Service (NPS) is heavily involved in the preservation of vernacular landscapes that range from small sites to large areas, most of which are historic agricultural properties. Although the systematic evaluation and management of the agency's varied vernacular and cultural landscapes is a recent occurrence, some earlier NPS holdings did include large areas of land that displayed significant evidence of manipulation by human populations. Since there were no systemwide policies to guide NPS managers at the time, most decisions occurred on a case-by-case basis.

Cades Cove

One infamous example of early NPS action took place at Cades Cove, Tennessee, a 2,500-acre historic district situated within Great Smokies National Park. The Cades Cove story marks one of the first times that the NPS, by exercising powers of eminent domain during the 1920s and 1930s, systematically removed significant numbers of residents from their land. Some six hundred people, most of whom had generations-long ties to Cades Cove, extending back to the early and mid–nineteenth century, began to be moved from their rural properties so the land could be incorporated into the recently designated national park. Although some farmers sold their properties directly to the NPS, others accepted less than the appraised value in exchange for leases or special permission to continue to live on the land. Such assurances were not legally binding, and in late 1935 the last twenty-one families were requested to vacate the Cove within one month; twelve families, however, eventually were allowed to remain on annual leases.[42]

Although private land ownership was not given consideration at Cades Cove, the NPS made an immediate decision to preserve the historic scene and several material cultural elements. The district, however, became a historical "exhibit" because it had such significant interpretive possibilities—including, according to the NPS, one of the foremost collections of American pioneer buildings. Ironically, to maintain a sense of "pioneer primitivism," only log structures were deemed worthy of preservation; virtually all of the frame buildings were destroyed. Likewise, the patchwork pattern of fields was considered unappealing by early managers, who recommended that all fences be removed from open meadows, that all cultivation on hillsides along roadsides be terminated, and that the grazing of animals occur on level land areas only. Since "the perpetuation of a *pastoral* scene presented fewer problems than did an *agricultural* scene," soil conservation and aesthetics, not historical authenticity, served as the primary management objectives.[43]

To maintain the historic landscape, albeit in a highly altered state, special grazing permits were issued to those leasees who continued to farm. They were given directions to follow crop rotation practices, to establish more meadowland, to eliminate row crops, and to increase beef cattle numbers. Changes in fencing arrangements, livestock watering plans, and drainage systems were introduced to improve conditions for lease holders. The result was a noticeable change in the appearance of the landscape. "By the late 1960's," an NPS report observed, "Cades Cove looked far different from the Cove of the 1930's and 1940's." Durwood Dunn's criticisms of these practices were much more sardonic: "Having destroyed the community of Cades Cove by eminent domain," he wrote in 1988, "the community's corpse was ... mutilated beyond recognition."[44]

National Seashores, Lakeshores, and Riverways

By the 1960s and 1970s, many new units were being added to the NPS system (often designated as National Seashores, Lakeshores, and Riverways), but few met the definition of *wilderness;* most had been heavily affected by humans before their identification as protected areas. In addition, the National Historic Preservation Act of 1966 gave legal stature to cultural resource protection throughout the NPS system. The NPS and other federal agencies were now forced to recognize that maintaining a balance between nature and culture was no longer just a theoretical issue: it was law. Nevertheless, certain NPS managers continued to follow previous practices; some demolished old structures or followed management guidelines that allowed the acceptable loss of historic structures, while others "allowed abandoned buildings to molder away until they became safety hazards—thus providing the rationale to destroy them."[45] The corollary with historic landscapes was the practice of ceasing management practices that fostered their preservation.

One NPS unit that utilized a different approach in managing agricultural landscapes, even before implementation of the 1966 act, was Point Reyes National Seashore in west central California. Designated by Congress in 1962, the preserve protects many miles of Pacific shoreline and some seventy-seven thousand acres of western Marin County's gently rolling landscape. Also included within the Point Reyes Seashore is a pastoral zone of seventeen thousand acres, most of which embraces an area originally subdivided into large ranches by the Mexican government during the 1830s. When the seashore was formed in 1962, the NPS allowed several existing dairy and beef ranches to continue as operating units. All of the ranches are restricted by a variety of legal constraints, including leases, special use permits, and reservations of use and occupancy. With some 6,500 cattle situated within the boundaries of the National Seashore in 1999, managers are now required to address a host of difficult problems; nonetheless, the five dairy farms that still function at Point Reyes (along with twenty-three beef cattle permits) represent a continuous, 150-year legacy of large-scale agriculture in Marin County.[46]

In 1984, Robert Z. Melnick and two collaborators prepared the first NPS manual that identified and documented vernacular and agricultural landscapes. Their report, *Cultural Landscapes: Rural Historic Districts in the National Park System,* reviewed a host of cultural landscape studies conducted by academics since the early twentieth century. Because these highly regarded studies were purely academic in scope and content, Melnick's report gave special attention to the development of criteria and methods for use in various NPS units. The Boxley Valley, a section of the Buffalo National River in Arkansas, was used as a case study site in the report.[47]

During the early 1980s, the NPS had proposed a nontraditional approach to rural landscape preservation for the Boxley Valley. Because of its unique natural features, the enabling legislation also gave recognition to the Boxley's cultural landscape, "a well-preserved example of a rural Ozark Mountains Valley as it has evolved over the past 150 years." To protect the "array of qualities" along the river, the NPS initially planned to purchase most of the 78,100 acres of land identified as Conservation Zones, followed by the leaseback of

LEGEND

⌇⌇⌇ RIDGELINE

🌿 WOODLAND

▦ FARMSTEAD

⊙ CONTRIBUTING STRUCTURE

✳ CONTRIBUTING SITE

▨ PINE PLANTATION

⋮⋮⋮ REMNANT ORCHARD

🌲 SUGAR MAPLE ROW

🌳 BLACK LOCUST GROVE

🌾 CONIFER WINDBREAK

▬▬ DISTRICT BOUNDARY

SCALE 0   1800'
     100' 500'

NORTH

FARMSTEADS
A. THORESON
B. WERNER/BASCH
C. CHARLES/HATTIE OLSEN
D. DECHOW/KLETT
E. KELDERHOUSE
F. BURFIEND/GARTHE
G. MILLER
H. BURFIEND
I. BARRATT
J. SCHNOR
K. LAURA BASCH
L. SCHMIDT/HAYMS
M. OLSEN/HOUDEK
N. HOWARD/BERTHA OLSEN
O. WEAVER
P. ECKHERT/BAUR
Q. MARTIN BASCH
R. MILTON BASCH
S. LAWR/CHAPMAN
T. GOFFAR/ROMAN

CONTRIBUTING SITES
1. WERNER FAMILY CEMETERY
2. PORT ONEIDA CEMETERY
3. ORIGINAL TOWNSITE
4. BURFIEND BURIAL SITE
5. FORMER FARMSTEAD LOCATION
6. FORMER CHURCH LOCATION

CONTRIBUTING STRUCTURES
a. BRUNSON BARN
b. PORT ONEIDA SCHOOL
c. BARRATT PIG BARN
d. ECKHERT CABIN
e. NORTH UNITY SCHOOL
f. DECHOW/KLETT SUGAR SHACK

Rural landscape features at the Port Oneida District, Sleeping Bear Dunes National Lakeshore, Michigan. The Port Oneida site, which includes some nineteen farmsteads, numerous contributing sites and structures, and thousands of acres of former agricultural land, represents one of the largest vernacular landscapes managed by the National Park Service. After years of neglect, efforts are now being made to maintain the character and appearance of the landscape and its associated features. Source: McEnaney, Tishler, and Alanen (1995), p. 54.

the better agricultural properties to residents. An additional 9,400 acres of land designated for Private Use Zones were scheduled for management by the purchase of scenic easements from property owners.[48]

Rather than acquiring development rights from Buffalo River residents, the NPS actually purchased most of the land outright, forced people off their properties, and eventually demolished the homes and outbuildings. Nevertheless, once it was realized that the Boxley's agricultural community faced virtual collapse because of land and farm abandonment, a 1985 NPS cultural landscape report recommended that the agency sell back its previously acquired land to the former owners. Now the goal became the perpetuation of "the Boxley Valley as an agricultural community in harmony with the historic scenery, natural resources, and appropriate visitor use." A few residents subsequently repurchased their original holdings, but several farmsteads are severely dilapidated and may be beyond repair.[49] Despite such qualifications, the Boxley Valley clearly represents the new management options the NPS is pursuing in several of its units that include vernacular landscapes: rather than stopping or modifying change, efforts are now being made to direct it.

Another clear example of the complex issues associated with vernacular landscape management is revealed at Sleeping Bear Dunes National Lakeshore in Michigan. As is typical, the original legislation that created the park emphasized the protection of outstanding natural resources; cultural resources were given little, if any, consideration. Although the 71,000-acre park was created to protect the "forests, beaches, dune formations and ancient glacial phenomena" of a linear mainland area and two large Lake Michigan islands, the unit also embraces thousands of acres of agricultural land and hundreds of farm buildings. Some farm residents quickly disposed of their land, selling to the NPS immediately after the park was created in 1970, and later most of the farmsteads and agricultural lands were abandoned. The general management plan for Sleeping Bear Dunes National Lakeshore, approved in 1979, recommended that most of the agricultural areas be returned to their natural condition, with management conforming to NPS wilderness policies.[50]

By the 1990s, as Sleeping Bear Dunes's abandoned agricultural holdings received more attention from NPS managers, a series of studies was commissioned to document the significance of the National Lakeshore's rural history and cultural landscapes. The initial report documented the evolution of agriculture throughout the overall region; it was followed by in-depth studies of three distinctive areas located within the boundaries of the National Lakeshore: Port Oneida (a mainland unit) and two Lake Michigan islands, South Manitou and North Manitou.[51]

Between the 1840s, when the first white settlers arrived, and 1970, when congressional action resulted in NPS designation, the Sleeping Bear Dunes area never advanced beyond marginal agricultural status. Nevertheless, the Port Oneida settlement zone, including its vernacular landscapes and farmsteads, is a premier example of a relatively intact rural settlement system that is unique to the entire NPS system. To date, the broad open landscape views have been maintained by a mowing regime that reinforces the historic scenes, but the crops, pastures, and animals once found throughout the entire district are no longer evident. Many buildings and farmsteads are boarded up, although a few are still inhabited under limited term leasing agreements. Because NPS funds for building and landscape maintenance are so limited, the integrity and character of Port Oneida remain under constant threat.[52]

Somewhat similar situations prevail at South and North Manitou Islands. Even though the general management plan for Sleeping Bear Dunes National Lakeshore identified both islands as "potential wilderness" areas, there was clear evidence of historic landscape features, including fields, orchards, farmsteads, logging and hunting camps, recreational homes, and life saving stations. South Manitou's historic agricultural properties were recognized in the form of a recommendation calling for modest maintenance of the cultural landscape, but subsequent studies have revealed the unusual and significant role of the island's former farmers, who raised most of the nation's Rosen rye seed from the 1920s to the 1940s. (The isolated location of the island prevented cross-pollination of the seed.) A recent historic landscape report for South Manitou Island even recommends that the farmsteads and landscapes associated with Rosen rye be evaluated for possible National Historic Landmark status, a designation that will require a complete rethinking and revamping of current management guidelines and funding priorities. On North Manitou Island, virtually none of the early NPS planning documents give any attention to the presence of previous human activities. In fact, the agency offered evidence that was self-contradictory in supporting its wilderness recommendations: "Except for previous logging and some agricultural use," a 1987 report concluded, "North Manitou Island is predominantly undisturbed." Despite the presence of some 125 years of Euro-American settlement, remnants of this history were termed "visual intrusions" that should be removed or allowed to deteriorate "naturally."[53]

Nevertheless, vernacular landscapes at Sleeping Bear Dunes and elsewhere in the entire NPS system are now receiving much more attention and consideration than at any time in the past. A notable example is provided south of Cleveland, Ohio, at Cuyahoga Valley National Recreation Area, where the Cuyahoga Countryside Conservancy was formed in 1999 to promote sustainable agriculture on 1,200 acres of land. Over the span of five years, the conservancy plans to recruit fifteen to twenty farmers who will engage in vegetable and fruit growing, certified organic farming, and the raising of free-range chickens, sheep, and goats.[54] In most cases, however, the "conflict" between wilderness and cultural resource management will continue to challenge NPS superintendents and managers well into the twenty-first century.

National Reserves

For various reasons including funding limitations, several recently authorized NPS sites are now managed as "public-private partnerships." An early example of such a partnership was initiated by a local community during the late 1970s at Ebey's Landing National Historical Reserve on Whidbey Island in the state of Washington. The term *National Reserve* was adopted to represent a way that resource protection could be achieved through a partnership of local, state, and federal units of government. Ebey's Landing Reserve was established in 1978 "to preserve and protect a rural community which provides an unbroken historical record from the nineteenth century exploration and settlement in Puget Sound to the present time."[55]

Very little land has been or is to be acquired through fee simple purchase by the NPS at Ebey's Landing. Instead, most activity has focused upon the purchase of scenic easements and development rights in critical areas. The foremost example of the application of these tools occurred in 1980, after the threatened sale of a 300-acre farm in the heart of the reserve that was to be subdivided into 5-acre parcels. To forestall the sale and simultaneously to maintain the rural character of the site, the NPS traded fee ownership of this land (with appropriate easements) in exchange for additional easements across adjoining lands. As stated in the Comprehensive Plan, had this development occurred, "the historic quality of the farm at the center of the Reserve would have been destroyed and both the visual and economic integrity of the rural farm community seriously diminished."[56]

Ebey's Landing National Historical Reserve, now administered by a trust board, has been relatively successful in protecting some of its most threatened and valuable holdings, but the future visual quality and appearance of the district remain vulnerable to development. Local zoning and state environmental regulations restrict some agricultural activities, and an advisory group reviews proposed alterations to farm buildings; the increasing scale of farming operations has contributed to the development of large new structures, feed storage units, and animal waste lagoons; and the easements do not require that the land be used for farming. Another major question concerns funding. Since the trust board must derive a considerable proportion of its financial support from local governments and voluntary contributions, these sources are subject to a host of political and economic conditions.[57]

Another reserve, the Pinelands or Pine Barrens of southern New Jersey, is located in the megalopolitan corridor of the United States, a most unlikely place to find a large vernacular landscape. Situated on a tract of some one million acres of southern New Jersey land, the Pinelands constitute the most extensive sparsely populated region of Megalopolis. Named for its predominant tree species, the pitch pine (*Pinus regida*), the region includes a labyrinth of marshes and bogs, as well as pine, cedar, and oak forests. Because these natural conditions served to limit development, the Pinelands escaped the extensive industrialization and high population densities that emerged throughout the remainder of New Jersey and much of the eastern seaboard. Already by the nineteenth century, journalists were expressing amazement that such a wilderness area could exist in the background of Philadelphia and New York City.[58]

In addition to its natural features, the people of the Pinelands (termed *Pineys*), through their folkways, social patterns, and economic activities, give the region an equally distinctive stamp of identity. In recognizing that the residents provide insights to both the past and the contemporary life of the region, the Pinelands National Reserve (PNR) was designated in 1978 as an "effort to safeguard natural and cultural resources while maintaining patterns of compatible human use and development." The Pinelands Reserve differs from natural preserves in that local people are considered an integral part of the environment and are encouraged to remain in the region and to continue their traditional land and resource use practices.[59]

The objective of the enabling legislation was to engender a "living landscape" that would be protected by its "traditional guardians," the residents of the region. Since no models existed by which to evaluate the traditional guardians or living cultural resources who resided in a nationally significant landscape, the American Folklife Center of Washington, D.C., was asked to conduct a field survey in 1983 that would give "special attention to the interplay of folk culture and natural resources and to the region's sense of place."[60]

The studies and surveys revealed that nature and culture in the Pinelands have converged around three phenomena: water, earth, and fire. To understand the Pine Barrens's people and their culture, the investigators developed the framework for a database that gave attention to stories associated with the landscape and to other "folklife expressions" that include important place-related information. The investigators also sought to identify certain regional cultural features that are powerful because of their symbolic "fit" with the landscape; examples of such phenomena range from the names on mailboxes to the associations between different ethnic groups and their uses of particular trees and plants.[61]

Despite the unique approach adopted to foster regional identity in the Pinelands, one investigator has asked whether such efforts to preserve cultural traits represent a search for characteristics and traditions that never existed in the past, much less in the present. Even more problematic is the possibility that "culture and traditions are invented, or at least transformed and magnified in the popular imagination, to create the idea of a simple and harmonious relationship between people and the environment." In addition, Pineys have been part of the larger metropolitan economic system for generations and do not understand why preservation sentiments should limit the number of economic and cultural options available to them in their home region. They fear becoming "museumized: classified, in essence, as an endangered species to be carefully managed along with the rest of the region's flora and fauna."[62] Although the marketing of the region's cultural image has not yet resulted in the development of a significant tourist industry, the lasting importance of preservation efforts in the Pinelands may lie in the recognition given to local cultural traits and the methods used to document them.

Industrial Landscapes

The designation, in 1970, of Lowell National Historical Park in Massachusetts marked the first effort by the NPS to recognize America's industrial history. Since then, several other sites have received attention from the NPS, including the remnants of a massive copper mining complex (Kennicott) within the boundaries of Alaska's Wrangle–Saint Elias National Park and Keweenaw National Historical Park (KNHP), a former copper mining and processing district situated at the northern tip of Michigan's Upper Peninsula. While the fate of Kennicott's historic structures and landscapes continues to be reviewed and debated, KNHP serves as an example of the public-private partnerships becoming increasingly evident in the NPS system. It was created by congressional action in 1992, and virtually all land and buildings within the authorized boundaries remain privately owned, although some key buildings and sites are beginning to be acquired by the NPS. A large portion of the park includes much of Calumet, a once-thriving town that served as the commercial center for a densely populated area of as many as 38,500 people in 1910 but that had declined to 5,450 residents by 1990.

The Keweenaw landscape also stands in marked contrast to traditional national parks. Instead of providing views of pristine natural or historical scenes, Keweenaw displays waste rock piles, abandoned commercial and industrial buildings, hundreds of small company-built houses (many in various states

Abandoned copper processing buildings and remnant landscape features at Kennicott, Alaska, situated proximate to the border with Canada's Yukon Territory. Located within Wrangle–Saint Elias National Park, Kennicott is one of the largest abandoned mining enclaves in the United States and is certainly the most isolated. Kennicott's huge scale, remoteness, climatic constraints, and advanced state of dilapidation pose a host of difficult preservation management problems. Photograph by Alanen, 1992.

of disrepair), and even a Superfund hazardous-waste site. After surveying the area in 1995, an unimpressed *Wall Street Journal* reporter claimed that Keweenaw may be the "bleakest" unit in the NPS system.[63] On the other hand, for those people interested in understanding the grittiness of industrial and mining history, Keweenaw represents America's earliest commercial copper mining region and serves as a stage where the evolution of extraction activities has been played out since the early 1840s. These activities include the effects of technological changes, the role of numerous European immigrant groups in mining, the vagaries of corporate paternalism, the distinctive architectural and landscape features associated with mineral extraction and processing, and the boom-and-bust cycles characteristic of many natural resource areas.

Keweenaw National Historical Park has also been criticized as a political pork barrel project where the primary objective is to improve economic conditions in a chronically depressed region. One venture that immediately sought to capitalize upon the perceived economic upturn is Mine Street Station, a retail shopping complex constructed upon mining ruins at the edge of downtown Calumet. Since the land is privately owned and the local zoning ordinance imposes few limitations, NPS managers could only recommend that the shopping center be "reflective" of the area's historic features. In keeping with the low-key nature of this suggestion, the developer agreed to do little more than provide some additional landscape buffering and visitor parking spaces for what he termed a "modern type commercial area." Unfortunately, "the promise of the park" has spurred an unregulated, modern-day period of growth in the immediate area that threatens the integrity of the historic resources. As noted by the park's first superintendent, these intrusions, which include typical examples of franchise architecture, huge signs, and parking lots, "are making the Keweenaw more and more like the rest of America."[64]

The Keweenaw situation also indicates that standard NPS guidelines and Section 106 review processes may cause problems in areas where median family incomes remain well below the state and national average. Because much of the original company-built housing stock in the Calumet area requires sig-

Recent commercial development at the edge of Keweenaw National Historical Park, Calumet, Michigan. Located in the heart of America's first commercial copper mining district—where the extraction of ore commenced during the 1840s—numerous church spires and remnant mining buildings still bear evidence of the booming mining economy that existed at Calumet until the end of World War I. Though designated a National Historical Park in 1992, the limited development controls outside the boundaries of Calumet generally have failed to recognize the historical integrity of the community and its landscape. Photograph by Alanen, 1996.

nificant upgrading to make the residences more habitable, the majority of homeowners are eligible for federally assisted rehabilitation grants to weatherize and upgrade their dwelling units and meet local building codes. Because many of the houses are located within the boundaries of existing or potential National Register districts, any work must satisfy the Secretary of the Interior's Standards for Rehabilitation (SOI Standards).[65]

As in many former company towns, some Keweenaw area residents typically cannot afford the costs of the regular, cyclical maintenance required by their dwellings; therefore, weatherization grants, along with private loans, are used to finance the installation of vinyl siding and replacement windows and doors. Because of these resident preferences, as well as prevailing socioeconomic conditions and the harsh climate, local agencies and citizens have proposed that the SOI Standards be relaxed. In considering possible modifications to the regulations, a 1995 review sponsored by Michigan's State Historic Preservation Office noted that several specific factors merit consideration at Keweenaw. After conducting their assessment, the agency determined that the basic, underlying goal of any housing preservation strategy in the area was obvious: "to keep people living in their houses." Recognizing that, in a region with a long history of corporate paternalism, "changes made to standardized, company-built houses represent a greater control over one's private life," the report also noted that "it may be important to allow owners to continue to modify their houses according to their own needs and preferences." The agency suggested that in the future the review process might emphasize the retention of neighborhood and streetscape patterns and rhythms rather than focusing upon individual dwellings. "The spacing of the buildings, regularity, and uniformity of forms are most important," the report concluded.[66] The agreement, nevertheless, failed to be adopted after the local administering agency concluded that additional layers of bureaucracy were being added to the review process.

Situations similar to those at Keweenaw point to a dilemma that seldom receives attention when vernacular environments are considered for preservation: the class and culture differences between residents and preservation professionals. Whereas residents usually want housing, communities, and landscapes that are comfortable and "socially satisfying," preservation professionals desire places that are "visually interesting" as they pass through or visit them.[67]

| Heritage Areas and Corridors

A recent form of preservation activity that often includes vernacular landscapes within its purview is the heritage area, "a region with a coherent and unified history that has made itself visible on the land, thus stamping the area with a distinctive sense of place." Since heritage areas often are based upon a unifying feature such as a waterway, railroad, or road, many are identified as heritage corridors. A smaller number are unified by a particular theme such as ethnicity, manufacturing, or mining, but even these areas are often linked together by corridors. Overall, heritage areas usually boast of a composite of resources, ranging from natural to cultural, historical, scenic, and recreational.[68]

The number of heritage areas in the United States has increased significantly since the National Trust for Historic Preservation initiated its Heritage Tourism program in 1990, followed by similar initiatives of the American Association of Museums and the National Conference of State Historic Preservation Officers. Some heritage areas and corridors are within or proximate to cities, several are located in less densely populated sections of the country, and others represent combinations of both urban and rural places. The Illinois and Michigan Canal National Heritage Corridor, situated in a metropolitan area, became, in 1984, the first NPS unit of this type. Since then, rural areas, villages, and small cities have been included in heritage corridors like Trails across Wyoming, which features the major wagon and railroad routes that played an important role in the settlement of the American West; the Chattahoochee Trace, a heritage tourism corridor in Alabama and Georgia that includes historic landmarks, scenic sites, and lakes; and Tennessee Backroads Heritage, which interprets the history of three counties along a transportation corridor dating back to prehistoric time.

In July 1998, the corridor concept was expanded even further when a panel appointed by President Bill Clinton selected fourteen of the nation's waterways as American Heritage Rivers. Battlefield sites are also being included within the purview of the corridor concept, as illustrated by recent efforts of the states of Illinois and Kentucky to create the Ohio River Civil War Heritage Trail. The corridor identifies and interprets thirty-three military, industrial, political, and commercial sites that were important during the conflict.[69] One of the largest programs is Silos and Smokestacks, a regional heritage tourism program embracing more than eighty sites, communities, and attractions in northeastern Iowa. Dedicating itself "to becoming the premier national and international destination for showcasing and interpreting American agriculture," Silos and Smokestacks in 1996 was designated the nation's first heritage tourism partnership to be sponsored by the U.S. Department of Agriculture.[70]

Most heritage areas and corridors, which require cooperation among several units of government and private organizations, are directed toward economic promotion and development. Silos and Smokestacks, for example, is seen as "a promising approach to revitalization that combines heritage tourism and small business development with preservation, recreation, natural resource conservation, interpretation, and education in a strategic effort to supplement and diversify—thereby enhancing—a community's overall economic activity." Likewise, the plan for Nebraska's River Country Heritage Tourism Region states that heritage tourism "goes beyond the academic study of history. Indeed, the concept is a formidable economic development tool for regions, linking resources in a way that increases their attraction to new markets of visitors." Farther to the north and proximate to the American-Canadian border, the Wild North Heritage Tourism Program proclaims that the project "is aimed at strengthening and diversifying the economy of northeastern Minnesota through tourism."[71]

Economic factors certainly need to receive significant attention if these and other preservation efforts are to succeed. Nevertheless, it would be unfortunate if heritage tourism, whether promoted or practiced within a corridor or some other configuration, is simply viewed as an economic panacea by governments and organizations seeking to capitalize upon the historic resources of a district or region.

| Conclusion

Vernacular landscapes are so ubiquitous in America that only a small number of preservationists have given them much consideration, and they are not generally included in the public's understanding of historic resources. Certainly, not all ordinary or vernacular landscapes can be preserved, nor should all of them be given such attention. And, of course, once a landscape is protected, it no longer is "ordinary." Nonetheless, some historic vernacular landscapes do merit preservation because they have outstanding educational, scenic, or cultural value. Those that have been preserved to date represent a spectrum, albeit limited, of America's ordinary places and areas.

Many of the vernacular landscapes discussed in this chapter are located in areas of the nation where economic limitations and distance from population centers have established their character and allowed them to exist in a relatively undisturbed form. In these places, local governments, groups, and individuals may not possess the necessary awareness, expertise, or monetary resources to carry out preservation activities—when and if they are warranted or deemed necessary. In addition, some forms of preservation treatment may compromise the authenticity and utility of vernacular landscapes that continue to function as working environments. On the other hand, in areas where the attractiveness of a vernacular landscape is responsible for the emergence

Main Street of Viroqua, southwestern Wisconsin. Small-town Main Streets are among the most common and numerous cultural landscapes still evident in several areas of the nation. Many Main Streets, however, are under siege as new commercial facilities emerge on the fringes of communities. The Main Street program, initially sponsored by the National Trust for Historic Preservation, has contributed to the development of numerous state-administered programs that provide assistance to small cities and towns seeking to revitalize declining or threatened downtown districts. Shortly after a Wal-Mart discount store opened just outside Viroqua in 1986, seven retail stores closed along three blocks of Main Street. Three years later, after Viroqua was selected as one of Wisconsin's first Main Street communities, the town embarked upon a program to co-exist, rather than compete, with Wal-Mart by attracting specialty businesses to vacant stores. In 1999, all of Viroqua's downtown commercial spaces were occupied (Jackson 1992; Mahan 1999). Photograph by Alanen, 1998.

of new (and often noncompatible) development, the very essence of the historic cultural landscape may be severely endangered. This is especially true in agricultural districts where local residents pursue employment in nearby towns and communities or retire from farming: buildings are vacated or modified, typical agricultural practices are discontinued, and land-use patterns change as fields are either abandoned or subdivided to accommodate new development.

As the homogenization of the landscape becomes increasingly evident throughout America, vernacular expressions undoubtedly will assume greater importance because of their ability to exhibit the characteristics and subtleties of the national cultural mosaic. Some vernacular landscapes will be preserved to portray the distinctiveness of different places as they existed at specific points in time, but the real challenge will be to develop both the will and the means to maintain those landscapes that continue to exist and evolve as places where people reside, work, and pursue their everyday activities. If we cannot maintain these evolving landscapes, the vernacular may become an endangered landscape form that belies the very terms *typical* and *ordinary.*

CHAPTER SIX

Asian American Imprints on the Western Landscape

GAIL LEE
DUBROW

Immigrants from Asia and the Pacific Islands have played significant roles in the development of the American West, yet the vast array of cultural resources associated with these groups has only begun to be documented in California, Nevada, Oregon, Idaho, and Washington. Many private individuals and public agencies in the region own properties that contain cultural resources associated with Asian Pacific Americans, but surprisingly few are aware of this fact. One reason is that immigrants from Asia and the Pacific Islands left remarkably few obvious cultural imprints on the built environment and landscape; instead, they tended to occupy and make practical alterations to standard American building types and landscapes (with a few notable exceptions). Another factor contributing to the relative invisibility of Asian Pacific American cultural resources has been that many preservation agencies, until recently, lacked the knowledge base and guidance needed to identify these resources effectively, evaluate their significance, and work with community groups to plan for their protection.

Though immigrants from Asia and the Pacific Islands to the United States constitute a diverse group encompassing a wide range of national origins, including China, Japan, Korea, the Philippines, Hawaii, Samoa, South Asia (India, Pakistan, Bangladesh, Sri Lanka), and more recently Southeast Asia, the existing base of knowledge about the cultural resources associated with Asian Pacific Americans is largely limited to the heritage of Chinese and Japanese Americans in the western states. This chapter synthesizes what is known about the cultural landscapes associated with these immigrant groups based on statewide preservation planning efforts and the documentation of individual properties, and it provides an agenda for enhancing the protection of these cultural resources.

While certain aspects of the built environment associated with immigrants from Asia and the Pacific Islands have been well represented in the nation's preservation programs, cultural landscapes figure prominently among the neglected classes of cultural resources that merit enhanced preservation planning efforts, particularly those located at town sites and in forests and rural settings. Recent preservation planning studies undertaken by state historic preservation offices, focusing on the contributions of Asian Americans, have begun to fill the gaps in our understanding of Chinese and to a lesser extent Japanese contributions to shaping the western landscape. Additional work is needed to understand fully the contributions of other Asian and Pacific American groups and to link that history to particular historic properties.

The best-known and most effectively preserved examples of cultural resources associated with Asian Pacific Americans are located in urban areas. These Chinatowns, Little Tokyos, Little Manilas, and Koreatowns embody patterns of segregation that are not merely social phenomena; they might also be understood as spatial expressions of racialized relations inscribed upon the urban landscape. These ethnic enclaves, in part the expression of community identity founded on common culture and language, also were forged as a result of restrictive immigration policies and pervasive discrimination in the sale and rental of property. Less familiar than the cultural resources associated with Asian Pacific Americans in urban areas, however, are examples of segregated Chinese and Japanese settlements in town sites and villages once associated with extractive industries. By looking outside the familiar urban districts at a broader array of settings, one finds previously overlooked evidence of Asian American cultural landscapes.

| Company Towns

Washington has several documented examples of company towns that contained segregated settlements of Chinese and Japanese workers, particularly in the fish canning and lumber industries. Asian immigrants formed the backbone of the labor force in Pacific Northwest canneries. Major employers, such as the Pacific American Fisheries located in Bellingham or the contractors who supplied the canneries with laborers, typically provided segregated bunkhouses for Asian workers ubiquitously known as *China houses*. A 1911 report of the U.S. Immigration Commission on the status of immigrants in industries noted that separate bunkhouses sometimes were provided for Chinese and Japanese workers, but often they were lodged in different parts of the

Bunkhouses for Asian workers in Pacific Northwest canneries ubiquitously were known as *China houses,* including these Filipino quarters at the P.H.J. Cannery of the Alaska Packers Association, Nushagak, Alaska, 1917. Source: Photograph by John Cobb. Courtesy of Special Collections, University of Washington Libraries. Negative UW13957; Cobb 4139.

same building. As Chris Friday explained in his history of Asian American labor in the Pacific Coast canned-salmon industry,

> Since Japanese crews were smaller and arrived later in the season than Chinese crews, and they were not represented by a contractor, only some of their bunkhouses had attached mess halls. For the same reasons, most were also considerably smaller than the Chinese bunkhouses. With the waning of Chinese numerical dominance in the crews after 1905, canners found that by building smaller compartments designed to house eight to sixteen workers within the larger bunkhouses, they could segregate the crew members without having to build and maintain separate facilities . . . Only occasionally might workers from different groups live together in the same room.[1]

The usual practice was for both groups to eat at separate tables in a common dining room.[2] The bunkhouses were inhabited primarily by single men, although they sometimes included a few families. A 1905 example of this building type still stands in the Washington town of South Bend in Pacific County.[3]

At some remote sites associated with the lumber industry, which once contained vital settlements of Asian immigrants, the structures have long since been demolished and the only signs of the workers' past presence are subtle clues in the landscape. The mill town of Barneston, established by the Kent Lumber Company in 1898 in the Cedar River Basin in western Washington, was one of many in the state that employed Japanese workers. The nearly twenty-seven hundred Japanese immigrants who were employed in Washington State's lumber industry in 1907 constituted more than 20 percent of the labor force. A statewide survey conducted two years later found approximately twenty-two hundred Japanese workers employed in sixty-seven mill and logging camps.[4]

The segregated settlement or camp of Japanese lumber workers that existed at Barneston was well documented in 1911 photographs taken by the Seattle Water Department (in conjunction with condemnation proceedings intended to protect the quality of the city's water sources). They show that Barneston's Japantown consisted of a cluster of simple gabled- and hipped-roof, wood-frame cottages set in a forest of fir and alder that had been badly scarred by lumbering. Workers rented homes from the company but made their own improvements to the landscape in conjunction with subsistence activities; they constructed chicken yards and cultivated strawberry patches in their home gardens.[5]

Despite the Japanese workers' subsistence activities, lumber mill towns were not self-sustaining communities, as the nearby town of Selleck, created in 1908 by the Pacific States Lumber Company, illustrates. Selleck contained a cohesive settlement of Japanese workers and their families on a peripheral site cleared for them by the company.[6] One former Selleck resident remembers that, although they had a general store, Japanese residents relied on monthly visits from representatives of major Asian importers with headquarters in Seattle. These door-to-door peddlers sold rice, *nori,* miso, tofu, *shoyu,* meat, and fish that enabled the Japanese to maintain their traditional dietary practices while working in remote areas of the Pacific Northwest. One man described such a town as consisting of "a smelly group of young bachelors some ten miles deep in the mountains with no amusement whatsoever except the sound of the wind echoing among the hills and the whine of the milling machines."[7]

Both Barneston and Selleck had some culturally distinctive community structures, such as Japanese-style bathhouses, the location of which suggests that they were principally intended for use by the single men who lived in

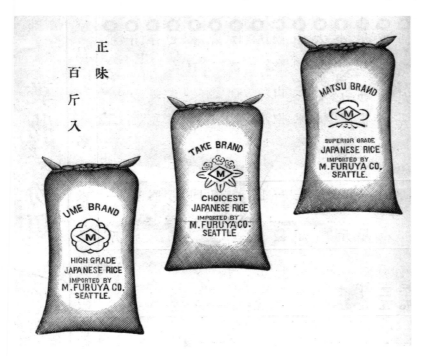

Importers such as the Furuya Company, with headquarters in Portland, Tacoma, Seattle, and Vancouver, supplied familiar foods to Japanese immigrants working in remote locations (1915). Source: *Catalog of the M. Furuya Company.* Courtesy of Frank Natsuhara.

nearby boarding houses. Families tended to have their own private *furos,* or soaking tubs, although children sometimes preferred the community facility because "it was bigger and you could swim in it."[8] The Japanese residents of Selleck built a language school as well. Despite the clear pattern of racialized segregation inscribed in the landscape, by the 1920s life in the Japanese camp had a bicultural character.[9] The most popular sport there, as in other Japanese American communities, was the favorite American pastime, baseball; nevertheless, segregated teams were the norm. Selleck's Yamatos played Japanese baseball teams from the nearby cities of Seattle and Tacoma as well as other western Washington mill towns.[10]

Although the structures associated with Barneston's Japantown have long been demolished, the remaining landscape elements, including several large stumps and a depression at the site of the millpond, are the only obvious marks signifying that the place once served as a lumber mill camp. Cultural debris located on the surface of the site, however, suggests the potential value of archeological excavation for better understanding the lives of Japanese American lumber mill workers during the early decades of the twentieth century.[11]

| Gardens, Farms, Water Systems, and Roads

One of the most systematic treatments of cultural resources associated with Chinese and, to a lesser extent, Japanese Americans in the West can be found in Eugene Hattori's and William White's contributions to the *Nevada Comprehensive Preservation Plan*,[12] which identifies farms and truck gardens, linear features such as ditches/flumes and railroads, placer mining sites, and temporary work camps as the most significant landscape elements.[13] The cited examples suggest that placenames can mark the past presence of Asian Americans; indeed, there are mountains, waterways, and town and garden sites throughout the West that carry the names China, Nippon, or other clear signifiers. In Elko County, Nevada, for example, the town site now known as Carlin historically was called Chinese Gardens because of the vegetable plots established by Central Pacific Railroad workers.[14] Modifications to local water systems, for the purposes of mining and gardening, often signify sites of Chinese settlement. Chinese workers in the railroad town of Elko established an irrigation system by constructing waterwheels in the Humboldt River to serve their "China Ranch" garden.[15] This technology reportedly was introduced into the western states by Chinese miners who constructed waterwheels "similar to those used by farmers in China. Mounted with buckets to scoop water from a stream or river, the wheel, as it turned slowly, emptied the buckets of water into a trough that carried the water to where it was needed."[16] Landscape features such as cabin sites, work camps, and garden sites, identified in the Lake Tahoe Basin, have been linked to Chinese labor in the lumber industry.[17] Companies of Chinese placer miners developed ditches, roads, and mines in the Tuscarora mining district, and in Mineral County, wood cutting and charcoal production camps run by the Chinese served local mining towns.[18]

Archeological investigations have revealed evidence of the activities of Chinese miners in the West. For example, remaining cultural features documented by Forest Service and University of Idaho archeologists at the Moore Gulch Chinese Mining site, located in Clearwater County, Idaho, mark Chinese efforts to adapt western river systems to accommodate extractive industries such as placer mining. So intensive were their efforts to extract gold from land often already worked over by white miners "that almost every drainage" studied by archeologists on the approximately 73-acre site "contains abundant evidence of early gold mining activity."[19] Among the remaining features of the cultural landscape are "numerous water diversion ditches, ground sluices, earthen dams, tailings and channels, and a timber 'corduroy' for an old wagon trail."[20] These types of sites are ubiquitous in the western National Forests. In Idaho, where the Chinese were the largest ethnic minority group during the mining boom, a systematic survey of nearly two hundred historic mining sites in the Warren Mining District revealed at least forty with some Chinese influence.[21] Elsewhere, the Chinese link to cultural resources associated with the mining boom has only been documented sporadically.

Chinese placer miners also have been associated with the design and construction of substantial engineering works in Washington state.[22] Along the Methow River, they built a three-mile system of ditches and flumes known as China Ditch to carry water to the gold-bearing sandbars on the west side of the Columbia River. After placer mining faded out, these ditches and troughs are known to have been reused by farmers and orchardists as primary irrigation systems. Although a 1948 flood destroyed the headworks, flumes, and canal, some traces of the original system are evident from a small section of the abandoned canal. Other types of historic properties identified with Chinese placer miners along the Columbia River include a dugout hillside home, with a fireplace at one end, bunks on the sides, and a roof piled with grass and dirt. Approximately twenty of the forty sites identified with the Chinese in Idaho's Warren Mining District contained evidence of earthen dwellings.[23] They generally appear in the forest "as square or rectangular shaped depressions covered in thick vegetation with collapsed rubble consisting of cobblestones or angular rock."[24]

Commercial activities such as terraced gardens that supported predominantly Chinese mining districts left their mark, as well, on the mountainous western landscape. In the period from 1870 to 1900, the north central Idaho mining district of Warren principally was populated by Chinese immigrants who worked placer deposits in Warren Creek and its tributaries. Fresh produce was transported to the town of Warren by packhorse from gardens located approximately sixteen pack-trail miles away. Jeffrey Fee has explained the cultural and economic significance of these gardens in light of the centrality of vegetables and fruits in the traditional Chinese diet, as well as the difficulty and expense of bringing fresh produce into this remote wilderness.[25] In these contexts, it is possible to appreciate more fully reports of the high quality of the vegetables produced by the Chinese gardeners who established terraces on the slopes of China Mountain and their tenacity in maintaining some traditional gardening and dietary practices.

At the Ah Toy site, named for its last known Chinese occupant, 116 earthen terraces have been identified on a mountainside that has a 30 percent slope.

The 3-acre garden produced vegetables, strawberries, apples, grapes, and rhubarb. Farther up the mountain, the 3½ acre Chi-Sandra Garden, containing 30 to 50 terraces, was located at a more isolated and protected site. The uppermost of the three gardens is the 12-acre Celadon Slope, where one of the few level surfaces above the South Fork of the Salmon River was chosen as the site for 30 terraces.[26] Although several of the terraces were spring-fed, gardeners drew water for most of them from ditches that channeled the flow from China Creek. These three terraced gardens are significant examples of the adaptation of traditional Chinese agricultural practices to the mountainous terrain of the western mining frontier. The remaining terraces and irrigation system, along with the grapevines and rhubarb that still grow at the Ah Toy site, are reminders of a time when these Chinese gardens served a population of six hundred to twelve hundred Chinese placer miners and other white miners in Idaho's Salmon River Mountains.[27]

Many western cities and town sites had outlying properties known as Chinese or China Gardens. One of the most notable examples was located in Walla Walla, Washington, a city that served as a center for Chinese farming. "At the turn of the century," according to historian Gail Nomura,

Walla Walla had a Chinese population of about 400 to 500, most of whom were engaged in vegetable farming on the outskirts of town. Called the "Chinese Gardens," Chinese farming colonies in the Walla Walla area rented productive agricultural land in the lowlands of the valley streams. At first they sold vegetables in the local market, but with the establishment of shipping houses in the early 1890s, Chinese gardeners began selling to the shippers for distribution to more distant markets. "Chinese greens" were sent to Seattle-area Chinese for years.[28]

Long dismissed as unskilled labor, the Chinese actually engaged in remarkable feats of engineering and construction, not only in the creation of terraced commercial gardens, but also as hired hands for ranches, railroads, and vineyards. Similarly, the endurance and skill of Chinese workers in extractive industries and agriculture merit greater recognition, since they were so often channeled into occupations and sectors of industry considered too marginal, dangerous, unbearable, or demeaning for white workers.

The State of California's survey of ethnic sites, *Five Views,* identified features that reflect the distinctive contributions of Chinese labor crews to the development of the state's economy and landscape. One of the best-documented examples of the masonry techniques of the overseas Chinese is a four-mile-long stone wall, constructed of uncut fieldstones with no mortar, running along the rolling hills of the Quick Ranch in Mariposa, California. Old stone walls located in the western states often are known by names that suggest an association with Chinese builders, yet these connections have been definitively established in only a few cases. Because the Quick Ranch has remained in the control of one family for six generations and written record of its 1862 construction survives, it has been possible to document the ranch's connection with Chinese builders.[29]

The contributions of Chinese laborers to the building of the western half of the first transcontinental railroad have been well established, and the rail line itself has left a permanent mark on the landscape. Yet it also might be understood as an ethnic cultural landscape because of the particular role played by Chinese crews in reshaping the mountainous terrain west of the Rockies. It was Chinese workers who carved the ledges on enormous outcroppings of rock to make way for the railroad. At Cape Horn, Sucheng Chan has written, "Chinese were lowered by rope in wicker baskets from the top of the cliffs. While thus dangled, they chiseled holes in the granite into which they stuffed black powder. Fellow workers pulled them up as the powder exploded. Those who did not make it up in time died in the explosion."[30] Chinese crews worked through the seasons under extreme conditions to clear and grade the rail line, even drilling through solid granite to make a path through the Sierra Nevada. Perhaps the traditional emphasis on group cooperation in Chinese culture allowed the railroad crews to complete these extraordinary projects.

Chinese immigrants participated in the harvest as seasonal laborers, but they also made significant contributions to the agricultural economy as tenant farmers, as Chan's interpretive history, *Asian Americans,* indicates:

In California's great Central Valley as well as smaller coastal valleys and plains, in Washington's Yakima Valley, Oregon's Hood River Valley, and in arable areas in other states west of the Rocky Mountains, Chinese leased land to become tenant farmers. For the most part, they specialized in labor-intensive vegetables, strawberries, and other small fruits, deciduous tree fruits, and nuts. In the Sacramento–San Joaquin Delta, a reclaimed marshland that is one of the most fertile agricultural areas of California, Chinese tenant farmers grew potatoes, onions, and asparagus—leasing large plots, many of which they had earlier helped to drain, dike, and put under the plow.[31]

Carey McWilliams credited Chinese workers with the transformation of "farming in California from wheat to fruit."[32] Historian Ronald Takaki suggests that this was possible because experienced Chinese farmers who became laborers in America "shared their agricultural knowledge with their white employers, teaching them how to plant, cultivate, and harvest orchard and garden crops."[33] In the fertile valleys of the western states, the development of the agricultural landscape was shaped by the knowledge and fueled by the labor of Asian immigrants.

Historian Patricia Nelson Limerick's 1992 meditation on the American landscape as experienced by people of Asian origin and descent, "Disorientation and Reorientation," published in the *Journal of American History,* raised the question of how to think about the experiences and perceptions of people who "discovered" that landscape from the west. Asian Americans clearly recognized the untapped economic potential of the landscape and had their own visions of order and standards of productivity. Yet an environmental perspective makes Limerick skeptical of past scholarship narrowly focused on Asian Americans' positive contributions to shaping the Western landscape, since these laudatory accounts have tended to gloss over the environmental consequences of stripping forests for timber, reclaiming delta land for agriculture, and excavating mountains for railroad tunnels: "Given the recognition of the various ways in which economic development exacted a heavy price from the physical environment, is a group's active role in the reshaping of the landscape and the domination of nature still an occasion for congratulations?"[34] Limerick offers a reminder that the intersection of ethnic and environmental themes requires a more nuanced reading than can be achieved through a defensive focus on ethnic contributions to history.

| *Social Relations Reflected in the Landscape*

Rising anti-Chinese sentiment during the last quarter of the nineteenth century created difficult conditions for Chinese working in many areas. In the process, the landscape associated with the Chinese was transformed into a battleground of contested meanings. For Chinese tenant farmers on Whidbey Island, off the western Washington coast, the aboveground "pits" in which they overwintered a portion of their potato crop represented wealth in the form of surplus produce held off the market until the right price could be obtained. In the eyes of exclusionists, those same pits represented a threatening transition from seasonal Chinese labor to year-round settlement; thus, the pits became targets of racially motivated bombings intended to drive Chinese farmers off the island.[35]

Careful examination of California's vineyards, frequently developed with the assistance of Chinese labor, provides an opportunity to look beyond the scenic qualities of the landscape to witness inequitable social relations encoded in seemingly natural settings. The Chinese worked at the Haraszthy Buena Vista Winery, in Sonoma. Beginning in 1857 they cleared land to enlarge the vineyard, blasted and excavated enormous hillside tunnels for wine storage, and performed backbreaking "stoop labor" in the fields. The force of social and labor relations in shaping the actual form of the landscape is rarely recognized, yet changing standards for pruning grapevines suggest that even the height that vineyard owners considered appropriate for plants may have varied according to their perception of the workers' status. The level of discomfort associated with particular methods of cultivation, in turn, may have shaped the ethnic composition of the agricultural labor force. "Although grape vines are now pruned to waist height, they were originally pruned to a foot and a half above the ground. This forced the picker to bend his back to a painful angle. Many non-Chinese laborers could not or would not perform stoop labor. About 1890, pruning customs changed, and there was much agitation to replace Chinese workers with white laborers,"[36] which was part and parcel of a broader reactionary movement in the western states pressing for Chinese exclusion.

If in certain time periods and places the form of the landscape could mirror the low status of Asian immigrants in America, discriminatory property laws threatened outright to dispossess them. Beginning in 1913 in California and sweeping the western states into the mid-1920s, laws and ordinances targeted Asian immigrants by prohibiting aliens ineligible for citizenship from owning land and in some cases even placing restrictions on their right to lease it. While not consistently enforced, these laws led farmers who had immigrated from Asia and the Pacific Islands to develop a variety of strategies for protecting their ability to operate. In response to the Alien Land Laws, Japanese American farmers struggled to keep their property by putting it in the names of children born in the United States (who were automatically accorded citizenship) or sympathetic white neighbors. Those who lacked the necessary means or method to own property often negotiated for a succession of leases. These complicated patterns of ownership and leasing make it a difficult but important task to document cultural resources associated with Asian Americans in agriculture. Not only are their farmsteads significant, but also several sites are associated with their efforts to challenge the legality of the Alien Land Laws. The Oyama property in Chula Vista was the basis for the 1948 U.S. Supreme Court ruling that upheld the right of minor children to own land, and litigation over the Sei Fujii property in Los Angeles resulted in California's Alien Land Law being declared unconstitutional in the 1950s.[37]

Asian Americans in Western Agriculture

Despite these formidable barriers, Asian Americans played a leading role in western agriculture. Beginning in 1893, the first Japanese immigrants settled in the White River Valley, an area of western Washington that would grow to have the largest number of Japanese farmers in the state. The concentration of Japanese immigrants in farming was due, in equal parts, to traditional skills, new opportunities, and exclusion from other occupations and industries.

Overt signs of ethnic identity were rare on the farms established by Japanese immigrants, as can be seen in this undated photograph of a farm in the Black River Valley of Washington. Source: Courtesy of Special Collections, University of Washington Libraries. Postcard collection.

Many of the Issei, or first generation of immigrants, came from Japanese farming families. Others acquired the necessary skills by working as farmhands or apprentices after coming to America. Population growth in the Puget Sound region led the Japanese in the White River Valley to enter dairy farming. Those who explored other economic alternatives, such as opening small businesses in nearby towns, soon found themselves subject to racial harassment.[38] So significant was their presence in dairy farming during the 1920s that Japanese farmers reportedly provided half of Seattle's milk supply.[39] While the appearance of most Japanese farmsteads differed little from that of property farmed by their white neighbors, Japanese architectural traditions occasionally were incorporated into new construction. Several western Washington barns intended to shelter dairy cows, built in the 1910s, incorporated the traditional *irimoya* (gable into hipped) roof form, though the structural system probably consisted of frame rather than post-and-beam construction.[40]

Gradually, the landscape associated with Japanese farmers in the White River Valley shifted away from dairying, which became less profitable, and over to raising berries and other produce, including lettuce, beans, cauliflower, peas, cabbage, celery, carrots, and radishes. By the beginning of World War I, Japanese farmers supplied 75 percent of the region's vegetables; made significant contributions in fruit production, particularly berries; and occupied 70 percent of the produce stalls in Seattle's Pike Place Market.[41] Agricultural properties significant in the history of the White River Valley are now threatened by the general decline of family farms, the aging of the immigrant farmers, and the pressures for commercial and residential development in the area.

Japanese immigrants also became a major force in California agriculture, first as farm laborers and later as tenant farmers. "Between 1900 and 1910," according to one study, "Japanese began to buy property and establish farms, vineyards, and orchards. All-Japanese communities developed in agricultural areas in central California, including Florin in Sacramento County (which the Japanese called *Taishoku*), Bowles in Fresno County, and the Yamato Colony at Livingston in Merced County."[42] Historic properties associated with these communities have been identified in the state's multiethnic sites survey. So profound was their contribution to California agriculture that by 1917 the Japanese reportedly produced "almost 90 percent of the state's output of cel-

The barn on Shigeichi and Shimanoko Hori's dairy farm in Kent, Washington, was one of several in the region that featured the *irimoya* roof traditional in Asian architecture (c. 1919). Source: Beikoku Seihokubu Hiroshima-Kenjinkai (1919), plate 121.

A rural farmhouse in Mountain View, California, where Japanese Americans, who were evacuated soon after (during World War II), raised truck garden crops (April 1941). Source: Courtesy of the Library of Congress.

ery, asparagus, onions, tomatoes, berries, and cantaloupes; more than 70 percent of the floricultural products; 50 percent of the seeds; 45 percent of the sugar beets; 40 percent of the leafy vegetables; and 35 percent of the grapes."[43] In his recent history of multicultural America, *A Different Mirror*, Ronald Takaki has credited Japanese pioneers in California with the transformation of "marginal lands like the hog wallow lands in the San Joaquin Valley, the dusty lands in the Sacramento Valley, and the desert lands in the Imperial Valley into lush and profitable agricultural fields and orchards."[44] Those looking for small signs of a distinctive Asian imprint on cultural resources associated with agriculture miss the larger picture: It simply is not possible to understand the agricultural landscape of the American West without observing the central roles Asian Americans played in creating it.

Although it would appear, with the exception of obvious examples such as Chinese terraced gardens, that Asian Americans typically did not leave many distinctive cultural imprints on the agricultural landscape, their past presence sometimes can be detected in culturally specific uses for seemingly ordinary outbuildings on rural properties. Hothouses, such as the ones remaining on the Hamakami Farm in western Washington (which at one time had approximately eighty acres in production), reflect a pattern of ethnic concentration in growing and cooperatively marketing certain crops, in this case hothouse rhubarb by Japanese and Filipino farmers.[45] Similarly, the presence of a wood-fired *furo,* or soaking tub, in either a freestanding outbuilding or a shed attached to a rural residence clearly marks the past presence of a Japanese household. In his personal history of Vashon Island, located in western Washington on Puget Sound, Fred Eernisse remembers that "every strawberry field that had Japanese tenants had a bathhouse containing a metal bathing tank that was heated from the outside with roots and wood from clearing land."[46] At least two remaining examples of the sheds that housed rural examples of family *furos* have been identified in western Washington, one on Bainbridge Island and the other in Auburn.[47]

| *Flower Fields, Nurseries, and Formal Gardens*

Commercial flower fields, nurseries, and formal gardens are three more examples of landscapes associated with Japanese Americans in the West. In 1892, the Japanese began commercial flower cultivation in Los Angeles. This operation, which started with field carnations, grew to include violets, chrysanthemums, roses, and garden plants. Originally these flowers were carried to market on the streetcar. "When a crop was picked, the small grower packed it into a large wicker trunk called a *yanagi-kori,* covered it with cloth, and carried it on his shoulder to the streetcar stop."[48] Growers turned to other means of transportation when the streetcar companies prohibited them from carrying the flowers on board. As documented in the multiethnic historical itinerary of Los Angeles created by the Power of Place project, historic properties associated with Japanese Americans in floriculture include not only the long-since-developed sites of the first flower fields, but also the cooperative Flower Market that growers established to distribute their products.[49]

Reaching beyond the basic productive aspects of farming, Japanese immigrants' vital presence in the nursery business suggests an interest in cultivating particular aesthetic qualities in the landscape. Early in the twentieth century on Bainbridge Island in Puget Sound, the nursery Bainbridge Gardens earned a reputation for founder Zenhichi Harui's cultivation of giant chrysanthemums, a prized flower in the residential gardens of many Japanese Americans. A knowledge of these and other varieties long cultivated within the Japanese American community is perpetuated by organizations such as the Evergreen Chrysanthemum Association of King County, Washington. Bainbridge Gardens is significant as one of only a few Japanese American nurseries that were reestablished in Washington after the profound disloca-

Giant chrysanthemums cultivated at Bainbridge Gardens, on Bainbridge Island, Washington, are a reminder of the horticultural knowledge possessed by Japanese Americans working in the nursery business and gardening. Shown are Mrs. Seko and Mrs. Harui of Bainbridge Gardens, 1936. Source: Courtesy of the Bainbridge Island Japanese-American Community Archives, Tsukada Collection.

tion of internment during World War II. Historian Patricia Limerick has found traces of an aesthetic imprint and an undercurrent of political resistance even in the most hostile of landscapes, most notably World War II internment camps. Although the creation of gardens in the camps frequently has been regarded by outside observers as evidence of Japanese Americans' compliance with wartime imprisonment, Limerick suggests a more complex reading of the landscape as "a symbol of defiance, a visible statement of an unbroken will," and a determined effort to make life bearable even in the most difficult of places.[50]

The numerous formal gardens established, inspired, or maintained by the Japanese on the western coast of the United States represent the most obvious examples of their influence on the landscape. The design of these gardens has been shaped by a coherent system of culturally specific aesthetic preferences, as revealed in the choice of forms and decorative details, as well as plant materials. Landscape features typically found in Japanese gardens include lanterns, water basins, bridges, gateways, walls, and fences. Stone lanterns are usually octagonal, hexagonal, or square and were originally used to provide light for the traditional nocturnal tea ceremony. Similarly, the water basin originated in the tea garden because of the Japanese custom of purification by rinsing the mouth and hands before entering the tearoom. The Japanese garden gate is typically a simple gabled structure topped by a tile, tree bark, or thatched roof. It is relatively narrow and often equipped with two wooden doors ornamented with bamboo. Garden walls are commonly constructed of clay, board, or stone and are viewed as important elements in composing the background of the garden, as well as enhancing the garden's vertical beauty. Fences are commonly constructed of bamboo and serve to lighten the mood

Japanese American nurserymen in Los Angeles County selling out their stock before being sent to internment camps (April 1942). Source: Photograph by Russell Lee. Courtesy of the Library of Congress. LCUSF 34-72385-D.

of the garden by not shutting away the scene beyond as completely as might a stone wall.[51] The first Japanese garden on the West Coast, which was created in 1894, survives in San Francisco, as do several others in California, Oregon, and Washington.[52]

| Traditional Cultural Practices

Traditional cultural properties are perhaps the most poorly documented types of landscapes associated with Asian Americans in the West. Scattered accounts, however, suggest the range of landscapes that might be considered significant in the preservation of traditional cultural practices. A lone photograph in the Bainbridge Island Japanese-American Community Archives

Dr. Kiyoichi Iwasa and Frank Kitamoto hunting for mushrooms in a western Washington forest (1940). Courtesy of the Bainbridge Island Japanese-American Community Archives, Shigeko Kitamoto Collection.

documents a 1940s mushroom-hunting expedition, probably in the vicinity of Port Townsend; perhaps the men pictured in the photograph were searching for the *shitake* or *matsutake* (wild mushrooms) prized in Japanese cooking. Today, south central Oregon forests such as the Winema and Deschutes supply about 8 percent of the world's supply of *matsutake* mushrooms, which grow in the roots of pine trees. A multimillion-dollar commercial market, which has developed during the past decade, has resulted in cutthroat competition that has made Northwest forests a more dangerous place for Japanese Americans and others hunting the mushrooms purely for personal consumption.[53]

In his history of the Washington lumber mill town of Port Blakely, on Bainbridge Island, Andrew Price alludes to traditional cultural landscapes associated with turn-of-the-century settlements of Japanese mill workers in the villages of Yama and Nagaya. One former resident recalled hunting "for the *matsutake* (wild mushrooms) and *warabi* (edible fern) on the hillsides" as a popular seasonal activity.[54] The villages' location on Puget Sound also provided the Japanese residents with easy access to many traditional foods. "Pleasant Beach wasn't far away, and the ladies made frequent trips there to get clams and *nori,* the seaweed that grew in the clean waters of Rich Passage. The *nori* was dried over lines strung on the porches at Yama. Once dried, it was heated in ovens until brittle and then crumbled over rice."[55] The coastline also provided urban residents with a taste of home, as church groups and prefectural associations headed to parks and beaches for summer picnics. As Masako Osada of Tacoma recalled,

we enjoyed our picnics, playing games and so on to our heart's content. Those who liked fishing caught rock-cod and roasted them immediately. And at low tide we caught butterclams, "geoduck" and so on. Squid were caught at Point Defiance on Puget Sound Bay, and we made them into *sashimi* or *shiokara,* or cooked them, thus appreciating the tastes of home. We had a song, a parody of *"Kusatsu Bushi,"* which goes:

> A nice place, Tacoma! Come over once.
> Mushrooms on the hill, octopus in the sea.

We caught octopus just like those we had in Japan. At least up to World War II, we had Japanese meals. I think it was after the war when we started eating Western food.[56]

As historian Chris Friday has documented, Chinese workers in the Pacific Northwest salmon canning industry also harvested coastal resources such as wapato (a bulbous root), seaweed, freshwater mussels, and saltwater clams to supplement the meager subsistence diet labor contractors provided.[57] The aquatic environment and landscape of the Pacific Coast contain many more examples of places that reflect the persistence and adaptation of traditional cultural practices, which have untapped potential to be designated and protected as historic resources.

| *Surveying Ethnic Resources*

The few known examples of cultural landscapes associated with Asian Americans are no reflection on the extent of their contributions to the western economy and relationship to the landscape. Rather, gaps in the coverage of many themes and property types associated with Asian Americans within historic preservation programs suggest the need for preservation agencies to work with members of Asian American communities to identify the wide array of cultural resources that remain undocumented. The only known statewide survey focusing on Asian American properties was undertaken by the California Office of Historic Preservation in conjunction with its multiethnic historic sites survey. That study's effectiveness in identifying properties points to the value of focused ethnic theme studies, as opposed to more broadly defined but geographically bounded surveys, as tools for identifying ethnic cultural resources.

While properties associated with Asian Americans can be identified in geographically defined surveys, especially in places that contained major settlements, experience has shown that many important properties will be missed without the active involvement of community elders. Gaps in the documentary record and the still-emerging status of scholarship in the field require preservation planners intent on documenting Asian American cultural resources to place greater emphasis on gathering oral history and employing public participation methods. One preservation student's afternoon drive with Koji Norikani, a long-term resident of Washington's historic White River Valley, resulted in the identification of numerous agricultural properties associated with Japanese Americans that had not been inventoried. Fred and Dorothy Cordova are among the most important sources for documenting Filipino history and cultural resources in the state of Washington; other communities have similar figures. In most cases, key people such as Mr. Norikani and the Cordovas have been involved in a variety of community history programs but have rarely been asked to link their knowledge to specific properties for the purposes of historic preservation. Past models of preservation planning, focused on identifying architecturally significant buildings, largely have relied on the expertise of design professionals. The identification of ethnic cultural resources, however, requires preservation planners to draw on knowledge based within ethnic communities.

Fortunately, there is now a body of work that provides a historic context for the protection of Asian American heritage in several western states. The need remains for more detailed work at the local level to outline relevant historical themes and to develop a predictive model of the property types that are likely to be found in local surveys. These preservation planning activities are critical because many of the undocumented resources lack obvious signs of an Asian imprint, making it easy for the unprepared surveyor to miss the more subtle clues of their connection to ethnic heritage.

The problem of effectively managing cultural resources associated with the history of Asian Americans begins, but does not end, with the need for more surveys. The limited base of knowledge about these property types creates further problems when it comes time for staff members in preservation agencies to assess the relative significance and integrity of individual property nominations for national, state, or local landmark designation. They quickly realize that there is a shortage of examples of any given property type to make the necessary comparative assessments. In the absence of a well-developed historic context for protecting Asian American resources or enough examples of cultural resources to draw upon for the purposes of comparison, preservation officials evaluating properties such as China houses at Pacific Northwest cannery sites have found it difficult to answer nagging questions:

—How significant was a particular cannery as a site of Asian American labor?

—How significant were bunkhouses as a property type associated with the labor history of Chinese and Japanese Americans?

—What features need to be present for an individual site, structure, or building to retain its integrity of feeling and association?

—What other examples of bunkhouses exist, and how significant is any particular example?

In the absence of this information, undue emphasis tends to be placed on the issue of physical integrity, which can be a problem for long neglected and undervalued aspects of ethnic heritage embodied in cultural resources. By defining the context, identifying the various property types associated with it, and conducting systematic surveys that provide a sufficient number of examples to develop a useful framework for evaluation, preservation planners will have the necessary tools to evaluate a particular resource against comparable properties within the same context. So few Asian American properties have been identified to date that it will take time to accumulate comparative examples. For that reason, preservation policies should be changed to favor the protection of extant properties until there are enough examples to allow comparative assessments of their relative significance and integrity.

Great gaps still remain in the National Historic Landmark Program, the nation's honor roll of historic properties. There the few designated properties only begin to hint at the richness of Asian American heritage. Intense efforts by Japanese Americans and their allies to gain public recognition of and restitution for World War II internment contributed to the gaining of National Historic Landmark status for the Manzanar War Relocation Center, situated in the vicinity of Lone Pine, California, and for the Rohwer Relocation Center Cemetery in Arkansas. Although the designation of these properties is an appropriate reminder that the unjust relocation and internment of Japanese Americans was a defining moment in American history, it has tended to overshadow other important goals, particularly the designation and protection of Nihonmachis or Japantowns that served as centers of Japanese American community life in the prewar period.[58] A National Historic Landmark theme study of American ethnic communities, which began in the 1970s, resulted in the identification of several prospective landmarks of Asian American heritage, including Chinatown in San Francisco and Little Tokyo in Los Angeles.

The introduction in 1981 of cumbersome new requirements for notifying the owners of properties under consideration for National Historic Landmark designation effectively doomed the Chinatown nomination, since it encompasses such a large number of properties. The designation of Little Tokyo, a significantly smaller district, finally was accomplished in 1995.[59] Despite these important gains, there has been no systematic effort to identify the properties that best mark the contributions Asian Americans have made to the nation's development, as has been done for properties associated with African Americans, women, and labor history.[60]

Even if such a systematic effort to identify nationally significant Asian American properties were to be initiated today, the process of evaluating the significance of prospective landmarks in relation to the National Historic Landmark program's standard of "overarching national significance" would raise some major problems that have been encountered before in the African American and women's history landmark studies. Aside from the most obvious properties, such as Angel Island and Manzanar, few seem to meet the standard of significance on initial inspection. The fact remains that the long history of discrimination, restriction, and oppression shaping ethnic communities of color, workers, and women tends to mitigate against many aspects of their lives being perceived as having that level of significance and works against the survival of many types of cultural resources associated with them. Beyond the ordinary forces that contribute to the erosion of the integrity of historic resources, resources associated with ethnic communities of color face some added challenges, since the devaluation of their historic experience has contributed to the long-term neglect of their cultural resources, further compromising the integrity of the surviving properties.

In the face of these challenges, one strategy for increasing cultural diversity in the roster of designated National Historic Landmarks seems promising: namely, nominating properties with a high degree of integrity that, while primarily significant in a local context, have the power to serve as outstanding representative examples of broader, nationally significant phenomena. Toward that end, Asian American properties listed on the National Register need to be evaluated for potential listing as National Historic Landmarks. Wider latitude within the National Register Program, which allows for evaluating the significance of historic properties at the national, state, or local level, has made it more amenable to listing Asian American cultural resources than the National Historic Landmark Program. The new inventories that emerge from local surveys and the properties otherwise identified as significant by ethnic communities will provide a sound basis for new efforts to nominate to the National Register properties significant in the history of Asian Americans.

These new nominations should fill gaps in the coverage of many themes associated with Chinese and Japanese American heritage and move beyond them to identify cultural resources associated with other Asian American groups. If we look beyond the built environment associated with major urban enclaves of immigrants from Asia and the Pacific Islands, varied cultural landscapes located in rural, wilderness, and small-town settings potentially merit listing on the National Register.

| Overlooking Ethnic Resources in Existing Historic Districts

New efforts to designate Asian American properties will improve their coverage in the National Register program and parallel programs at the local level. This goal, however, also could be advanced by documenting the hidden ethnic heritage associated with some properties declared significant and listed on landmark registers for other reasons. Many historic districts associated with extractive industries such as mining or lumbering, for example, were designated at a time when there was less appreciation of the significance of Asian American labor, and their official boundaries were defined in ways that unnecessarily excluded nearby sites of segregated Asian American settlement.

Dayton, Nevada, provides one example of the possibilities for redefining existing historic districts to make them more historically accurate and culturally inclusive. Recognized as significant in association with the theme of mining, Dayton was home to the first Chinese immigrants in Nevada, who were recruited to construct a canal and then remained to rework the placer mines. Economically central but racially segregated, Dayton's Chinese population resided in a quarter that lies outside the established boundaries of the town's National Historic Landmark District and Comstock Historic District.[61] Similarly, the site of the settlement of Japanese workers at the western Washington lumber mill town of Selleck lies outside the boundaries for the Selleck Historic District, which is listed on the National Register and as a designated King County Landmark. The district is considered one of the most intact examples of a lumber mill town. Its boundaries stop short of the Japanese site because all of the above-ground resources were demolished a long time ago. Since Asian American cultural resources generally were devalued until recently, leading to their destruction, one compensatory strategy might be to extend the boundaries of historic districts such as this one to encompass related sites primarily of interest for archeological reasons, thus enhancing the opportunities for public interpretation of Asian Americans' historic presence.[62]

In other cases, individual property nominations that have overlooked important links to Asian American heritage, or aspects of it, might be amended.

Staff members at the King County Landmarks and Heritage Commission recently supported the development of a new landmark nomination in connection with the history of Japanese American tenant farmers at the Neely
Mansion, long recognized as the home of a white pioneer family who settled
in Auburn in the 1890s and "significant as the most elaborate piece of crafts-
man architecture in unincorporated King County."[63] The farm's later development and economic contributions, however, were primarily due to the
labors of the Japanese and Filipino families who leased it for the greater part
of the twentieth century. This property is an outstanding representative example of the broad pattern of leasing and operation by Japanese and Filipino
immigrants typical in the White River Valley and elsewhere in the West. It was
only through detailed interviews and site visits that their association with the
property could be documented. In the process, an abandoned shed was identified as the shelter for a *furo* that dates to the period of Japanese occupancy
before the 1940s. As a result of these efforts, the shed itself has been designated
as a County Landmark and plans have been initiated to integrate the newly
discovered cultural resource into the Neely Mansion Association's program of
public interpretation.[64] As this example illustrates, the process of amending
landmark nominations is not merely a symbolic gesture. It can contribute to
the protection of neglected cultural resources and the seeding of new interpretive programs.

Ironically, it may also be necessary to reexamine historic properties long
recognized as significant in Asian American heritage because of features that
were overlooked when they were originally documented, as is doubly illustrated by the example of the Panama Hotel in Seattle. A single-room-occu-
pancy, workingman's hotel, the Panama is one of many structures contributing to Seattle's International District. As has been common practice in many
places, the surveys conducted in preparation for the historic district nomination did not extend into the buildings' interiors. Consequently, the district
nomination overlooked two significant cultural resources. Half of the
Panama Hotel's basement contains the only known intact example of an urban bathhouse, the Hashidate-Yu, which is extraordinarily well preserved. As
Max Fukuhara recalled,

soaking in the large and hot *furo* eased the pain of aching muscles and joints, melted
away the stresses of the day and simply felt just great. Often it was a communal experience, providing a forum for trivial or serious discussions. Sometimes after athletic
events such as ballgames, martial arts tournaments, etc., the *furo* would be over-
crowded with guys who assembled here to wash up, unwind and rehash the "what ifs"
or indulge in other small talk. Families went to the bath houses together—fathers with
sons on the mens' side and mothers with daughters on the ladies' side.[65]

One of the most distinctive ethnic markers in the rural landscape associated with Japanese Americans was the family *furo*, or soaking tub. The shed that housed a *furo* on the property of the Neely Mansion in Auburn, Washington, recently was declared a King County Landmark. Photograph by Dubrow, 1994.

Out of use for nearly half a century, the bathhouse silently conveys the vitality of Japanese American community life in the prewar period. The basement of the Panama Hotel also contains a significant number of fully packed trunks stored by Japanese Americans on the eve of internment and never reclaimed. Taken together, the trunks and bathhouse are poignant reminders of the losses Japanese Americans sustained, at the individual and community level, as a result of relocation and internment.

While the incorporation of Asian architectural styles or decorative features helps to identify Buddhist temples in surveys of ethnic cultural resources, interior features frequently are missed, such as wood-fired stoves whose top openings are sized to fit the large woks and rice steamers used in community celebrations. As a result, these interior features often are threatened in the process of modernization. Similarly, commercial buildings that left few permanent ethnic imprints on their exterior, such as newsstands and confectionaries, but that housed important ethnic businesses in their day can only be discovered by conducting systematic research in special collections or through oral history interviews. Important cultural resources such as these receive no recognition or protection unless they are documented in the preservation planning tools used by cultural resource managers.

Standard "windshield surveys" of buildings, used by preservationists, fail to identify significant historic resources located within them. A survey of properties contributing to the historic character of Seattle's International District overlooked the oldest intact U.S. example of a Japanese bathhouse, the Hashidate-Yu, in the basement of the Panama Hotel. Photograph by John Stamets, 1995.

Preservation planning agencies generally operate within extremely tight budgets, making it easy to contemplate but difficult to implement proposals for covering new ground, much less retracing old paths. An untapped resource for accomplishing both goals is the establishment of new working partnerships with ethnic community groups engaged in other forms of heritage preservation, such as oral history programs, and forging new alliances with university departments and programs in American ethnic studies. In addition to enhancing the ability of preservation agencies to protect the nation's multicultural heritage, such an approach is likely to have the added benefit of widening the constituency for and ultimately expanding the leadership of the historic preservation movement in the United States.

CHAPTER SEVEN

Ethnographic Landscapes
Transforming Nature into Culture

DONALD L.
HARDESTY

The cultural practices and beliefs of living people per-
meate American landscapes with meaning that is often
imperceptible and incomprehensible to others. Ari-
zona's Canyon de Chelly National Monument, for example, is a landscape that
means quite different things to the Navajo who live there and to visitors who
carry other cultural traditions.[1] The Navajo see the canyon as filled with places
that are sacred or have traditional importance. Such places include springs,
mountains, rock outcrops, abandoned Navajo dwellings, and ancient pueblo
ruins. The places are associated with Navajo origin stories, spiritual beings and
events, and materials needed for rituals, health, and well-being.

Most visitors to Canyon de Chelly, on the other hand, see an entirely different landscape. To them, the landscape lacks the intense cultural meaning
assigned by the Navajo to specific places in the canyon. Instead, it is appreciated for its scenic value, its wilderness value, its solitude, its archeological
value, or a host of other meanings. Landscapes viewed in this way, through the
eyes of specific cultures, are *ethnographic landscapes.* Unlike vernacular landscapes, which generally reflect, often unintentionally, repetitive human activities such as farming or mining, ethnographic landscapes mirror the systems
of meanings, ideologies, beliefs, values, and world-views shared by a group of
people. The group thinks of itself as having a common identity, whether it be
ethnicity, nationality, class, gender, or something else. An ethnographic landscape, for example, could be a Euro-American town green in New England as
well as Canyon de Chelly in the Navajo culture.

In a very real sense, ethnographic landscapes reflect a distinctive way of
transforming nature into culture. The transformation, among other things,
affects land-use practices, responses to landforms and other features of the

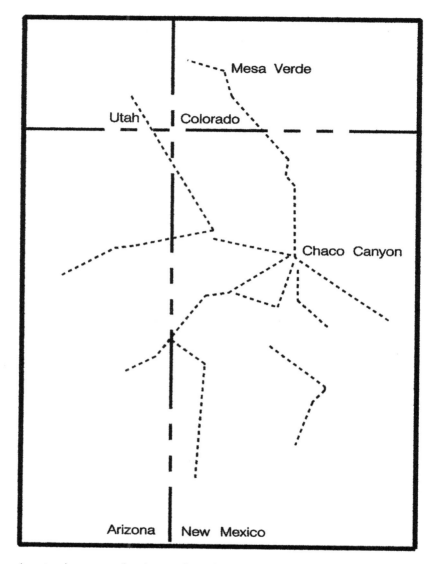

An extensive system of ancient roads at Chaco Canyon, New Mexico, originally developed by the Anasazi Indians, continues to carry cultural meaning among contemporary Pueblo peoples. Shown here is a reconstruction of the road system as it appeared in A.D. 1050. Source: Based on data in Thomas (1998), p. 137. Cartography by Julie Goodman.

natural environment, and the layout or spatial organization of landscape components such as roads, buildings, boundary markers, ditches, vegetation related to land use, and topographic features. Ethnographic landscapes reflect not only quite different histories and cultural traditions but also the continuing process of world-making. Thus, Gisli Palsson observes that "humans *make* their worlds in the sense that their reality is inevitably mediated by their cultural context."[2] What this implies is that the process of landscape transformation is dynamic and ongoing, involving not only past history but also current events. Ethnographic landscapes change as people themselves and their cultures change.

In America, ethnographic landscapes have been and continue to be created by Native Americans and more recent immigrants from Europe, Africa, Asia, and other places. The mix of American cultures and ethnic groups coming at different times means that the same landscape may be simultaneously significant to people carrying quite different cultural traditions. Canyon de Chelly, for example, has strong cultural and historical associations with the Navajo, several Pueblo groups, other Native American groups, and non-Indian visitors.[3] Although associated with living people by definition, ethnographic landscapes often incorporate archeological remains that carry cultural meaning. The landscape of New Mexico's Chaco Canyon contains the remains of a vast road network of ancient Anasazi origin that appears to reflect the spiritual and origin legends of some modern-day Pueblo groups who consider themselves to be descendants of the Anasazi. Some archeologists believe that the roads are symbolic expressions of the Anasazi's "cosmological landscape."[4] The roads connect Great Houses with sacred places, such as peaks with shrines, lakes, and Great Kivas.

| *Transforming Nature into Culture*

The making of ethnographic landscapes is but one part of world-making, in which people transform the world about them into their image.[5] Transforming nature into culture involves several actions and processes. Perhaps the best-known example of culture-specific ways of responding to landforms and other landscape features is *fengshui,* "an esoteric set of theories and practices grounded in indigenous philosophies and human experiences . . . used in China to probe the landscape and to discern from the irregularity and asymmetry of mountains and waters appropriate locations for specific human occupancy."[6] Fan Wei describes the traditional practice of *fengshui* in China as organized around the cardinal directions and divination.[7] In its most common form, the practice of *fengshui* uses the concepts of *yin* and *yang* to locate

The Mormons of Utah and adjacent states transformed nature into culture by using a grid system to lay out and organize their villages and farms. This man is regulating the flow of water in a ditch that still functioned as part of an orthogonal irrigation system in Alpine, Utah, in 1977. The traditional Mormon land-division pattern is currently changing in areas experiencing rapid urbanization and suburbanization. Photograph by Alanen, 1977.

places (*xue*) that control vital life forces (*shenqui*). Settlements placed close to *xue* give "advantage and general good fortune" to those who live there.

Chinese immigrants to America certainly brought with them the principles of *fengshui,* but the extent to which landscapes and architecture actually reflect the concept is debatable. Archeologist Roberta Greenwood, for example, cautions against the wholesale application of *fengshui* to the interpretation of Chinese American ethnographic landscapes and architecture by noting that Sanborn fire insurance maps show that buildings in nineteenth- and twentieth-century Chinese settlements in California cities, contrary to *fengshui* principles, were "contiguous, arranged in straight lines, were not square, were frequently in low-lying areas subject to floods (Napa, Ventura), and opened in other directions as often as south. The 'joss house' (Chinese temple) at Riverside was at the north end of Mongol Street, where it was 'supposed' to be, but the one in San Bernardino was at the east end of Chinatown . . . and the one in Ventura . . . was actually at the extreme south of the community, facing east."[8] Greenwood attributes the deviation from "ideal" landscapes and architecture in California urban places "to high density with the constraints of low cost, vernacular western building practices."[9] The Chinese immigrants often reused existing buildings, lived in low-cost places such as those near railroads or on lands subject to flooding, and settled in places forced upon them by the dominant white society. All of these places are urban landscapes, of course, and *fengshui*-dominated landscapes may be more common in rural places in the American West.

Another example of the transformation of nature into culture is provided by the Mormons. Of all the nineteenth-century utopian communities in America, Mormons emerged as the most successful and continue to have a prominent place in contemporary society. After establishing a settlement on the shores of the Great Salt Lake in Utah in 1847, the Mormon community set about rapidly transforming the landscape in distinctive ways. Anthropologist Mark Leone has described the key features of the Mormon landscape.[10] Settlement patterns reflect Mormon ideology in the farm-village and the grid. Early church authorities, for example, dictated village life rather than scattered homesteads. The Mormon prophet Joseph Smith drew up the Plat of the City of Zion as the blueprint for laying out the farm-village. Among other things, the plat reflected the Mormon ideal of social equality. The plat used the grid system to divide the village into building lots and farm plots of equal size, and Mormon settlers selected farming plots and building lots by drawing lots to assure equality. In addition, a grid-type irrigation network made certain that everyone received equal shares of water. Leone noted that "the canals flowed down the streets on the side. A grid made water dispersal efficient by packing farm land in the village close, and choosing lots by chance meant that water rights could not provide a basis for social inequality. Land and water, the two key sources of wealth for farmers in a semidesert, were distributed in equal amounts based on chance."[11]

At first impression, small components would seem to be relatively unimportant when "reading" ethnographic landscapes. In the Mormon landscape, however, Leone found that *fences* carry enormous cultural meaning: "The whole living space of agrarian Mormons and of Mormons today in towns throughout the Great Basin is parceled out by fences. The Mormon's physical world is divided or compartmentalized by interior walled spaces, yards full of fences, and gridded towns with gridded fields. This is the cultural environment the Mormon was and is born into and raised in."[12] A fence surrounds every Mormon house, farm plot, and lot. Traditionally, picket fences enclosed lawns and gardens, barbed wire and brush enclosed pastures outside of town, and hedgerows and tree rows enclosed large farm fields. Mormons used fences to help redeem the earth, to return it to the state of the original Garden of Eden, in preparation for the Second Coming of Christ.

When a Mormon raises a garden or lawn behind a fence, he has shown that he subdued a piece of the earth and made a bit of the desert bloom. He has helped redeem the earth. Growing a garden or a lawn is a challenge that he has met. He has made something more beautiful, more orderly, and more refreshing; something neater, cleaner, and more desirable. He has created a semblance of the divine. By managing, manipulating, and grooming the earth, he has imitated God and proven that he is worthy; he is a saint. A Mormon who creates something green has shown his inner state. In this context, fences are valuable because of what they preserve behind them. What they preserve in addition to a subsistence base is a man's right to a place in the Kingdom of God. One local Mormon summed it up: "The state of a man's yard is the state of his religion."[13]

| Reading Ethnographic Landscapes

Whatever their origin, ethnographic landscapes have culture-specific characteristics that often are unfamiliar to the eyes of the Western world. Reading the landscape demands attention to these qualities. The cultural meaning of ethnographic landscapes is expressed not only in large-scale patterns and processes of land use, spatial organization, and responses to the natural environment, but also in buildings, structures, objects, circulation networks, boundary markers, vegetation related to land use, clusters of landscape features, archeological sites, and small-scale components such as cairns or isolated milling stones.[14]

Identifying the landscape processes and components with enough cultural significance to make them part of an ethnographic landscape is a key problem. What is included and what is excluded from an ethnographic landscape is another issue. One view focuses upon *explicit* awareness and recognition of landscape features by members of the cultural community, excluding from the landscape places not connected to the community by practice, beliefs, or mention in oral traditions. Thomas King, however, favors an alternative view that allows for the possibility of a previously unrecognized place being included in an ethnographic landscape: "One can imagine . . . cases in which the knowledge-bearer, viewing a rock or a spring, a hill or a ruined structure (for the first time) makes a previously unmade connection, recognizes a characteristic that matches some template in the mind, that enables him or her to connect the place with a tradition, a practice, a belief, a piece of the group's cultural history."[15] In a sense, then, an ethnographic landscape is not only the product of cultural awareness but also an unrealized potential, a landscape in the process of becoming cultural.

In general, the components of ethnographic landscapes may be either material or nonmaterial and may or may not be physically modified by human activity. Rock art panels and the archeological remains of ancient buildings or structures, for example, may carry significant cultural meaning. The same significance may be attached to visible landforms or other landscape features with no evidence of human modification. Other components of ethnographic landscapes may be "less clearly delimited 'empty' spaces and could not be identified without the specialized knowledge maintained in the community."[16] Lynn Sebastian gives a good example of the latter:

> In one New Mexico case, an electrical substation was built on a seemingly "empty" piece of ground, but in fact, this was the location where a Hispanic community traditionally held the costumed dance known as "Los Matachines." Other Hispanic traditional cultural properties might include the remnants of traditional land-use patterns—long-field systems, community ditches—or the shrines, descansos, roadside crosses, moradas, and other properties associated with folk religious traditions and practices that are central to the unique culture of Hispanic New Mexico.[17]

Dorothea J. Theodoratus, while working on the controversy over Native American claims about the effect of the proposed Gasquet-Orleans Road through public lands, also documents the importance of the intangible aspects of ethnographic landscapes in her study of the world-views of the Yurok, Karuk, and Tolowa, who lived in northern California: "I learned about the fine points of meaning beyond topographical features for sacred sites (ambiance such as sight, sound, and smell, as well as concepts of distance between interconnecting topographical features were important)."[18]

The specific components of ethnographic landscapes include a wide variety of places, with or without material expression or human modification and with a continuum of sacred to secular meanings. A good place to live is one of the most visible and culturally variable landscape components. Where to establish settlements and residences is a central concern of all societies and must be interpreted with a cultural context. *Fengshui,* as discussed above, is perhaps the best example. In discussing the problem of interpreting the significance and boundaries of archeological sites, Theodoratus also observes that Me-Wuk descriptions of a traditional village site in the central Sierra Nevada "included the village itself but also included as part of his home, areas of particular meaning separate from the archeological site (e.g., food collecting and processing areas, and trails with connections to other villages)."[19]

Places containing subsistence resources make up another and related component of ethnographic landscapes. Pinyon pine forests provided a critical food resource for the indigenous peoples of the Great Basin and figure prominently in the cultural traditions of the region. Catherine Fowler describes the role of the pinyon complex in the Great Basin by noting that the seeds of the single-needled pinyon (*Pinus monophylla*) and double-needled pinyon (*Pinus edulis*) were intensively harvested in the late summer, especially during years of abundance (which occur in cycles of three to seven years), and then roasted, shelled, and eaten plain, parched, or in a mush or gruel.[20] Archeological evidence of the pinyon complex in the Great Basin extends back several thousand years, and, historically, families owned pinyon groves in some places. Emphasizing the blending of secular and sacred meanings of the pinyon forests in Great Basin cultures, Fowler commented that "certain ceremonialism was associated with pinyon harvesting. Several months before harvest time, prayers were offered to 'fix' the crop. Round dances were held at the time of harvesting, and special prayers of thanksgiving were offered over the first seeds collected. The prayers ensured good harvests of other seeds and game for the remainder of the year."[21]

The importance of plants and animals in other culturally significant activities cannot be overestimated as a component of ethnographic landscapes. In the Great Basin, for example, big sagebrush (*Artemisia tridentata*) plays sig-

A forested area along the Indian River (Sitka, Alaska) in the 1820s. To the Kiks.ádi clan of the Tlingit Indians, the river (called *Kasdehin*) served as the site for ancient interactions with the Frog people; the frog continues to serve as the primary crest for the Kiks.ádi. (See p. 19 of this volume.) Source: Litke (1987), p. 210.

nificant roles in a variety of rituals and ceremonies.[22] Burning the plant purifies the living in the presence of ghosts or when a person dies, in girls' puberty ceremonies celebrants use the plant for costuming or for other purposes, and crushed sage may be "a medium through which messages are taken to the spirits, for example, as an offering in the spring to ripen the pine nuts or as an offering for health after a specific illness."[23] Landforms and other places associated with healing and general well-being make up a related component of ethnographic landscapes. Theodoratus gives the example of Coso Hot Springs in Owens Valley, California, as a mythological place with implications for the health of the Owens Valley Paiute-Shoshone: "Coso holds meaning for life before there were people—when animals and Sun held the worldly balance of life. Some creatures (bear and frog) remained there after people came, and the locality holds strong in the minds of Owens Valley people for its physical and mental health potential and the camaraderie experienced when present there."[24] In another example, the Blackfeet traditionally used the Badger–Two Medicine area of Montana for vision quests.

It is well established that high mountain peaks have traditionally been used for seeking visions, and continue to be used for that purpose. Napi, the incarnate Creator, told the first dreamer to seek a place several days away from other people; that is, a remote area. He gave instructions for a sweat lodge ritual as part of the quest. The activity requires the presence of particular rocks and pure water. The best location of a dream bed is one that requires great bravery, either due to its proximity to fierce predators, such as grizzlies, or because of the situation of the dream bed on a high, narrow ledge. The Badger–Two Medicine area offers many such locations.[25]

| *Landscapes in Collision*

People create ethnographic landscapes in their own cultural and social images. When people carrying different cultures come into contact, either living together in or visiting the same geographical region, worlds collide. The social and political controversies created by the collision often involve the maintenance of ethnic or cultural identities. In America, the controversies typically have to do with conflicting cultural meanings that dictate, permit, or prohibit alternative uses, treatment, or concepts of landscape. The alternatives involve such activities, philosophies, and attitudes as recreation, social bonding, profit making, respect, vandalism, scientific management, wilderness, multiple use, worship, submission, comfort, fear, and domination. Theodoratus gives a good example of the conflict between different cultural images of the Mount Shasta landscape in northern California. The Wintu, who traditionally occupied the area, object to the construction of a new ski lift on the mountain at upper Panther Meadow Spring.

A foggy view of Mount Shasta, California, in the early twentieth century. Tourists have been part of the Mount Shasta environment for more than a century, but some activities currently pursued by nonnative groups—ranging from downhill skiing to the practice of New Age religion—are of great concern to the native Wintu people. Source: Special Collections Department, University of Nevada, Reno Library.

> The ski lift is but one of the concerns here; the Wintu are also troubled by nudists and New Age religious practitioners who stuff their sacred spring with crystals, plant flowers, and otherwise destroy the natural habitat with their activities. Further, Mount Shasta houses "little people" whose residence undergoes constant disturbance. On another level of meaning it is even more difficult for non-Natives to comprehend that Native concepts extend to the mountain even when it is not visited physically. Since it is the most supreme figure in the non-ordinary world, it embodies the peak level of every aspect of Wintu life and the point of death which moves a Wintu into the afterworld.[26]

Conflicting cultural interpretations of landscapes are further illustrated by a recent study of traditional land use by the Timbisha Shoshone Tribe. Their traditional homeland includes what is now Death Valley National Park in California. Catherine Fowler and her colleagues found that the tribe objects to the common use of language and images in literature about Death Valley that stress death and bleakness. "To them, it is a living valley, a place that they have called home for untold generations. It is a place where many living things are to be found, a joyous place where life has been and can continue to be celebrated. Their religion teaches them not to dwell on death, but to look at life, including the life in this 'living valley'."[27]

A 1993 article in the *New York Times* underlines the conflict between indigenous Americans and self-exploring New Age religious practitioners, such as members of the Church of Gaia: Council of the Six Directions, who often use the symbols and landscape images of traditional Native American cultures. John Lavelle, a Santee Sioux and director of the Center for Support and Protection of Indian Religions and Indigenous Traditions, is quoted as follows: "This is the final phase of genocide. First whites took the land and all that was physical. Now they're going after what is intangible." In addition, the article cites a "declaration of war," approved by the National Congress of American Indians in December 1993, against people exploiting sacred rituals, including "non-Indian 'wannabes,' hucksters, cultists, commercial profiteers and self-styled New Age shamans."[28]

Placenames also reflect colliding ethnographic landscapes. John E. Cook of the National Park Service argued, in 1991, that the replacement or loss of culturally unique placenames is "one of the most tragic losses to cultural identity." Traditional placenames not only offer support for surviving members of cultural communities, but also deprive future generations of insight into the cultural meaning of ethnographic landscapes.

Worse yet is the erasure of place names with official sanction. Alaska's cultural landscapes have been heir to the irresistible urge of many early geographers and explorers to name a prominent landscape feature after their boss or sponsor (or lady friend), not even questioning as to an original place name and its cultural meaning. Old sourdough gold-panners may presumably be excused, since their often colorful place names (or corrupted versions of aboriginal names) did not have direct access to official government publications. How much of this cultural-landscape information has been irretrievably lost across our entire Nation is impossible to estimate.[29]

Among the more enduring consequences of worlds in collision is the vandalism of ancient graves and archeological sites for fun and profit. The high prices commanded by the 1971 sale of Native American antiquities at a famous New York auction house marked the beginning of a large-scale assault upon the ethnographic landscapes of indigenous Americans that continues to the present. Private collectors, museums, and commercial art dealers all share the blame, although the American Association of Museums explicitly rejects as unethical the acquisition of artifacts of illegal or questionable origin. The conflict between Native Americans and the scientific community of professional archeologists and biological anthropologists over the issue of skeletal remains and cultural items, including funerary objects, sacred objects, and objects of cultural patrimony, reflects another dimension of the same collision. Legislation such as the Native American Grave Protection and Repatriation Act (NAGPRA) passed by Congress in 1990 and implemented in 1993 requires museums and other repositories to return items to the tribes and other Native American entities if requested. In a somewhat different vein, the vandalism of a sacred place in Montana by two brothers during a "sibling bonding" experience illustrates yet another dimension of conflicting cultural meanings of landscape.

Public land management policies that prevent access to culturally meaningful landscapes also illustrate the conflict between the cultures of politically dominant and subordinate groups in America. Federal regulations typically prohibit motor vehicle access to designated wilderness areas or sensitive riparian zones and often prevent Native Americans, because of age, infirmity, or distance, from reaching ethnographic landscapes contained therein.[30] Fowler and her colleagues found that the Timbisha Shoshone Tribe had many concerns about restricted access to traditional places and resources within what they considered to be their traditional homeland in Death Valley National Park.

The anger formerly expressed by the parents of the present elders at restrictions on hunting and gathering is still with some people today, if not specifically, in general. Very few have ever participated in a hunt for bighorn sheep, something that is now only cultural memory. Few have gathered the many and varied plant resources of their ancestors. More have participated in pine nut and mesquite collecting activities, or in rabbit or bird hunting. Most feel strongly that at least those aspects of life should not become cultural memory. Although people still go to gather pine nuts and wild spinach, and would like to take mesquite, it is hard to do so if one is made to feel like a trespasser on one's own lands. Some are not against the present system of obtaining permits; others are, as they are advised by California Indian Legal Services to ignore the process. Generally, the people feel that they are not the ones in control of these lands, and yet they have been taught that these are their lands, they always have been, and always will be.[31]

The tribe fears that the passage of the Desert Protection Act in 1994 and Death Valley's recent change in government status from a national monument to a national park will bring even more limitations. Park boundaries have been expanded to include places that are now used for hunting, camping, fires, and water access. As a response to these issues, the tribe affiliated with the Western Shoshone National Council, which has attempted to regain federal lands under the Treaty of Ruby Valley of 1873.

Finally, the confidentiality of culturally sensitive information about ethno-

Devils Tower, in northeastern Wyoming, reveals the cultural clash that can occur when a landscape feature pits two different groups against each other. To several Great Plains native peoples, Devils Tower is a sacred center that should be limited to traditional and spiritual ceremonies during the month of June; to elite rock climbers, however, the monolith represents one of the premier climbing challenges in the United States. Photograph by Alanen, 1980.

graphic landscapes is another critical issue emanating from worlds in collision. Consider the following example:

> Most tribes in Wyoming and Montana are extremely reluctant to divulge information about sacred sites. Some tribes, like the Eastern Shoshone of west central Wyoming, provide information because their spiritual leaders have concluded that Shoshone sacred sites will be gradually destroyed unless white people are informed about them. In contrast, the Kootenai of northwestern Montana are strictly prohibited from discussing their sacred sites to anyone outside their tribe and have reportedly allowed sacred sites to be physically destroyed rather than provide information that might have helped to preserve sites in the first place.[32]

Preserving the Identity of Ethnographic Landscapes

Ethnographic landscapes in America are diverse, created not only by indigenous Americans but also by a wide variety of more recent immigrants from Europe, Africa, Asia, and other places. How to preserve this diversity in the face of efforts by politically dominant groups to impose uses, treatments, and concepts reflecting their own cultural meaning on all American landscapes is an enormous problem. At present, the preservation of ethnographic landscapes most often takes place within the statutory and regulatory framework established by federal, state, and local governments. The key statutes are the National Historic Preservation Act (NHPA), the National Environmental Policy Act (NEPA), the Federal Land Management Policy Act (FLMPA), the American Indian Religious Freedom Act (AIRFA), the Native American Grave Protection and Repatriation Act (NAGPRA), the Alaska Native Claims Settlement Act (ANCSA), the Alaska National Interest Lands Conservation Act (ANILCA), and the Archaeological Resources Protection Act (ARPA).

Within this context, ethnographic landscapes are significant as "traditional cultural properties" because of their association "with cultural practices or beliefs of a living community that a) are rooted in that community's history, and b) are important in maintaining the continuing cultural identity of the community."[33] Section 101(d)(6) of NHPA, added in 1992, specifically states that Native American sacred sites are eligible for the National Register of Historic Places. Despite the common perception that ethnographic landscapes and other traditional cultural properties are protected only as "sacred sites" under AIRFA, the fact that many cultures offer no distinction between sacred and secular makes it possible to protect ethnographic landscapes as historic places under NHPA as well.[34] In addition, ANILCA brought the landscapes of traditional Alaskan cultures under the protection of federal laws and policies by creating new national parks, national monuments, national preserves, national wildlife refuges, and National Wild and Scenic Rivers within the region.

The process of Section 106 review and compliance with NEPA provides one tool for preserving ethnographic landscapes within the existing statutory and regulatory framework.[35] Section 106 requires, among other things: (1) an inventory and documentation of historic properties that may be affected by a proposed federal project, (2) a determination of their eligibility for listing on the National Register of Historic Places, and (3) consideration of the effect of the proposed project upon historic properties. Without question, Section 106 provides the most widespread set of laws and implementing regulations with potential application to the preservation of ethnographic landscapes. The process, however, has several drawbacks. It takes place late in the planning stage, often much too late to do anything about effects upon larger entities such as ethnographic landscapes. For this reason, some argue for the concept of holistic and ecosystem planning from the beginning of the project's inception to assure "that traditional cultural properties can be thought of as components of the total landscape, rather than isolated spots that must be 'dealt with' as a final obstacle to construction."[36]

In addition, it is difficult to inventory and document ethnographic landscapes, much less determine their importance to a cultural tradition. Clearly, many culturally meaningful properties associated with an ethnographic landscape cannot be identified with the traditional methods of a pedestrian survey and a search of historical documents. The properties may or may not be tangible, and they may or may not have evidence of human modification. Interviews with living people carrying the cultural tradition may provide the necessary information. Even here, however, what information is received often depends upon exactly who is asked. Not every member of a community, for example, has equal access to its cultural knowledge, nor is the same cultural knowledge sacred or even important to all members of the community. At what point of community consensus should a property be considered sufficiently significant to be eligible for listing on the National Register? In addition, some cultural knowledge is so sacred that it cannot be divulged to the public at large. Notwithstanding all of these shortcomings, however, the Section 106 process is probably the most effective tool for preserving ethnographic landscapes in America.

Another approach to the preservation of ethnographic landscapes is a change in management procedures to involve native peoples more fully. Consider, for example, the Medicine Wheel National Historic Landmark controversy in Wyoming. The Medicine Wheel is a large circular rock alignment with radiating spokes high in the Bighorn Mountains in an area with archeological evidence of occupation as early as seventy-five hundred years ago. Most Native Americans in the region revered the Medicine Wheel as "a uniquely important and powerful spiritual site that figures prominently in tribal oral and ceremonial traditions." In 1988 the Bighorn National Forest proposed access road and facility improvements at the Historic Landmark to accommodate increased tourism. Although not previously involved in cultural resource management issues, Northern Arapaho tribal elders protested the plan, arguing that the improvements would "disturb, or possibly destroy, the spiritual integrity of the Medicine Wheel."[37]

For the first time, the elders consulted with the Wyoming State Historic Preservation Office and received assistance in applying the appropriate federal statutes and regulations to the case. The event set in motion a new era of cooperation among the Native American communities, the state, and the federal land-managing agencies. Another example is the increased involvement of government agencies with Alaskan indigenous peoples to include such innovations as "working with native organizations to develop cultural landscape maps, which were based upon information from village elders."[38]

Finally, public education is an approach to the preservation of ethnographic landscapes that takes place outside the framework discussed above. An example is the Ak-Chin Him Dak ecomuseum near Phoenix, Arizona. An ecomuseum is "a new model for a community museum that originated in France. It is organized around a holistic, integrated concept of territory, culture, and people. Its goals are cultural identity and community development."[39] Nancy Fuller of the Smithsonian Institution has described how the museum works:

The plan called for tribal leaders, elders, project staff and advisors to visit museums and archives in the United States and Canada to see existing models firsthand, and to get a sense of the problems and potential solutions that accompany the operation of such facilities. The goal of this phase of training was to convey a vision of a community museum as a place to serve community needs, and to establish a community image of the Ak-Chin actively performing museum and archives work. During their investigation, they looked at the inter-relationship of culture to the other factors in a community such as geography, politics, generations, neighbors, and economics. Then they examined how the expressions of their culture were reflected in the Ak-Chin Indian community. Then, they studied ways that their culture could manifest itself and be reflected in a community operated facility.[40]

Both indoor and outdoor exhibits organized around ethnographic landscapes can be an effective part of such ecomuseums. The exhibits, for example, might include dioramas, walking tours, or driving tours of landforms, rock art panels, archeological sites, plants and animals, trails, shrines, and other components of the landscape, along with culturally meaningful placenames on the signage used for interpretation. In this way, the ecomuseum supports the cultural identity of the local community and, at the same time, exposes museum visitors carrying other cultures to the cultural meaning of different ethnographic landscapes.

| Summary and Conclusions

American landscapes must be understood within the context of a vast variety of cultural traditions. Culture transforms nature into its own image, creating distinctive ethnographic landscapes. Such landscapes are pregnant with cultural meanings and uses. Conflicts arise when people carrying different cultural traditions perceive of and attempt to use the same place—including plants, animals, water, landforms, and other landscape components—in incompatible ways. In America such diverse groups as wilderness enthusiasts, the tourist industry, and New Age religions, all based in a Euro-American cultural tradition, have intensified the conflict by advocating nontraditional land-use practices in the traditional homelands of Native Americans. The preservation of rapidly disappearing ethnographic landscapes is a critical need in contemporary America. Ways to meet the need include protection of such landscapes under existing federal laws and policies as traditional cultural properties, more involvement of native peoples, and public education.

CHAPTER EIGHT

Integrity as a Value in Cultural Landscape Preservation

CATHERINE
HOWETT

Integrity as a concept is rather like the great triumvirate of beauty, truth, and goodness; ordinary people have a sense that they know intuitively what the terms mean and leave to philosophers the task of wrestling with definitions and subtle distinctions. The *American Heritage Dictionary* seems to confirm this perception, since its three definitions of the word *integrity* are followed by the injunction "See Synonyms at *honesty*." Honesty is, after all, a down-to-earth, comprehensible virtue, more black and white than gray in its ethical and emotional coloration, at least when it describes a quality of specific human thoughts, speech, or actions. Similarly, the first definition of integrity—"rigid adherence to a code of behavior; probity"—applies to a human way of acting in the world. The two remaining definitions, however, define integrity as a term applied to things, not people: "the state of being unimpaired; soundness" and "completeness; unity." The word has its etymological roots in the Latin *integritas*, meaning "completeness, purity," itself derived from *integer*, meaning "whole."

Perhaps some of the problems that arise in using integrity as a criterion in evaluating historic cultural landscapes derive from this duality; a word that in the first instance describes, with a fair measure of clarity and precision, a trait of human character—"rigid adherence to a code of behavior"—is also invoked as a standard for nonhuman entities, although its sense in that application is radically different from the first. The integrity of things-in-the-world is rooted in a physical condition of soundness, completeness, or wholeness, not in an intangible human attribute. One might presume that measuring the integrity of things would consequently be easier than deciding whether, for example, a given person acted with integrity in a particular situation. Is it not easier to say with certainty that a broken pot lacks integrity than to evaluate human motivations and actions? Perhaps not, if the broken pot is a rare example of the art of some ancient civilization; even if pieces are missing, scholars may recognize a high degree of integrity in the restored vessel. Making good judgments about the integrity of objects, structures, or sites most often requires a level of educational achievement or professional competence that is scarcely analogous to awareness of the personal or communal moral standards by which to judge human actions. Twelve ordinary citizens constitute a jury because the law presumes that their common humanity enables individuals to determine the guilt or innocence of the accused. Judging the wholeness, soundness, or unity of complex cultural entities represents an entirely different sort of challenge.

Nevertheless, integrity as a concept and as a descriptive (even a prescriptive) value has become firmly entrenched within philosophical, scientific, political, and legal discourses. The environmental philosopher Holmes Rolston III has suggested that Aldo Leopold's call for a "land ethic"—identified by actions that tend to preserve the "integrity, beauty, and stability of the biotic community"—at the conclusion of *A Sand County Almanac,* first published in 1949, may mark the beginnings of the widespread contemporary acceptance of the notion that integrity is a characteristic of healthy natural systems and, by extension, of cultural systems as well.

Leopold's hope for integrity has, in ensuing years, even become the law of the land, with legislation sometimes employing that very phrase, sometimes using related concepts such as environmental quality, land health, and resource sustainability, not only in the United States but in Canada and elsewhere. In this perspective the National Forest Management Act, the Wilderness Acts, national parks legislation, and legislation about clean water and air, old-growth forests, acid rain, pesticide and herbicide pollution, overuse of fertilizers, loss of wetlands, soil conservation, fire policy, ecosystem management—all of these, if we put them under one umbrella idea, are about the integrity of the environment.[1]

This enthusiasm for a concept of integrity that ultimately derived from an ecological model—the unity or completeness of natural systems seen as "places of adapted fit with many species integrated into long persisting relationships, life perpetually sustained and renewed [through] cycling and recycling of energy and materials"[2]—has had significant philosophical implications for cultural landscape preservation. Since the National Park Service (NPS) administers the National Register of Historic Places, the same scientific model that had demonstrated its validity most often in natural-systems applications in park management was transferred to cultural resource management. Even in scientific applications, however, the restoration or maintenance of integrity as a goal of government policy has frequently been problematic: "No matter how often the goal of 'integrity' is enunciated, what appears to be constant is the emergence of two related problems: a) a lack of definition for the concept in all regulatory acts, and . . . b) a corresponding lack of prescriptive, binding force, easily traceable to the concept's imprecision."[3]

Integrity as a National Register Criterion

The National Register brings the criterion of integrity to bear on the most critical part of the nomination process, the evaluation of significance:

The quality of significance in American history, architecture, archaeology, engineering, and culture is present in districts, sites, buildings, structures, and objects that possess integrity of location, design, setting, materials, workmanship, feeling, association, and:

A. that are associated with events that have made a significant contribution to the broad patterns of our history; or
B. that are associated with the lives of persons significant in our past; or
C. that embody the distinctive characteristics of a type, period, or method of construction, or that represent the work of a master, or that possess high artistic value, or that represent a significant and distinguishable entity whose components may lack individual distinction; or
D. that have yielded, or may be likely to yield, information important in prehistory or history.[4]

This statement balances a requirement of integrity in seven possible categories with a requirement for significance based either on association with important historical events or personages or on the intrinsic value of the site as a historical resource. The logical structure of the paragraph suggests that the integrity of the resource has priority over the other values; in other words, no matter how historically important a site or structure may have been, if its present condition fails to meet standards of integrity under the seven categories of location, design, setting, materials, workmanship, feeling, and association, it cannot qualify for listing in the National Register of Historic Places. National Register Bulletin 15 states that a property need not possess integrity in all seven respects, but "to retain historic integrity . . . will always possess several, and usually most, of the aspects."[5]

The charges of a lack of conceptual precision in governmental statements of policies and goals related to integrity seem to be legitimate when one moves from these criteria to the definition of integrity in Bulletin 15 that is meant to elucidate them: "Integrity is the ability of a property to convey its significance."[6] Here is a perplexing tautological tangle: the significance of a resource is to be determined on the basis of its integrity; integrity is recognized in the way that the resource conveys its significance. Whatever happened to unity, completeness, and soundness as the essential sense of the word *integrity* as it applied to things and places? What happened has to do not just with the persistent difficulty, noted earlier, of determining the precise definitions of large qualitative abstractions, but also with the temptation to assume that a common understanding of the meanings of these terms already exists. As it turns out, what the National Park Service understands by integrity really does have to do with the unity, completeness, or soundness of the resource being evaluated: Bulletin 16A advises that integrity is "the authenticity of a property's historic identity, evidenced by the survival of physical characteristics that existed during the property's prehistoric or historic period."[7]

This definition is a good deal easier to understand because it at least seems to confirm ordinary usage; that is, integrity has to do with the unity or completeness of something. In the case of historic cultural landscapes, according to the NPS, the physical record must be sufficiently intact—still on the ground, so to speak—to allow todays' visitors to experience an environment that existed at a specific time in the past. And this is the way that the evaluation of the integrity of a site is addressed in practice. In a case study in cultural landscape analysis at the Vanderbilt Estate at Hyde Park, New York (a property administered by the NPS), Patricia M. O'Donnell described integrity as "the extent to which the character, organization, and details of the historic landscape are retained." Referring to the NPS definition, she maintained that it "implies that a series of comparisons should be made between the historic period or periods and the present," specifically with respect to nine categories of "character-defining elements" set forth in the then-current NPS document *Draft Guidelines for the Treatment of Historic Landscapes.*[8] Although at first glance O'Donnell's observation about the need to compare the historic period to the present may seem perfectly obvious, the criterion of integrity—an essential determinant of the significance of any historic cultural landscape being considered for National Register listing—has been inextricably joined to the notion of a specific historic period that defines the limits of the interpretive program for the site. The measure of the site's integrity with respect to features extant in the historic period and still extant will in turn determine the most appropriate "treatment" of the four possible approaches recognized by the NPS: preservation, rehabilitation, restoration, or reconstruction.

| *Integrity Defined by the Interpretive Period*

Because the development of special criteria for the nomination of historic landscapes to the National Register and the production of guidelines for their treatment have been relatively recent NPS projects, it is possible to trace the adjustments and refinements to theory and recommended practice that have emerged from the recognition that many historic landscapes were not well suited to analysis using preservation criteria derived largely from architectural models. The notion of historic period illustrates this difference strikingly. Quite early in landscape preservation discussions, scholars and practitioners called attention to the problem of landscapes that are fundamentally dynamic biotic systems subject to continual change. In a 1976 essay in *Landscape Architecture*, James Marston Fitch urged landscape architects interested in the management of historic landscapes to abandon "anti-temporal postures" and face the fact that, unlike architects, they must work with "living tissue" at "two different time scales: changes in size, scale, and form of individual plants; and changes in the very species and varieties in use at any given historical period. This means that very few historic landscapes . . . have a physiognomy corresponding to the ambitions of the original designers." He warned against an even more subtle flaw "embedded in restorations of entire towns like Williamsburg . . . namely that time is not only artificially stopped but the cumulative record of historical evolution is artificially compressed and foreshortened in space."⁹ Writing in the same magazine eleven years later, Patricia O'Donnell and Robert Z. Melnick were still at pains to point out that landscape had to be understood as process as well as product: "The most important difference between preserving landscapes and preserving structures and objects is the dynamic quality of the land—it continuously changes and grows. Recognizing this quality reveals the fallacy of trying to freeze a landscape at a moment in time."¹⁰

In spite of this awareness of the difficulties involved in selecting and interpreting a particular period within the past life of a historic landscape, NPS guidelines—and the landscape preservation community generally—accepted the idea that recommendations supporting well-defined interpretions dated *nothing earlier than (year) and nothing later than (year)* were an essential outcome of the research and analysis phase of a master-planning project for a historic site. Applying this standard to vernacular and rural cultural landscapes proved especially difficult, a case tellingly argued by Melody Webb in her 1987 essay "Cultural Landscapes in the National Park Service"¹¹ and acknowledged in the expanded definition and discussion of *period of significance* that appeared in the 1990 National Register Bulletin 30 on the subject of rural historic landscapes.

Period of significance is the span of time when a property was associated with important events, activities, persons, cultural groups, and land uses or attained important physical qualities or characteristics. Although it may be short, more often it extends

many years, covering a series of events, continuum of activities, or evolution of physical characteristics. Properties may have more than one period of significance. . . .

    A property's periods of significance become the benchmark for measuring whether
subsequent changes contribute to its historic evolution or alter its historic integrity.[12]

The emphasis in this definition has clearly shifted to the evolutionary nature of the historic landscape; indeed, *historic integrity* was now defined in the
same Bulletin 30 as "a measure of a property's evolution and current condition." These guidelines sought to broaden the concept of integrity by recognizing that the completeness of the physical remains surviving from the historic period may reflect not a static order of landscape elements organized in
a fixed pattern that was continuously in place between the interpretive dates,
but rather an assemblage, arrangement, and function of parts that was subject to change over time within those same dates. This modification represented an important refinement of the concept of integrity and of the period
of significance within which integrity is to be measured. Although the emphasis was now on continuity over time, an awkward accommodation had to
be made to the requirement of a distinct break between past and present time;
if the continuity in land use and in the character of the landscape extends even
to the present day, it is recommended that "fifty years ago may be used for the
period of significance if a more specific date cannot be identified."[13] Such a
decision would, in effect, freeze time arbitrarily at a point fifty years before the
site's nomination to the National Register.

    Nevertheless, the change in the way that a site's integrity with respect to the
whole complex of landscape features surviving from a historic period of significance is to be evaluated and subsequently treated and managed is very apparent. This change was noted in an issue of *Landscape Architecture* devoted
to the theme of landscape preservation:

Landscape restorations once were pegged to a specific year or period. In projects ranging from small gardens to whole river valleys, preservationists and landscape architects
now pursue a more enveloping approach: interpretation of the "cultural landscape."
. . .
    Leading the way with projects at National Historic Sites and parks, the National
Park Service . . . has established rigorous standards for research and practice. Historic
landscape treatments now seek to explain how a place evolved, while recommending
how to manage it in ecologically sensitive ways.[14]

The same article called the NPS's 1993 *Draft Guidelines for the Treatment of Historic Landscapes* "the most influential publication" currently aimed at the need
to "clarify the steps toward restoration integrity," and the NPS restoration
project at Fairsted, the Frederick Law Olmsted National Historic Site in
Brookline, Massachusetts, is described as "showcasing" the *Guidelines.*[15]

A look at the decisions being made by the NPS for the Olmsted site, however, raises some doubt about the usefulness of this project, exemplary as it may be in other respects, as a case study that reinterprets traditional definitions of historic period by embracing a more evolutionary or diachronic perspective. An earlier (1982) study had recommended a circa 1960 interpretive date for the site, resulting in the removal of such later features as a swimming pool and formal garden. Then, in the late 1980s, the NPS moved the interpretive date back to the period of the 1920s, when the firm begun by the senior Olmsted was still very active, adding to the house and office, and when, according to Lauren Meier, historical landscape architect for the site, the landscape retained "a high level of integrity from Olmsted Sr.'s design influence."[16] Furthermore, rich archival documentation existed for this period.

The scope of work involved in "returning the site to its earlier, more evergreen and picturesque design" does not support, however, the view that the existing landscape possessed a high level of integrity related to that earlier time period,[17] in spite of the standard established in Bulletin 15: that, "ultimately, the question of integrity is answered by whether or not the property retains the identity for which it is significant."[18] Azaleas and "volunteer" maples will be removed, and 250 to 450 shrubs and 70 trees will be added to the less than two-acre site.[19]

John Charles Olmsted died in 1920; Frederick Law Olmsted Jr. died in 1957. Given the virtual impossibility of choosing an interpretive period closer to the tenure of the senior Olmsted, who died in 1903, and given also the plenitude of photographic and other documentation available, it seems that the NPS has opted to "take the landscape back" to the 1920s through a much more dramatic intervention than the earlier plan to interpret the 1960s would have required. The most compelling reason for doing so must be, first of all, that the changes can be supported by documentation (the 1994 NPS publication *Protecting Cultural Landscapes: Planning, Treatment and Management of Historic Landscapes*, which replaced the *Draft Guidelines*, is rigorous in demanding that a highly inclusive range of possible modifications to a historic site be supported by adequate documentation) and, second, that the educational thrust of the interpretive program is better served by a landscape that can be identified with the Olmsted family, rather than merely with their professional successors. These justifications for changing the choice of the historic period to be interpreted are probably legitimate, but they are also traditional within the context of the landscape preservation movement in this country. It is not at all clear in what ways such a project represents an innovative approach to the problem of interpreting evolutionary change over time as an alternative to locking a period landscape into place.

| *Documentation as Evidence of Integrity*

What the Fairsted project does do, however, is illustrate the possibility that in certain cases a determination of satisfactory integrity may be based less on what remains intact from a period of significance than on the quantity and quality of documentation for that period. The unity, completeness, and soundness of the physical evidence, in other words, may not be confined to the site itself, but in practice will extend to the supporting archival materials. Without acknowledging the significance that this alternative method of evaluation implies for the accepted understanding of site integrity, the 1994 publication *Protecting Cultural Landscapes* recognized this approach, as the earlier *Draft Guidelines* had done as well, under the treatment category of restoration:

> When the most important goal is to portray a landscape and its character-defining features at an exact period of time, restoration is selected as the primary treatment. Unlike preservation and rehabilitation, interpreting the landscape's continuum or evolution is not the objective. Restoration may include the removal of features from other periods and/or the construction of missing or lost features and material from the reconstruction period. In all cases, treatment should be substantiated by the historic research findings and existing conditions documentation.[20]

The weight of this "hard" evidence—as opposed to what is frequently a subjective critical evaluation of whether enough of some past landscape fabric survives in situ to warrant the judgment that a property possesses integrity relative to the period of historic significance—has the almost irresistible appeal of science itself.[21] It introduces factual, quantifiable, and measurable support for a preservation strategy; a datable picture or plan seems to offer "proof" that at least has the potential to authenticate the historic truth of whatever course of action is implemented.

A recent example of the discovery of what appeared at first to be extraordinary documentation of a significant original eighteenth-century American garden illustrates all too well, however, how even such apparently solid evidence may still fall far short of a standard of proof as to what actually existed during the interpretive period. The garden in question is associated with Tryon Palace in coastal New Bern, North Carolina, a stately brick residence that also served as government house for Royal Governor William Tryon in 1767–70, when the stirrings of revolution were already creating political and social unrest in the colony—so much so, in fact, that Tryon seized an opportunity to become colonial governor of New York barely a year after moving into the palace overlooking the Trent River. This original edifice—"finished within in a very elegant manner"—was subsequently destroyed by fire in 1798.[22]

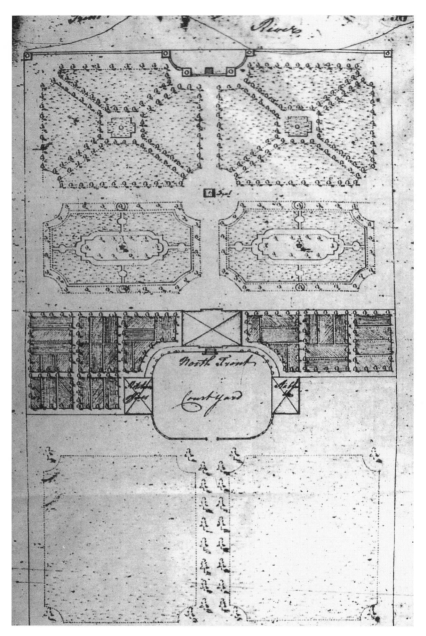

Site plan of Tryon Palace Garden, North Carolina, 1783, tentatively attributed to Claude Sauthier, with annotations in the hand of John Hawks. The parterre garden in this drawing appears on the riverfront side of the palace, whereas two 1769 plans of New Bern by Claude Sauthier show parterre gardens on the opposite side, flanking the entrance drive. Source: Archives of General Miranda, Collections of the Academia Nacional de la Historia de Venezuela, Caracas.

In the twentieth century, many North Carolinians, and especially civic-minded women's groups—undoubtedly influenced by the same Colonial Revival enthusiasms that inspired not just John D. Rockefeller's restoration of Williamsburg but a myriad of smaller projects, such as the Garden Club of America's research and publication of the two-volume *Gardens of Colony and State*[23]—lobbied for reconstruction of the Tryon Palace complex. In 1939, a fairly complete set of plans and drawings made by the architect John Hawks had been located in the collections of the New York Historical Society. Also extant were two maps of New Bern commissioned by the English crown from the French cartographer Claude Sauthier and dated 1769, both of which showed the grounds of the Governor's Palace in some detail, although the pattern of the parterre gardens shown in the two plans differed slightly. With a generous gift from a private donor to support reconstruction, the North Carolina legislature moved in 1945 to acquire the property and begin work; funding of the project was substantially increased by a bequest from the same donor at her death in 1951. The same architectural firm responsible for Williamsburg was hired to oversee the palace reconstruction, and landscape architect Morley Williams, joined by his wife Nathalia Williams, was given the task of producing a site plan based on whatever evidence might be uncovered by those responsible for historical research of the property.

Early on, however, the usefulness of the two contemporary Sauthier maps in providing documentary evidence of the disposition of the landscape was apparently challenged by scholars who believed the garden illustrations may have been merely *staffage,* invented by Sauthier to embellish his drawings in a conventional way. They also argued that there had been too little time, given Tryon's brief tenure at the site, for such elaborate gardens to have been established, especially since the costs associated with the buildings and furnishings had already occasioned much public criticism of the governor's extravagance. According to Curator of Gardens Perry Mathewes, the Tryon Palace Commission therefore decided to ignore the Sauthier parterres and commission Williams to design a landscape "like those which flourished from 1760 to 1770 at comparable estates in Great Britain."[24] With this imaginative license to create a period look for a property meant to serve the needs of historic tourism, the landscape architects laid out a sequence of garden spaces (allée, kitchen garden, privy gardens, "wilderness," etc.) and designed historic features (e.g., a dovecote and a smokehouse). The master plan, over a period of more than twenty years, had to accommodate a series of significant changes, including the addition of two memorial gardens honoring donors.

The administrators of Tryon Palace Historic Sites and Gardens recognized, of course, that the grounds surrounding the reconstructed palace did not reflect an original plan; even beyond the fact that the size of the property and its boundaries were quite different from the eighteenth-century configuration, the landscape plan was a twentieth-century invention in what has come to be described as the Colonial Revival style. Moreover, the administrators were increasingly sensitive to issues of current historic landscape preservation philosophy, which raised such questions as whether plant choices in the kitchen garden should be restricted to species in use in the eighteenth century, while other gardens within the Williams plan now functioned as seasonal display gardens—spring bulbs, fall chrysanthemums—that had become highly popular annual programming features.

Adding spice to this stew of uncertainty was the knowledge that, as early as the 1940s, research of the site had uncovered an intriguing reference in the diary of a Spanish traveler, Francisco de Miranda, who reported having been given, on the occasion of a visit to New Bern in 1783, "an exact plan of the [Tryon Palace] edifice and gardens" by the building's architect, John Hawks. The historian who published this discovery noted that "if Miranda's plan could be recovered, it would be an unquestionably authentic diagram of exactly how the gardens were laid out by this early American designer and landscape architect."[25] In other words, the possibility existed that the Tryon Palace site might prove to be one of the best-documented eighteenth-century landscapes in America. The discovery of the architectural drawings in Hawks's own hand had made possible the reconstruction of the palace; might not the Miranda plan provide a sketch, also in the architect's own hand, of his plan of the surrounding landscape? And would not such a plan, by adding immeasurably to the completeness of the historic record, enhance the historicity—and by extension the integrity—of a landscape reconstruction based on it?

Although early efforts to locate the diary had ended in failure, in 1991 Tryon Palace administrators finally succeeded in obtaining a copy of the Miranda drawing and text from the National Academy of History in Caracas, Venezuela. Perry Mathewes has recently described how the recovery of what appeared to be "Tryon Palace's Rosetta stone, . . . the magic blueprint for restoring a garden," at first generated considerable media attention and public excitement but has since proven to be anything but the "unquestionably authentic" plan that had been anticipated. Instead, according to Mathewes, "the new plan raised more questions than it clearly answered."[26] For one thing, more recent scholarship has challenged the notion that the cartographer Sauthier routinely used representations of landscape simply as graphic embellishment. Adding to the interest of this reappraisal is the still more intriguing observation that, while the notes on the Miranda drawing appear to be in Hawks's hand, the plan drawing of the landscape bears marked similarity to the graphic style of Sauthier, even though the parterre garden on the Miranda plan is on the opposite side of the palace from the gardens depicted on the 1769 maps of New Bern.[27]

In the end, what analysis of the Miranda manuscript and drawing has unquestionably provided is not proof of the form and substance of an original landscape design, much less of an actual eighteenth-century landscape that existed on the site. Even if authorship of the drawing, now tentatively attributed to Sauthier, is reliably established, it remains impossible to know whether any of the three plans represents an as-built record of Governor Tryon's palace grounds. None of these caveats, however, compromises in any way the richness and complexity that recovery of the Miranda documents has added to the historic record of Tryon Palace, to the *story*—including the historic twentieth-century effort to rebuild and interpret it—that the place has to tell. The challenge for the interpretive program will be to make these historic puzzles and pursuits more vivid and interesting to visitors and more revelatory of our human need continually to pursue a more authentic and profound understanding of past times and places than the physical experience of a reconstructed eighteenth-century garden might have been, quite apart from the philosophical or ethical implications of a decision to dismantle or destroy the physical record and, in so doing, the *integrity* of the twentieth-century designs.

| *"True" History/"False" History*

Since the early 1970s, the preservation movement in the United States has struggled to set forth the philosophical foundations of preservation practice. The growing list of NPS National Register Bulletins, the publications and activities of the National Trust for Historic Preservation, the proliferation of academic courses and degree-granting programs, as well as the expansion of preservation practice within the design disciplines, have all helped to form a body of theory and to generate a lively intellectual discourse. The need for more rigorous scholarly research and more careful documentation to support planning and design decisions has been the rallying cry of this entire movement. Within the domain of landscape preservation, archeological and archival studies assumed a new importance even for small organizations and individuals who aspired to a high standard of quality in a preservation project. Perhaps it should not be surprising that this commitment to enhancing the authoritative reliability of the data upon which the decision-making process depends has created in some quarters—and certainly in the tone and tenets of the most recent NPS publications—the expectation that landscape preservation methods and outcomes can achieve a quasi-scientific empirical certitude.

The reaction against the Colonial Williamsburg Restoration—a preservation project so celebrated and so popular as a tourist destination for more than half a century that a tide of reaction was almost inevitable—must surely have contributed to the fear of "false history" that now looms like a dark specter over every preservation undertaking, encouraging the pursuit of a more "scientific" basis of credibility. In a scathing 1992 indictment of the American taste for theme-park entertainment environments, "festival marketplaces," and architecture that "treat[s] history as a stylistic grab bag," Ada Louise Huxtable seemed to blame everything that is wrong with American urban design and contemporary architecture on the preservation movement, starting with Willamsburg:

The replacement of reality with selective fantasy has been led first by the preservation movement and then by a new, successful, and staggeringly profitable American phenomenon: the re-invention of the environment as themed entertainment. The process of substitution probably started in a serious way at Colonial Williamsburg, predating and preparing the way for the new world order of Disney Enterprises. Certainly it was in the restoration of Colonial Williamsburg that the studious fudging of facts received its scholarly imprimatur and history as themed artifact hit the big time.[28]

Huxtable is hardly alone in raising serious questions about the efficacy of removing 731 buildings at Williamsburg in order to restore 81 that met the cutoff date of 1770, then rebuilding 413 from scratch on the original sites. But "studious fudging" implies deliberate deceit. It has become fashionable to portray the entire Williamsburg venture as a conspiracy of wealth and class—WASPs celebrating the nation's Anglo-Saxon cultural roots in the face of a tide of immigration from southern Europe and elsewhere—a perception that does a disservice to the professional integrity (illustrating nicely the first sense of the word) of those involved.

There is plenty of evidence to suggest that the Williamsburg restorers were, in fact, serious and dedicated professionals struggling to determine the most appropriate values and directions for a project of unprecedented scale and novelty. As early in the process as December 1928, landscape architect Arthur A. Shurcliff expressed to colleagues his concern that two extremes had to be avoided in designing the grounds around individual properties at Williamsburg:

One is putting in and planting the whole scheme too poorly and poverty looking, the other is making them look too flossy . . . It would be a mistake to go to the extreme of making the grounds too good looking, too much boxed, too many flowers, too many trees, because they wouldn't be appropriate to the simple, little weather-beaten and rather poor looking houses, and the small amount of money that we know the old people living in those houses spent in the old days, so in making these estimates I have tried to err on the side of making those places look a little bit thin.[29]

If in the end things had, indeed, gotten "too flossy," it was not because the historians, archeologists, and other experts assembled to work on the project were any more careless of the truth, naive, prejudiced, or driven by the force of cultural mythmaking than we are today. The latest myth is the one that Huxtable implicitly embraces, namely, that it is possible to create "real" environments that are devoid of the "dream, invention, wish-fulfillment" that she deplores and that she contrasts with Utopian modernism, in which social purpose, form, and function were revered as the holy trinity of style.[30]

Huxtable's lament over the death of the modern movement in architecture and urban design offers a clue to her quarrel with the entire preservation movement and at the same time, perhaps, an insight into the current paranoia about "false history" within preservation circles. Early modernism espoused a purism that demanded the rejection of historic precedent and the messy eclecticism of past styles; it actually defined the present—"modernity"—by its radical separation from the past. One would almost think, in reading the Huxtable essay, that there had never been, centuries before Williamsburg, vibrant cultures that chose to imitate—yes, and to re-create to the best of their imperfect knowledge—the environments and architectural styles of earlier peoples and earlier times. It is as the inheritors of modernism that the preservation movement continues to tolerate the misconception that a line, a date, divides the present from the past and that from our vantage point within the present it is possible to describe the past accurately, analyze it objectively, and interpret it with fidelity to some absolute standard of truth or reality. Based on this false assumption, critics like Huxtable strike a moral posture, corrupting the meaning of integrity as it is applied to the built environment by implying that most contemporary architecture and most historic preservation projects lack integrity in the sense of honesty, thus impugning the moral rectitude of those whose aesthetic sensibilities are different from the critic's own.

Yet well before many people outside the academy had become aware of deconstructionist challenges to the notion that a "text" (object, place, or narrative) is able to communicate unambiguous essential meanings, David Lowenthal had forced historians and preservationists to acknowledge two painful realities: (1) that it is impossible to know, much less to experience or to reconstruct, the past and (2) that historical bias in recording, describing, and interpreting the past is inevitable.

No historical account ever corresponds precisely with any actual past. . . .

So-called primary sources come no closer to the reality of the past than derivative chronicles do. No process of verification can totally satisfy us that we know the truth about the past, for we accept or reject an account solely on the basis of its internal plausibility and its conformity with other known or trusted accounts. . . .

The past we know or experience is always contingent on our own views, our own perspective, above all our own present. Just as we are products of the past, so is the known past an artifact of ours.[31]

Lowenthal is certainly not hostile to the mission of the historian or of the preservationist, but he insists—and in this effort anticipated the current effort to broaden the range of cultural groups whose experiences are interpreted through historic sites—that preservation is itself a form of history making and hence inescapably an expression of contemporary culture devoid of that distanced objectivity associated with science.

The very "speculation and conjecture" proscribed within the NPS guidelines have frequently been the hallmark of exceptionally fine historical writing; why might not the same opportunity be available to the most creative and well-trained minds within the discipline of preservation? The warnings against "false historicism"—characterized by the introduction of *any* undocumented element within a restored or reconstructed historic landscape—reflect a widespread overreaction to the legitimate demand for good scholarship, painstaking research, and careful documentation in the treatment of historic landscapes. The problem is that many legitimate exceptions to the rules being set forth will occur to informed readers; in other cases, the recommended actions seem inconsistent with the philosophical premises espoused in the definitions of each treatment type.

Because both the preservation brief *Protecting Cultural Landscapes* and the final version of the *Guidelines* provide fewer specific examples of inappropriate design strategies than the 1992 *Draft Guidelines* did, the practical implications of the demand for documentary or physical evidence for every design element included within a restored or reconstructed historic landscape may be less apparent to readers. Hence, a look back at the earlier draft version is enlightening, since there is nothing in the more recent publications to suggest that the same examples do not apply. For each of the four potential treatments of a historic landscape, the *Draft Guidelines* and the final version use a two-column format of "Recommended" and "Not Recommended" actions or omissions. Under the treatment of restoration, for example, the "Recommended" column in the 1992 draft advocated the replacement of missing vegetation features, "matching the original design intent and appearance during the historic period," provided there is "historical, pictorial, or documentary evidence." The parallel "Not Recommended" column warned against "creating non-historic 'period gardens' such as kitchen gardens or building grounds intended to evoke the historic period for which insufficient historical information exists."[32] The final version states simply that "installing vegetation that was thought to have existed during the restoration period, but for which there is insufficient documentation; or planting vegetation that was part of the original design but was never installed, thus creating a false historical appearance" is not recommended.[33]

Similarly, under the reconstruction treatment category the 1992 *Draft Guidelines* warned against "replacing a vanished vegetation feature using speculative evidence," an example of which would be "replanting a kitchen garden without sufficient information regarding its exact configuration and historic plant materials."[34] This means that the evocative kitchen gardens within round paling-and-board fences recently developed as part of the interpretation of the nineteenth-century slave quarters at Carter's Grove in Virginia, for which the archeological evidence hardly supplies this level of "exact" information, would be tarred with the "false historic appearance" brush. Quarters existed at this place on the property, but the form of the gardens and the choice of vegetation is based on an understanding of what was typical for such housing within the region and the historic period. The fact is that the number of historic gardens and landscapes for which documentation of either the "exact configuration" (the landscape plan) or the actual list of "historic plant materials" exists is very few indeed.

The final version of the *Guidelines* seems equally demanding of highly precise documentation of plant choices, allowing substitution only in cases where the original plant is known but compelling reasons obtain for using an improved substitute, which must duplicate the appearance of the original in "habit, form, color, texture, bloom, fruit, fragrance, scale and context."[35] Anything less constitutes, in a sense, a form of inappropriate reconstruction: "Executing a design for the landscape that was never constructed historically" is bad practice. Reconstructions of any kind, moreover, must be "clearly identified as a contemporary recreation."[36]

One example of recommended/not recommended actions that seems inconsistent with the philosophy set forth in the definitions of the treatment types relates to the insistence upon the unity of "associated historic resources" in determining the period of interpretation in landscape restoration or reconstruction. The concepts of multiple periods of significance and of evolution over time seem to be contradicted by strictures against "selecting a

Slave quarters at Carter's Grove, Colonial Williamsburg, Virginia. These three photographs, which provide views of the reconstruction of the quarters, illustrate the use of garden forms and plantings associated with the regional practice of the period but not necessarily documented by archeological evidence. Sources: *Top left,* photograph by David Doody, 1995 (copyright by Colonial Williamsburg Foundation, negative 1995-DMD-411,6s); *bottom left,* photograph by Carl Lounsbury, 1988 (copyright by Colonial Williamsburg Foundation, negative 1988-VEP-889,16as); *right,* photograph by Vanessa Patrick, 1992 (copyright by Colonial Williamsburg Foundation, negative 1992-CRL-971,32s).

restoration period for the landscape and its vegetation features that presents a time frame that is different than its associated historic resources, or conversely, restoring a building to a different period than the landscape" or "selecting a period for the reconstruction of the landscape and its structures that presents a time frame that is different than its other associated historic structures."[37] This restrictive language from the *Draft Guidelines* is still reflected in the limited options enforced within the treatment categories of the final version. Preservation and rehabilitation admit the possibility that "changes to a property that have acquired historic significance in their own right" should be "retained and preserved," but restoration and reconstruction both demand the removal of features not belonging to the interpretive period.[38]

The same *Landscape Architecture* article celebrating current preservation projects that seemed to "raise new contextual questions"—with the implication that these directions were inspired or at least supported by the *Draft Guidelines*—described the landscape plan being developed for the National

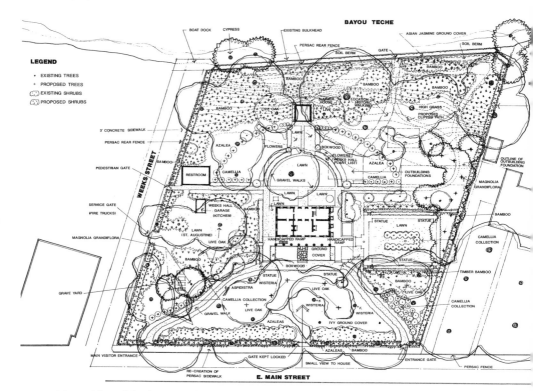

Master Plan of Shadows-on-the-Teche, New Iberia, Louisiana, during the Weeks Hall period, c. 1922. The master plan incorporates elements of the Weeks Hall plan, while retaining such features of earlier periods as the fence, documented in an 1861 painting by Adrien Persac, that was reconstructed by the National Trust after it assumed ownership of the property. Weeks Hall had eliminated the central walk and substituted a screen of bamboo for the wooden fence and gate seen in the Persac painting. Source: Plans by Emerson Associates, Baton Rouge, Louisiana, and Balmori Associates, New Haven, Connecticut, for the National Trust for Historic Preservation, 1992.

Trust property Shadows-on-the-Teche in New Iberia, Louisiana. Here the decision has been made to restore the remarkable early twentieth-century residential garden of a fourth-generation descendent of the family that built the house early in the nineteenth century, when the property (now just 2½ acres and urban) was part of a 200-acre holding. Weeks Hall, the heir, was himself a zealous antiquarian who spent a lifetime "restoring" and furnishing the mansion; the interior is today restored and interpreted using the prosperous antebellum years as the period of greatest significance. The temporal disjuncture between the house and the landscape that Hall designed in response to the reduced scale of the site and the drastic changes in its setting constitutes, in a sense, the actual historic record, but so does the white wooden fence, not a part of the Weeks Hall design, that the National Trust partially reconstructed after assuming ownership in 1958, using the evidence of a circa 1861 painting of the front facade. This, too, will be retained, in a landscape that its designers hope will achieve a sense of historic layering, rather than a sharply defined and absolutely faithful recreation of one or more past landscapes.

Layering as a concept can probably be traced to Kevin Lynch's insightful meditation on the expression of time in environmental design, including historic landscape preservation, *What Time Is This Place?*, first published in 1972. Lynch described layering as "a deliberate device of aesthetic expression—the visible accumulation of overlapping traces from successive periods, each trace modifying and being modified by the new additions, to produce something like a collage of time."[39] The term has been frequently associated in recent years with the metaphor of the landscape as palimpsest, a document in which the remnants of earlier, partially erased or effaced texts underlie the most recently inscribed surface. The analogy with the way that contemporary environments are physically superimposed over the fabric of past landscapes is apt. Even when preservationists think in these terms, however, it has been difficult to discover legitimate ways to define—and then to reveal through design and the interpretive program—the reality of this sequential piling-up of landscape layers in a single place. It is a Western habit of mind to conceive of time as a horizontal, not a vertical, progression; that is how we imagine time-logic, chronology, and that is why we are comfortable using the language of cutoff dates and spatially isolating the historic periods being interpreted at a historic site.

Rethinking the Integrity of Cultural Landscapes

Precisely because getting at the "truth" of history is so conditioned by everything from ingrained cultural predispositions to willful determination that a favored reading of the past should be taken as the only authoritative one, the best course is to acknowledge up front the limitations on what can be known or recovered and how it is communicated. History had its beginnings, after all, in oral tradition, in storytelling. The rhetorical and poetic dimensions of history are still what move human hearts and enlighten human understanding. That is what Kevin Lynch was trying to explore in his study of the way that contemporary places can be made to resonate with a sense of historic time. Cultural landscape preservation, as a form of history telling, is not less than science; it is more than science.

This is not to say that those within the discipline of landscape preservation should retreat from the hard-won recognition that the quality of a preservation project is absolutely dependent upon the quality of the research and scholarship that inform the decision-making process. But we must be cautious about institutionalizing one or another particular method, a dubious achievement that would be less likely to help us avoid error than to assure that future experience and practice will discover the shortcomings of a too-stringent set of rules of procedure. We need particularly to abjure the conception of landscape preservation as a pseudoscience, even while respecting the legitimately scientific studies that it embraces as components of the work. The concept of integrity borrowed from ecology is appropriate as a guiding metaphor as long as the value of unity or completeness or wholeness in the historical record is used to describe a dynamic process over time rather than a static inventory. Under the rubric of that metaphor, the present as the vantage point from which the past is discovered and made more real and accessible should be the focus of interpretation.

Ada Louise Huxtable is afraid that "the blend of new and old, real and fake, original and copy, in even the best . . . restorations defies analysis";[40] in other words, it is virtually impossible to help visitors at historic sites achieve a clear understanding of the premises, scope, and character of the preservation work at which they are looking. This view merely accepts the limitations of current interpretive programs and needlessly despairs of the public's ability to appreciate the issues and options involved. The time has long since passed when poorly trained docents, trite texts, and amateurish slide shows should be tolerated; this is the area in which standards need most to be elevated. Extraordinary educational and interpretive models are emerging at sites around the country, particularly where curators and administrators are willing to take risks. Daring to acknowledge, for example, that the Carter's Grove mansion has as much to tell visitors about the twentieth-century Colonial Revival as about the original eighteenth-century plantation house and redoing the interiors to encourage them to see the way in which the McRae family chose to reveal, to suppress, or to manipulate elements of the past is a case in point. The same willingness to address the messy complexity of history in a lively way is reflected in the surrounding landscape of Carter's Grove, which simultaneously interprets a seventeenth-century settlement unknown until its archeological discovery less than twenty years ago, a large eighteenth-century kitchen garden on the important river-facing facade of the house, and the reconstructed nineteenth-century slave quarters mentioned earlier.

Perhaps the whole field of cultural landscape preservation needs to be renamed *cultural landscape interpretation*. It would be helpful, certainly, to unload the inaccurate connotations of *preservation* and put the emphasis on an expanded understanding of *interpretation,* which in fact begins with the research phase, is inseparable from every design decision, and is then documented through the interpretive program that visitors experience. Then, perhaps, the profession and the public alike will come to recognize the creative and artistic dimensions of this interpretive process—open to experiment and innovation, to critical discourse and debate. Great art of any kind takes chances, breaks out of conventional ways of approaching the work, surprises and delights, sometimes even shocks. If we saw our task from the beginning as transformative—artfully to transform the raw data, the physical facts, the historical record, into a comprehensible vision with potential meaning for men and women today (even if the meaning has to do with the discovery of otherness, difference, the mysterious or finally unknowable)—we might be less afraid to expand rather than to restrict the options for interpretation. A disciplining set of "do nots" ("Not Recommended" has the force of "Do Not" among those seeking to follow the highest standards) will in the end produce an orthodoxy with respect to the treatment of historic landscapes that inhibits the development of new and better ways of recovering the past as a visible and meaningful presence in the lives of people today.

To speak of the integrity of historic sites is rightly to define their potential to provide that important and meaningful physical reality; they are more or less complete fragments of the record, and we want to hold on to as much as we can of what might help us to make sense of the past. But the quality and importance of any preservation project is determined not by the integrity of the site, but by the quality of what is made of the site through interpretation of its history. That is the added value that can turn even a precious few evocative fragments, transformed by intelligence and imagination, into significant history; without it, even historic sites of exceptional integrity will remain sterile.

Notes

INTRODUCTION | *Why Cultural Landscape Preservation?*

1. *New York Times,* 19 August 1984, 29 October 1986.
2. Bird 1981; Goldberger 1980; Carmody 1982. The comment about the "grass museum" was provided by Gerri Weinstein-Bruenig in an interview with Arnold Alanen on 20 January 1998; Ms. Weinstein-Bruenig was director of horticulture for Central Park from 1979 to 1985.
3. This book uses a broad interpretation of preservation when considering and defining the processes that contribute to preservation action. Cultural resource and cultural landscape preservationists, however, distinguish among preservation, restoration, rehabilitation, and reconstruction. From a technical standpoint, *preservation* is the most conservative approach to resource and landscape treatment, since it emphasizes the retention of the greatest amount of historic material; *restoration* and *reconstruction* typically occur only when sufficient evidence to document the former form and content of a resource or landscape exists; and *rehabilitation,* which lies somewhere between preservation and restoration, is the more common approach, since it retains the character-defining features of a property while simultaneously making it functional for contemporary uses (see Birnbaum, with Peters 1996; MacDonald and Alanen 1999; and Howett, this volume). The restoration-preservation debate is an especially lively issue among restoration ecologists, who focus upon the repair of damaged natural landscapes, and it often is a point of contention among art historians, who have differing views about the restoration of historic works of art. For a discussion of these debates, refer to M. Hall (1999).
4. Robert E. Cook (1996) posed a similar question in his essay, "Is Landscape Preservation an Oxymoron?"
5. Lamme 1989, 182.
6. Ibid., 85. This is not to say that historic restoration and preservation activities in the United States began at Williamsburg. Mount Vernon, Va. (1853), and Santa Fe, N.M. (1912), serve as especially noteworthy examples of two earlier architecturally motivated endeavors; see Murtaugh (1988) and C. Wilson (1997).
7. Lamme 1989, 183.
8. Clay 1976.

9. Page, Gilbert, and Dolan 1998; Melnick, Sponn, and Saxe 1984. For recent assessments of designed landscapes situated within national parks, refer to Carr 1998 and McClelland 1998.

10. Birnbaum 1994, 1–2. In addition, the NPS has identified several subcategories that often pertain to cultural landscapes; examples include rural historic districts, historic mining sites, historic engineering sites, and so forth. Ethnographic landscapes also need to be distinguished from the "traditional cultural properties" discussed in National Register Bulletin 38 (Parker and King 1992). Traditional cultural properties embrace a broad range of property types, which can include battlefield sites, objects such as Native American medicine bags, and structures and land-use patterns in communities. Ethnographic landscapes, on the other hand, are larger places or locations that carry cultural meaning or values and may include buildings, sites, or objects; however, it is possible that they may not be associated with other tangible traditional cultural properties.

11. UNESCO 1994, 11. To make the definitions more understandable, we made slight changes to the exact wording presented in the UNESCO document.

12. Mitchell 1995.

13. Sauer 1925, 343.

14. Johnston 1991; Wagner and Mikesell 1962, 10–11.

15. Jackson 1984, 8, xii; also see Jackson 1997.

16. Groth 1997, 1, 3.

17. Jackson 1976, 194.

18. Birnbaum, with Peters 1996.

19. Fitch 1982.

20. Jackson 1980.

21. Groth 1997, 1. It is also unlikely that many Americans are aware of provisions in the National Historic Preservation Act of 1966 which set forth a process (Section 106) that federal agencies and affiliated applicants must follow in determining what effect their actions will have on properties included in or declared eligible for the National Register of Historic Places; the law requires that the agencies seek to reduce, if not avoid, future actions that have potentially negative consequences for historic resources. For further information refer to Murtach 1988, esp. pp. 64–72.

22. Jackson 1994, 85; Cronon 1995, 85.

O N E | *Considering Nature and Culture in Historical Landscape Preservation*

I extend my thanks to Kenneth Helphand and Polly Welch, both of the University of Oregon, and to Simon Swaffield, of Lincoln University (New Zealand), for their careful reading of previous drafts of this chapter and their especially insightful and helpful comments.

1. Lowenthal 1985.

2. See, e.g., Rolvaag 1927 and Appleton 1975.

3. Rolvaag 1927; Kolodny 1984.

4. Sauer 1925; Appleton 1975; Blouet and Lawson 1975; Cronon 1995.

5. Nevius 1976.

6. Thayer 1994.

7. Williams 1985.

8. Wilson 1991.

9. Bahre and Lawson 1975.

10. Cronon 1983; Silver 1990.

11. Lowenthal 1985.

12. Brown 1994.

13. See, esp., Brown 1994.

14. Ibid.

15. Abbey 1990.

16. Nevius 1976.

17. Hutchings 1990 (1886); Clark 1910; Foley 1912; Matthes 1950; Russell 1992 (1959); Orland 1985; Nash 1989; Runte 1992 (1990); Demars 1991.

18. Runte 1992 (1990), 16.

19. Evernden 1992, 35.

20. Ibid., 19.

21. Tuan 1984.

22. Cooper 1982 (1841), 35.

23. Deakin 1967 (1852).

24. Noguchi 1897, 29.

25. Runte 1992 (1990).

26. Lane 1919, 4.

27. Demars 1991.

28. Sargent 1975; Demars 1991; Gramann 1992.

29. Land and Community Associates 1994.

30. This phenomenon was already evident in a guidebook to Yosemite prepared by the Geological Survey of California in 1869.

31. Matthes 1950.

32. Hall 1921; Matthes 1950; Russell 1992 (1959).

33. Hill 1916.

34. Heady and Zinke 1978, 1.

35. Golden 1997.

36. Interviews with Yosemite National Park staff, conducted by Land and Community Associates, 1994.

37. Stornoway 1888; National Park Service 1931.

38. Orsi, Runte, and Smith-Baranzini 1993.

39. See, e.g., Malin 1984 and O'Brien 1984.

40. Limerick 1987.

41. Wilson 1922; Worster 1993.

42. Runte 1992 (1990), 227.

43. I thank Kenneth Helphand for this concept.

T W O | *Selling Heritage Landscapes*

1. Bowen 1990, introduction, n.p.

2. Murtagh 1988.

3. National Trust for Historic Preservation, n.d.

4. "Heritage Tourism Defined," 1993, 2.

5. George Gallup Organization 1986; also see Barthel 1996.

6. See, e.g., "Focus on Landscape Preservation"—a theme issue of *Historic Preservation Forum* (1993)—which contains six articles on the subject.

7. Personal communication from Kent Millard, National Trust for Historic

Preservation, Texas/New Mexico Field Office, Ft. Worth, to R. Francaviglia, 4 January 1994.

8. Lowenthal and Prince 1965, 126.

9. David Kammer, "Mora County, New Mexico: New Perspectives on a Historical Cultural Landscape," paper presented to the Western History Association, Tulsa, Okla., 15 October 1993.

10. Jackson 1990.

11. Francaviglia 1978a.

12. "Bisbee, Arizona, Copper Queen Hotel," two-sided, sixfold brochure, n.d.; obtained by R. Francaviglia from the Copper Queen Hotel, Bisbee, Ariz., December 1993.

13. "Main Street—Making Downtown Come Alive," six-page brochure prepared by the National Trust for Historic Preservation, Washington, D.C. (c. 1990).

14. Southeastern Arizona Governments Organization 1982.

15. "Pioneer Arizona Living History Museum," seven-page synopsis, n.d.; provided to R. Francaviglia, December 1973.

16. Bowen 1990, 175.

17. Porter 1990, 9.

18. Francaviglia 1991.

19. Francaviglia 1981, 1996.

20. Personal communication from Ann McBride, Old Tucson, Ariz., to R. Francaviglia, 7 January 1995. A total of 466,785 people visited Old Tucson in 1992, and 477,220 visited in 1993.

21. Bowen 1990.

22. Francaviglia 1989.

23. "Recall the Past, Live the Present, Dream the Future," Disney America's brochure, 1993, 6 pp.

24. Francaviglia 1978b.

25. Kammer 1993, "Mora County, New Mexico."

THREE | *The History and Preservation of Urban Parks and Cemeteries*

1. *New York Times,* 8 June 1965, 24.

2. Cramer 1993; Toth 1991.

3. LANDSCAPES 1990.

4. Keller and Keller 1987; Birnbaum with Peters 1996.

5. Birnbaum 1994; Birnbaum with Peters 1996.

6. Beveridge and Schuyler 1983; Schuyler and Censer 1992.

7. Schuyler 1991.

8. Rosenzweig and Blackmar 1992, 410–11.

9. Ibid.; Rogers 1987.

10. M. Brigid Sullivan, "Measuring the Economic Benefit of Your Park," presented at the National Recreation and Parks Association Congress for Recreation and Parks, San Jose, Calif., 20–25 October 1993. Sullivan was director of the Louisville and Jefferson County Parks Department, Louisville, Ky.

11. Keller 1993, 26–27.

12. Olmsted quoted in Schuyler 1986, 120; Beveridge and Schuyler 1983, 213; Beveridge 1995.

13. Caro 1974, 451.

14. Hayward 1991.

15. Rogers 1987.
16. Hawes 1982, 32.
17. Ibid.
18. O'Donnell 1993.
19. Hayden 1995.
20. Olmsted quoted in Schuyler and Censer 1992, 630; Gompers quoted in Smith 1992, 67.
21. Smith 1992.
22. Hawes 1982, 18.
23. Rosenzweig and Blackmar 1992.
24. Black quoted in Caro 1974, 561.
25. Schuyler and Censer 1992, 42, 613.
26. Schuyler and Censer 1992.
27. Schuyler 1986, 45–46, 54; Downing quoted in Schuyler 1996, 187–91.
28. "Central Park," 1873, 529.
29. LANDSCAPES 1991.
30. Olmsted 1871, 18.
31. Sennett 1990, 29.
32. Rowe and Koetter 1978.

F O U R | *Appropriating Place in Puerto Rican Barrios*

The research for this chapter was supported by the Bronx Council on the Arts and by a Rockefeller-Schomburg Fellowship. The Bronx Council on the Arts has been the prime sponsor of the *Casita* Project. Bill Aguado, executive director, and Betty Sue Hertz, artist and coordinator of the *Casita* Project, have been the movers behind the effort to disseminate and support the work of casita builders. The *Casita* Project has sponsored several exhibits, including one at the Experimental Gallery of the Smithsonian Institution in Washington, D.C., in 1991 and another in the Bronx Museum of the Arts later during the same year.

1. Bhabha 1994, 1.
2. See Aponte-Parés 1997.
3. See, e.g., the special section "Then and Now, 100 Years of New York City" in the *New York Times* of 25 January 1998. If one were to understand the presence of Puerto Ricans and other Latinos in the history of New York from this document, their history seems to begin in the 1980s, rather than the 1890s.
4. Building casitas is a collective effort of neighbors in different neighborhoods of New York City. Since the recording of casitas began some ten years ago, many have been destroyed by fire or through the direct actions of the city government, which fears that they will be generalized as squatters' settlements. Villa Puerto Rico, one of the oldest casitas in the South Bronx, was rebuilt in 1991. *Casita Culture,* a video produced by Kathy Hukum for the Smithsonian Institution, records the building of Villa Puerto Rico.
5. King 1991.
6. The term *vernacular architecture* tends to oversimplify complex cultural expressions of a society. In Puerto Rico, as elsewhere, the transformation of pre-Columbian habitat to a vernacular form took different routes. Each was colored by factors including location and geography (e.g., rural versus urban, coast versus mountain), the economic status or class of the inhabitant, the colony/metropolis relation-

ship, and the development level of the metropolis (i.e., technology, commercial/market relationships to other metropolises, etc.). In this chapter I look at the transformation of the Taíno hut into the casita, a particular expression of the Puerto Rican popular dwelling that is most common among the working classes and the poor. See Lewis 1983, Segre 1984–85, Bertelot and Gaumé 1982, and Aponte-Parés 1990.

7. Boddy 1992, 134.

8. In 1987 it was estimated that over 25 percent of all New Yorkers were poor; however, among Hispanics and African Americans the rates approached 32 percent and 43 percent, respectively. Poverty was also geographically uneven. In 1986, when close to 26 percent of all renter households lived below federal poverty or near-poverty levels in the Bronx, the comparable figures for Hispanics and African Americans approached 45 percent in the Bronx, 37 percent in Brooklyn, 21 percent in Queens, and 27 percent in Staten Island. Even within the boroughs, the disparity was significant. (Figures are derived from Michael Stegman, "Housing Vacancy Report," New York Department of Housing Preservation and Development, April 1988.)

9. Friedmann and Wolff 1982.

10. During the past three decades, Puerto Ricans, African Americans, and other minorities have been displaced from key districts in New York City to other areas of lesser economic value. Nevertheless, new arrivals—mainly other blacks from the Caribbean, other Caribbean Latinos (i.e., from the Dominican Republic), and Asian/Asian Pacific peoples—have repopulated other middle-class districts in the city.

11. Friedmann and Wolff 1982, 319.

12. Ibid., 326.

13. Davis 1992, 155.

14. Zukin 1991, 17.

15. Boyer 1992, 118.

16. Riley 1992, 17.

17. Anderson 1991.

18. Gómez-Peña 1993, 20.

19. The contribution made by Puerto Ricans to the built environment of New York City has not been studied. In fact, for the new majority of New Yorkers—people of color and new immigrants—the built environment of the city has no apparent relationship to their history; in other words, they are guests in someone else's city. Except for a recent attempt by New York City's Landmarks Commission to begin to recognize important places in the South Bronx, Queens, and Harlem, preservation efforts have been directed primarily toward the preservation of the history of European descendants. Even those buildings being preserved in the Bronx have little association with the history of Puerto Ricans in New York City.

20. Davis 1992, 164.

21. Hobsbawm and Ranger 1992.

22. Sánchez 1992, 37.

23. Gómez-Peña 1993, 16.

24. Zukin 1991, 17.

25. Abad 1992, 14.

26. These areas include all of the Caribbean islands; the coastal, southern, and Gulf states in the United States; and the Caribbean-facing areas of South and Central America.

27. Zukin 1991, 12.

28. Aponte-Parés 1990; Quintero-Rivera 1988; Rigau 1992; Sepúlveda 1989; Sepúlveda and Carbonell 1987.

29. The Puerto Rican cultural critic Guillermo Ramírez has been unable to identify another similar event in African culture in the Americas. In fact, he argues that *El Velorio* depicts a Spanish religious custom; to prove his point he lists other Spanish paintings of the period that are similar to Oller's (Ramírez, n.d.).

30. In 1905, the Puerto Rican Ramón Frade completed *El Pan Nuestro,* which codified the image of the *jíbaro* in the twentieth century. In this painting of a poor peasant, one can see an isolated *bohío/*casita clinging to a steep mountain slope in the distance. Such isolation, as depicted in the painting, allowed the continuity of a peasant culture in Puerto Rico throughout most of the twentieth century in what otherwise is a highly urban society.

31. Zukin 1991, 7.

32. During a 1991 visit to Puerto Rico, I had an interesting and revealing experience. In the middle of the Plaza de Cabo Rojo, a very old town on Puerto Rico's southern coast, townspeople had placed an "authentic" vintage 1930 casita. I asked a group of women seated on park benches nearby about the reasons behind such an occurrence. They reported that there had just been a town festival celebrating Puerto Rican culture and that, when they were searching for a "universal symbol" of Puerto Rican culture for the earlier part of the century, the casita won by acclamation. They found and rebuilt one in the middle of the plaza.

33. Flores 1993, 39.

34. Rodríguez Castro 1993; Sanchez 1994.

35. At the time of the demolition, I was working for the Office of Manhattan Borough President Ruth Messinger. As the borough president, Messinger made every attempt to preserve a major portion of the ballroom. When her office commissioned a well-known architectural preservation firm to evaluate the building's soundness, I became her lead staff person in this project and spent over a year negotiating with the city and others, but to no avail. The Municipal Arts Society and other groups pressured the Office of the Mayor to reconsider the demolition of this historic landmark. The groups were unable to convince city government, and only the facade of a small portion was preserved. Out of this experience Landmarks Harlem, a historic preservation group, was formed. Landmarks Harlem has now emerged as a major preservation group for African Americans and has argued for the preservation of African American history in Harlem and elsewhere in upper Manhattan. However, no preservation group emerged in the Latino community.

36. For the many important sites that recorded the history of Puerto Ricans and other Latinos during the early part of the twentieth century, see the work of Jesús Colón (1982) and Bernardo Vega (Andreu Iglesias 1984). The Center for Puerto Rican Studies at Hunter College has records of this earlier history.

37. Hayden 1995, 11.

38. Boyer 1983, 287.

39. Zukin 1995, 2.

40. Ibid., 20.

F I V E | *Considering the Ordinary*

1. Stilgoe 1982, 3; Conzen 1978, 154; Rapaport 1969. For examples of some books that use *common* and *ordinary* in their titles to identify the vernacular landscape, see Meinig 1979, Stilgoe 1982, and Groth 1997.

2. Wyatt and Midwest Vernacular Architecture Forum 1987. Additional informa-

tion about the fate of the bulletin was provided by Barbara Wyatt. Although never published in its final form, the draft copy has been used by the NPS and other preservationists to address vernacular architecture.

3. For additional examples of landscape preservation methods in rural areas, refer to Stokes, Watson, and Mastran 1997.

4. Jackson 1984; Jackson 1986b, 145.

5. Brunskill 1978; Jackson 1986, 145; Oliver 1997.

6. Oliver 1997, 1:xxiii.

7. Kammen 1980; Foner 1990.

8. Glassie 1968, 33.

9. "Raw Vision's Definitions" 1993; Kimmelman 1997, C-37; Sancar and Koop 1995, 143; House 1996, 58.

10. Riley 1987, 130; Jackson 1984, 151; Jackson 1986a.

11. Hunt and Wolschke-Bulmahn 1993, 3.

12. McClelland et al. 1990, 1–2.

13. Porter and Lukermann 1975.

14. Barthel 1984.

15. Land and Community Associates 1977a, 3; 1977b, 2.

16. Barthel 1984; Land and Community Associates 1977a, 4.

17. Barthel 1984.

18. Ibid.; Hayden 1976, 254.

19. Barthel 1984, 161.

20. Dunbar/Jones Partnership, "Amana Colonies: Amana Colonies Tour, Iowa County, Iowa," fieldtrip guide for annual meeting of the Council of Educators in Landscape Architecture, Iowa State University, Ames, Iowa, 1995.

21. Egerton 1977, 39.

22. Ibid.; Brachey and Brachey 1995; Stokes, Watson, and Mastran 1997; Ehrenkrantz Group 1985.

23. Brachey and Brachey 1995; "Rugby Colony Master Plan" 1986, 110.

24. Current 1977, 56.

25. William Tishler and Erik Brynildson, "Namur Belgian-American District: National Register of Historic Places Inventory—Nomination Form" (Madison: Preservation Division, State Historical Society of Wisconsin, 1985); *Door County Advocate* (Sturgeon Bay, Wis.), 19 December 1990, 1; Calkins and Laatsch 1986.

26. For further explanation of the Section 106 process, refer to note 21 of the introduction to this volume.

27. Wisconsin Department of Transportation (WDOT), Minutes of Transportation District 3, 17 August 1994 (on file with WDOT, Green Bay office).

28. Alanen 1995. Although Finnish immigrants established the first permanent settlement in the area, *embarras* is a French word that refers to hindrance or encumbrance. The term was used by French voyageurs who, during the 1600s, described the narrow passages along waterways that caused difficulties for canoe travel.

29. *Duluth News-Tribune*, 6 June 1993, 15 June 1997.

30. Paddock 1991, 2.

31. Michael Koop, "Rural Finnish Log Buildings of St. Louis County, Minnesota: National Register of Historic Places Multiple Property Documentation Form" (St. Paul: State Historic Preservation Office, Minnesota Historical Society, 1988).

32. Ibid.

33. Trustees of Reservations 1992.

34. Land Trust Alliance 1998.

35. Ibid.; Sorensen, Greene, and Russ 1997; American Farmland Trust 1997, 83; Copps 1995, 125.

36. American Farmland Trust 1997; Hart 1991, 18.

37. Hayward 1993; Schneider 1994, 10A.

38. Bidwell et al. 1996; Hayward 1993.

39. Bidwell et al. 1996; Schneider 1994.

40. Schneider 1994, 10Y; Glen Chown, "Agricultural Land Protection: Linking Projects and Policy Reform," presentation at the National Land Trust Rally, October 17–20, 1998, Madison, Wis. (Chown is executive director of the Grand Traverse Regional Land Conservancy.)

41. Brooke 1998, A1, A1B; P. Galvin quoted by Skow, 69.

42. Dunn 1988; National Park Service 1988.

43. National Park Service 1988, 40.

44. Ibid., 47; Dunn 1988, 256.

45. Webb 1987, 82.

46. Livingston 1993.

47. Melnick, Sponn, and Saxe 1984.

48. National Park Service 1985, 1; Westmacott 1994.

49. National Park Service 1985; Westmacott 1994; Webb 1987, 87.

50. National Park Service 1979.

51. Haswell and Alanen 1994; McEnaney, Tishler, and Alanen 1995; Williams, Alanen, and Tishler 1996; MacDonald and Alanen 1999.

52. McEnaney, Tishler, and Alanen 1995. Because of concerns over the deteriorating buildings at SBDNL, especially the Port Oneida district, in 1998 concerned citizens formed a nonprofit organization, "Preserve Historic Sleeping Bear." Adopting a grassroots approach, the organization is encouraging historic preservation partnerships between the NPS and other institutions, implementing educational programs, and conducting outreach and fund-raising activities.

53. Williams, Alanen, and Tishler 1996; National Park Service 1987, 21, 30.

54. *Beacon Journal* (Akron, Ohio), 14 May 1999.

55. McKinley 1993, 44.

56. National Park Service 1980, ii.

57. Westmacott 1994; McKinley 1993.

58. Hufford 1985; Mason 1992.

59. Hufford 1985, 11.

60. Ibid., 12; Hufford 1986, 8.

61. Hufford 1985, 1986.

62. Mason 1992, 203.

63. Noah 1995, B10.

64. Ibid.; William Fink, "Killing the Goose That Laid the Golden Egg," *Daily Mining Gazette* (Houghton, Mich.), 29 June 1996.

65. Bureau of Michigan History, "Keweenaw National Historical Park: Housing Preservation Issues Workshop," 1995, manuscript report on file in State Historic Preservation Office, Lansing, Mich.; Alanen and Franks 1997.

66. Bureau of Michigan History, "Keweenaw National Historical Park."

67. Alison K. Hoagland, "Industrial Housing and Vinyl Siding: Historical Significance Flexibly Applied," 1997, unpublished paper available at Michigan Technological University, Houghton, Mich.

68. Shelly S. Mastran, "Heritage Areas: New Partnerships for Saving Cultural Landscapes," paper presented at the annual meeting of the Association of American Geographers, Chicago, 15–18 March 1995.

69. Comp 1994; personal communication from Mike Cassady, American Heritage Rivers Progam, to author, 27 May 1999; *Chicago Tribune,* 14 February 1999.

70. Silos & Smokestacks Board of Trustees 1997, 1.

71. Silos & Smokestacks Board of Trustees 1997, 3; Shukert 1995, 1; Iron Range Resources and Rehabilitation Board (IRRRB), "Request for Proposals: Preservation Management and Marketing Plan," 1996, prospectus developed by IRRRB, Eveleth, Minn.

six | *Asian American Imprints on the Western Landscape*

I thank Eugene Hattori, Dolores Hayden, Gene Itagawa, David Streatfield, John Tchen, and the editors of this collection for their constructive comments in preparing this chapter.

1. Friday 1994, 112–13.

2. U.S. Immigration Commission 1911.

3. Dubrow, Nomura, et al. 1993, 137.

4. U.S. Immigration Commission 1911, 347.

5. Paul Olson files, cited by Lynn Getz in "Barneston," in *Cedar Riverside Watershed Cultural Resource Inventory* (Seattle: Seattle Water Department, 1987).

6. Morda C. Slauson, "One Hundred Years on the Cedar" [Renton, Wash.], 1967, reproduction of typescript, Special Collections, University of Washington.

7. Memorandum from Nancy Ishii to Marie Ruby, Seattle Water Department, 11 May 1994; interview with Kay Abe by Nancy Ishii, 1 June 1993. The information, cited in Ed Suguro, "Old Sawmill Towns Remembered," *Northwest Nikkei* (Seattle), May 1994, was confirmed in an interview with T. Z. Maekawa. Also see Ito 1973, 403, quoting Shoichiro Katsuno, who worked at Kereston in 1908–9.

8. The Rev. Joseph Sakakibara, quoted in Suguro 1994, 15.

9. Memorandum from Ishii to Ruby (see n. 7); interview with Tamako Kawamura by Nancy Ishii, 27 July 1993.

10. Suguro 1994, 7, 15; Bradley Bowden and Lynn L. Larson, "Cultural Resource Assessment, Japanese Camp and Lavender Town, Selleck, King County, Washington," unpublished report prepared for the King County Cultural Resources Division by Larson Anthropological/Archaeological Services, 1997, p. 14.

11. For additional information on Barneston, see Richard Gilbert and Mary Woodman, "Barneston's Japanese Community: A Report Prepared for the Seattle Water Department," unpublished paper prepared for the class Introduction to Preservation, Preservation Planning and Design Program, College of Architecture and Urban Planning, University of Washington, 1995.

12. Hattori 1991; White 1991.

13. White 1991, 38, 33–35. One additional landscape feature was identified in this study, the principles of site selection and orientation defined by *fengshui.* "Site selection for the construction of a dwelling and arrangement of structures upon the landscape is influenced by tradition and cosmology," the report noted. "A correctly placed building followed rules associated with an area's geomorphology, exposure and water supply. An orientation to the south to southeast was considered as most favorable" (38, 34). This landscape feature, however, remains to be linked to specific cultural resources

associated with Asian Americans in Nevada. On *fengshui,* also refer to chapter 7 of this book.

14. White 1991, 38, 21.

15. Ibid., 38, 22.

16. Chan 1991, 29.

17. White 1991, 38, 20.

18. Ibid., 38, 23, 28.

19. "Moore Gulch Chinese Mining Site, Vicinity of Pierce, Idaho," National Register of Historic Places Inventory-Nomination Form, 1982 (on file in the National Register of Historic Places, National Park Service, Washington, D.C.).

20. Ibid.

21. Fee 1991, 77.

22. Dubrow, Nomura, et al. 1993, 135.

23. Fee 1991, 78.

24. Ibid.

25. Ibid., 69–71.

26. Ibid., 87.

27. Kate O'Brien Reed, National Register of Historic Places nomination forms for the following properties in the Payette National Forest, Warren, Idaho, which were included as part of a Multiple-Property Listing prepared in 1989 and approved in 1990: "Chinese Sites in the Warren Mining District": "Ah Toy Garden," "Celadon Slope Garden," "Chi-Sandra Garden," and "Old China Trail"; the "Chinese Cemetery" was added to the listing in 1994. (The nominations are on file in the Idaho State Historic Preservation Office, Boise.)

28. Gail Nomura cited in Dubrow, Nomura, et al. 1993, 13.

29. California Department of Parks and Recreation 1988, 133–34.

30. Chan 1986, 31.

31. Ibid., 32.

32. Takaki 1993, 199, citing McWilliams 1939; also see Chan 1986.

33. Takaki 1993, 199.

34. Limerick 1992, 1031.

35. Dubrow 1999.

36. California Department of Parks and Recreation 1988, 135.

37. Ibid., 194–95.

38. Flewelling 1990, 89.

39. Takami 1992, 12.

40. Beikoku Seihokubu Hiroshima-Kenjinkai 1919, pl. 121.

41. Takami 1989, 3; Nomura 1993, 13.

42. Waugh, Yamato, and Okamura 1988, 164.

43. Chan 1991, 38, citing Japanese Agricultural Association 1918, ii (chart).

44. Takaki 1993, 270.

45. Japanese leadership in the hothouse rhubarb industry is documented in Japanese-American Citizens' League, White River Valley Chapter, 1986.

46. Fred Eernisse, "Arie Eernisse and His Time," 1967, 57, in the Community History file of the Vashon Island Library, Vashon Island, Washington.

47. For additional information on the extant shed in Auburn, see the proposed addendum to the King County Cultural Resources nomination for the Neely Mansion, prepared by graduate students in the Preservation Planning and Design Program of the University of Washington, 1994. Also see Mildred Tanner Andrews, "The Hori

Foroba aka the Hori-Acosta Bathhouse," King County Landmark Registration Form, 1996, on file in the King County Cultural Resources Division, Seattle.

48. Hayden, Dubrow, and Flynn 1985, esp. sect. 7, "The Flavor of Flowers." For expanded treatment of this subject, see Hayden 1995, 210–25, and Yagasaki 1982.

49. Hayden, Dubrow, and Flynn 1985.

50. Limerick 1992, 1046.

51. Shigemori 1949, 73–98.

52. According to landscape historian David Streatfield of the University of Washington, other surviving Japanese gardens in California include the Hakone Gardens in Saratoga, which were created for Isabel Stine by an Imperial gardener in 1917; the San Mateo Japanese Garden and Arboretum, designed by Nagao Sakurai in 1966; UCLA's Hannah Carter Japanese Garden, designed by Nagao Sukukari for Mr. and Mrs. Gordon Guiberson; part of the Huntington Gardens, in San Marino, designed in 1912 by William Hertrich, who used structures from a failed commercial tea garden; and part of a small private garden at El Cerrito in Hillsborough, designed by Japanese gardeners in 1912 for the Eugene De Sabla estate. Farther north, individual Japanese gardens survive in Portland, designed by P. Takuma in 1967, and in Seattle, designed by Juki Iida in 1957.

53. Ed Penhale and Pin Sisovann, "There's Money to Be Made Stalking the Wild Matsutake Mushroom—and Hundreds in on the Hunt," *Seattle Post-Intelligencer,* 9 October 1997, A1, 16.

54. Price 1989, 130.

55. Ibid., 139.

56. Ito 1973, 805.

57. Friday 1994, 54.

58. The narrow focus on properties associated with Japanese American relocation and internment was a result of politics rather than sound professional judgment. The designation of World War II internment camps was the result of a congressionally mandated study on that subject. National Historic Landmark Program staff argued for a broader focus that would include Japanese American community life in the prewar period, but their recommendations were not followed.

59. As of 1985, Manzanar was the only National Historic Landmark associated with Asian American heritage located outside Hawaii. Since that time, four more properties significant in Asian American heritage have been accorded National Historic Landmark designation: Locke Historic District, Sacramento County, Calif. (1990); Harada House, Riverside County, Calif. (1990); Rohwer Relocation Center Memorial Cemetery, Desha County, Ark. (1992); and Little Tokyo Historic District, Los Angeles, Calif. (1995). The history of the National Historic Landmark theme study on ethnic communities was recounted by Jim Charnelton, who worked on the study during his tenure in the History Division of the National Park Service (personal communication to Gail Dubrow, 22 November 1995).

60. Efforts to increase the number of National Historic Landmarks associated with African Americans and women are reported in the following sources: Afro-American Bicentennial Corporation 1973, 1976; Miller 1992, 1993. A congressionally funded initiative in the area of labor history was nearing completion when this chapter was being completed. Early publications related to this study include Grossman 1994; the spring 1995 issue of the journal *Labor's Heritage* has several articles devoted to this subject, including two by Archie Green (Green 1995a, 1995b).

61. White 1991, 38, 26.

62. Bowden and Larson 1997 (see n. 10).

63. Mary A. Mendenhall, "The Neely Mansion aka the Aaron Neely, Sr., Mansion." Nomination for the King County Register of Historic Places; on file with the King County Cutural Resources Division, Seattle.

64. For additional information on the extant shed in Auburn, see the proposed addendum to the King County Cultural Resources nomination for the Neely Mansion and the King County nomination form for the Hori Furoba prepared by Mildred Tanner Andrews (see n. 47).

65. Max Fukuhara, "Memories of Hashidate Yu." Unpublished handout distributed at a tour of the Panama Hotel, Seattle, 1997, 1.

SEVEN | *Ethnographic Landscapes*

1. Cowley 1991; Mitchell 1987; National Park Service 1990.
2. Palsson 1990, 7.
3. Cowley 1991, 10.
4. Wicklein 1994, 36–41.
5. Palsson 1990.
6. Wei 1992, 35.
7. Ibid., 39–43.
8. Greenwood 1993, 386.
9. Ibid., 395.
10. Leone 1973, 1979.
11. Leone 1973, 196.
12. Ibid., 199.
13. Ibid., 198–99.
14. McClelland et al. 1990.
15. King 1993, 63.
16. Sebastian 1993, 23.
17. Ibid.
18. Theodoratus 1993, 46.
19. Ibid.
20. Fowler 1986.
21. Ibid., 65.
22. Ibid.
23. Ibid., 97.
24. Theodoratus 1993, 46.
25. Greiser and Greiser 1993, 10.
26. Theodoratus 1993, 47.
27. Fowler et al. 1995, 138.
28. *New York Times,* 27 December 1993.
29. Cook 1991, 39.
30. Laidlaw 1991.
31. Fowler et al. 1995, 136.
32. Chapman 1991, 21.
33. Parker and King 1992, 1.
34. Sebastian 1993.
35. Ibid.
36. Downer and Roberts 1993, 12.

37. Chapman 1991, 19.
38. Cook 1991, 39.
39. Fuller 1991, 36.
40. Ibid., 37.

E I G H T | *Integrity as a Value in Cultural Landscape Preservation*

1. Rolston 1994, xi.
2. Ibid., xii.
3. Westra 1994, 31.
4. National Park Service 1991b, 2.
5. Ibid., 44.
6. Ibid.
7. National Park Service 1991a, 4.
8. O'Donnell 1992, 38. The *Draft Guidelines* were still under review when O'Donnell's article appeared. The categories of "features which define the character of historic landscape" defined in the *Draft Guidelines* were topography, vegetation, natural systems, circulation, structures, site furnishings and objects, water features, spatial relationships, and surroundings (9–10). This list was simplified by grouping the same features under just seven categories in Preservation Brief 36, *Protecting Cultural Landscapes: Planning, Treatment and Management of Historic Landscapes,* by Charles A. Birnbaum, published in September 1994. The list of "character-defining features" was simplified still further in the *Secretary of the Interior's Standards for the Treatment of Historic Properties with Guidelines for the Treatment of Cultural Landscapes,* finally published in 1996: "Land use patterns, vegetation, furnishings, decorative details and materials may be such features" (Birnbaum with Peters 1996, 4).
9. Fitch 1976, 277, 279.
10. O'Donnell and Melnick 1987, 136.
11. Webb 1987.
12. McClelland et al. 1990, 21.
13. Ibid.
14. McCormick 1994, 75.
15. Ibid.
16. Lauren Meier quoted in McCormick 1994, 76.
17. McCormick 1994, 76.
18. National Park Service 1991b, 45.
19. Ibid.
20. Birnbaum 1994, 15.
21. Bulletin 15 states that "the evaluation of integrity is sometimes a subjective judgment, but it must always be grounded in an understanding of a property's physical features and how they relate to its significance" (ibid., 44).
22. Entry dated 23 November 1787, journal of William Attmore of Philadelphia, in Lida Tunstall Rodman, ed., "Journal of a Tour to North Carolina by William Attmore, 1787," *James Sprunt Historical Publications* 17 (1922), quoted in *A Documentary History of the Gardens at Tryon Palace,* compiled by Perry Mathewes (unpublished report) (New Bern, N.C.: Tryon Palace Historic Sites and Gardens, 1998), 31.
23. Lockwood 1934.
24. Quoted in Mathewes, 3.
25. Dill 1942, quoted in Mathewes, *A Documentary History,* 40.

26. Mathewes 1998, 4–5.
27. Ibid.
28. Huxtable 1992, 24.
29. Arthur A. Shurcliff quoted in Hosmer 1985, 57–58.
30. Huxtable 1992, 28.
31. Lowenthal 1985, 214–16.
32. National Park Sevice 1992, 70.
33. Birnbaum with Peters 1996, 112.
34. National Park Service 1992, 89.
35. Birnbaum with Peters 1996, 136.
36. Ibid., 134, 129.
37. National Park Service 1992, 69, 95.
38. Birnbaum with Peters 1996, 18, 50.
39. Lynch 1980, 171.
40. Huxtable 1992, 24.

References

Several chapters in this volume cite such sources as unpublished manuscripts, National Register nominations, anonymous and local newspaper articles, brochures, personal communications, and interviews; these sources are included with the endnotes for individual chapters.

Abad, Celedonio. 1992. "El Espacio Conquistado." In *La Casa de Todos Nosotros.* New York: Museo del Barrio.

Abbey, Edward. 1990. *The Monkey Wrench Gang.* Salt Lake City: Dream Garden Press.

Afro-American Bicentennial Corporation. 1973. *A Summary Report of Thirty Sites Determined to Be Significant in Illustrating and Commemorating the Role of Black Americans in United States History.* Report prepared for the National Park Service by the Corporation.

————. 1976. *Summary Report of a Three Year Study by the Afro-American Bicentennial Corporation of Sites Determined to Be Significant in Illustrating the Role of Afro-Americans in United States History.* Report prepared for the National Park Service by the Corporation.

Alanen, Arnold R. 1995. "Back to the Land: Immigrants and Image-Makers in the Lake Superior Region, 1865 to 1930." In *Landscape in America,* edited by George F. Thompson. Austin: University of Texas Press.

Alanen, Arnold R., and Katie Franks, eds. 1997. *Remnants of Corporate Paternalism: Company Housing and Landscapes at Calumet, Michigan.* Calumet, Mich.: Keweenaw National Historic Park.

American Farmland Trust. 1997. *Saving American Farmlands: What Works.* Washington, D.C.: American Farmland Trust.

Anderson, Benedict. 1991. *Imagined Communities: Reflections on the Origin and Spread of Nationalism.* London: Verso.

Andreu Iglesias, César. 1984. *Memoirs of Bernardo Vega: A Contribution to the History of the Puerto Rican Community in New York.* Translated by Juan Flores. New York: Monthly Review Press.

Aponte-Parés, Luis. 1990. "Casas y Bojios: Territorial Development and Urban Growth in Nineteenth-Century Puerto Rico." Ph.D. diss., Columbia University.

———. 1997. "What's Yellow and White and Has Land All Around It? Appropriating Place in Puerto Rican Barrios." In *The Latino Studies Reader: Culture, Economy, and Society,* edited by Antonia Darder and Rodolfo D. Torres. New York: Blackwell.

Appleton, Jay. 1975. *The Experience of Landscape.* London: John Wiley & Sons.

Bahre, Brian W., and Merline P. Lawson, eds. 1975. *Images of the Plains: The Role of Human Nature in Settlement.* Lincoln: University of Nebraska Press.

Bahre, Conrad Joseph. 1991. *A Legacy of Change: Historic Human Impact on Vegetation in the Arizona Borderlands.* Tucson: University of Arizona Press.

Barthel, Diane L. 1984. *Amana: From Pietist Sect to American Community.* Lincoln: University of Nebraska Press.

———. 1996. *Historic Preservation: Collective Memory and Historical Identity.* New Brunswick, N.J.: Rutgers University Press.

Beikoku Seihokubu Hiroshima-Kenjinkai. 1919. *Soritsu Nijunen Kinen Shiatoru Beikoku Hiroshima Kenjinkai.* Tokyo: Beikoku Seihokubu Hiroshima-Kenjinkai.

Bertelot, Jack, and Martine Gaumé. 1982. *Kaz Anitiyé: Jan Moun Ka Rété—Caribbean Popular Dwelling.* Point-à-Pitre, Guadaloupe: Editions Perspectives Créoles.

Beveridge, Charles E. 1995. *Frederick Law Olmsted: Designing the American Landscape.* New York: Rizzoli.

Beveridge, Charles E., and David Schuyler, eds. 1983. *The Papers of Frederick Law Olmsted.* Vol. 3, *Creating Central Park, 1857–1861.* Baltimore: Johns Hopkins University Press.

Bhabha, Homi K. 1994. *The Location of Culture.* New York: Routledge.

Bidwell, Dennis P., Joanne Westphal, John Wunsch, and Valerie Berton. 1996. *Forging New Directions: Purchasing Development Rights to Save Farmland—How Peninsula Township, Michigan, Designed and Built Support for Farmland Protection.* Washington, D.C.: American Farmland Trust.

Bird, David. 1981. "Repairs at Wollman Rink Renew a Thirty-Year Dispute." *New York Times,* January 20.

Birnbaum, Charles. 1994. *Preservation Brief 36. Protecting Cultural Landscapes: Planning, Treatment and Management of Historic Landscapes.* Washington, D.C.: National Park Service, Preservation Assistance Division.

Birnbaum, Charles, with Christene Capella Peters, eds. 1996. *The Secretary of the Interior's Standards for the Treatment of Historic Properties with Guidelines for the Treatment of Cultural Landscapes.* Washington, D.C.: National Park Service, Cultural Resource Stewardship & Partnerships, Heritage Preservation Services, Historic Landscape Initiative.

Blouet, Brian W., and Merline P. Lawson, eds. 1975. *Images of the Plains: The Role of Human Nature in Settlement.* Lincoln: University of Nebraska Press.

Boddy, Trevor. 1992. "Underground and Overhead: Building the Analogous City." In *Variations on a Theme Park: The New American City and the End of Public Space,* edited by Michael Sorkin. New York: Noonday.

Bowen, John. 1990. *America's Living Past.* New York: M&M Books.

Boyer, Christine M. 1983. *Dreaming the Rational City: The Myth of American City Planning.* Cambridge: MIT Press.

———. 1992. "The Imaginary Real World." *Assemblage* 18:115–27.

Brachey, Doug, and Dawn Brachey. 1995. *Rugby: Tennessee's Victorian Village.* Rugby, Tenn.: Historic Rugby.

Brooke, James. 1998. "Rare Alliance in the Rockies Strives to Save Open Spaces." *New York Times,* 14 August.

Brown, Richard Maxwell. 1994. *No Duty to Retreat: Violence and Values in American History and Society.* 2d ed. Norman: University of Oklahoma Press.

Brunskill, Robert. 1978. *Illustrated Handbook of Vernacular Architecture.* 2d ed. London: Faber & Faber.

California Department of Parks and Recreation. 1988. *Five Views: An Ethnic Survey of California.* Sacramento: Office of Historic Preservation.

Calkins, Charles F., and William G. Laatsch. 1986. "Belgians." In *America's Architectural Roots: Ethnic Groups That Built America,* edited by Dell Upton. Washington, D.C.: Preservation Press.

Carmody, Deirdre. 1982. "Cutting of Central Park Trees Angers Birders." *New York Times,* May 3.

Caro, Robert A. 1974. *The Power Broker: Robert Moses and the Fall of New York.* New York: Alfred A. Knopf.

Carr, Ethan. 1998. *Wilderness by Design: Landscape Architecture and the National Park Service.* Lincoln: University of Nebraska Press.

"Central Park." 1873. *Scribner's Monthly* 6 (September): 523–39; 6 (October): 673–91.

Chan, Sucheng. 1986. *The Bittersweet Soil: The Chinese in California Agriculture, 1860–1910.* Berkeley: University of California Press.

———. 1991. *Asian Americans: An Interpretive History.* Boston: Twayne.

Chapman, Fred. 1991. "Native Americans and Cultural Resource Management: The View from Wyoming." *Cultural Resources Management Bulletin* 14, no. 5: 19–21.

Clark, Galen. 1910. *The Yosemite Valley: Its History, Characteristic Features, and Theories Regarding Its Origin.* Yosemite Valley, Calif.: Nelson L. Salter.

Clay, Grady, ed. 1976. "Whose Time Is This Place? The Emerging Science of Garden Preservation." *Landscape Architecture* 66 (May): 217–18.

Colón, Jesús. 1982. *A Puerto Rican in New York and Other Sketches.* New York: International Publishers.

Comp, T. Allan, ed. 1994. *Regional Heritage Areas: Approaches to Sustainable Development.* Washington, D.C.: National Trust for Historic Preservation.

Conzen, Michael P. 1978. "Analytical Approaches to the Urban Landscape." In *Dimensions of Human Geography: Essays on Some Familiar and Neglected Themes,* edited by Karl W. Butzer. Chicago: Department of Geography, University of Chicago.

Cook, John E. 1991. "The Cultural Legacy of America's National Parklands." *Cultural Resources Management Bulletin* 14, no. 5: 38–41 (reprinted from *National Forum,* spring 1991).

Cook, Robert. 1996. "Is Landscape Preservation an Oxymoron?" *George Wright Forum* 13, no. 1: 42–53.

Cooper, James Fenimore. 1982 (1841). *The Deerslayer.* New York: Collier Books.

Copps, David H. 1995. *Views from the Road: A Community Guide for Assessing Rural Historic Landscapes.* Washington, D.C.: Island Press.

Cowley, Jill. 1991. "Canyon De Chelly: An Ethnographic Landscape." *Cultural Resources Management Bulletin* 14, no. 6: 10–11.

Cramer, Marianne. 1993. "Urban Renewal: Restoring the Vision of Olmsted and Vaux in Central Park's Woodlands." *Restoration and Management Notes* 11 (winter): 106–16.

Cranz, Galen. 1982. *The Politics of Park Design: A History of Urban Parks in America.* Cambridge: MIT Press.

Cronon, William. 1983. *Changes in the Land: Indians, Colonists, and the Ecology of New England.* New York: Hill & Wang.

———. 1995. "The Trouble with Wilderness; or, Getting Back to the Wrong Nature." In *Uncommon Ground: Toward Reinventing Nature,* edited by William Cronon. New York: W. W. Norton.

Current, Richard N. 1977. *Wisconsin: A Bicentennial History.* New York: W. W. Norton.

Davis, Mike. 1992. "Fortress Los Angeles: The Militarization of Urban Space." In *Variations on a Theme Park: The New American City and the End of Public Space,* edited by Michael Sorkin. New York: Noonday.

Deakin, Motley F., ed. 1967 (1852). *The Home Book of the Picturesque; or American Scenery, Art, and Literature, Comprising a Series of Essays by Washington Irving, W. C. Bryant, Fenimore Cooper, and Others.* Gainesville, Fla.: Scholars' Facsimilies & Reprints.

Demars, Stanford E. 1991. *The Tourist in Yosemite.* Salt Lake City: University of Utah Press.

Dill, Alonzo T. 1942. "Tryon's Palace: A Neglected Niche of North Carolina History." *North Carolina Historical Review* 19 (April): 119–67.

Downer, Alan S., and Alexandria Roberts. 1993. "Traditional Cultural Properties: Cultural Resources Management and Environmental Planning." *Cultural Resources Management Bulletin* 16 (special issue): 12–14.

Dubrow, Gail. 1999. *A History of the Chinese on Ebey's Prairie, Whidby Island, Washington.* Seattle: Pacific Regional Office, National Park Service.

Dubrow, Gail, Gail Nomura, et al. 1993. *The Historic Context for the Protection of Asian/Pacific American Resources in Washington State.* Olympia, Wash.: Office of Archaeology & Historic Preservation.

Dunn, Durwood. 1988. *Cades Cove: The Life and Death of a Southern Appalachian Community, 1818–1937.* Knoxville: University of Tennessee Press.

Egerton, John. 1977. *Visions of Utopia: Nashoba, Rugby, Ruskin, and the "New Communities" in Tennessee's Past.* Knoxville: University of Tennessee Press.

Ehrenkrantz Group. c. 1985. *Master Plan for the Development, Management, and Protection of the Rugby Colony Historic Area: Morgan and Scott Counties, Tennessee.* Nashville: U.S. Army Corps of Engineers.

Evernden, Neil. 1992. *The Social Creation of Nature.* Baltimore: Johns Hopkins University Press.

Fee, Jeffrey M. 1991. "A Dragon in the Eagle's Land: Chinese in an Idaho Wilderness, Warren Mining District, ca. 1870–1900." Master's thesis, University of Idaho.

Fitch, James Marston. 1976. "Preservation Requires Tact, Modesty, and Honesty among Designers." *Landscape Architecture* 66 (May): 276–80.

———. 1982. *Historic Preservation: Curatorial Management of the Built World.* New York: McGraw-Hill Book Co.

Flewelling, Stan. 1990. *Farmlands: The Story of Thomas, a Small Agricultural Community in King County, Washington.* Auburn, Wash.: Erick Sanders Historical Society.

Flores, Juan. 1993. *Divided Borders: Essays on Puerto Rican Identity.* Houston: Arte Publico Press.

"Focus on Landscape Preservation." 1993. *Historic Preservation Forum* 7 (May–June): 1–69.

Foley, D. J. 1912. *Yosemite Souvenir and Guide.* Yosemite National Park, Calif.: Yosemite Falls Studio.

Foner, Eric. 1990. *The New American History.* Philadelphia: Temple University Press.

Fowler, Catherine S. 1986. "Subsistence." In *Handbook of North American Indians,* vol. 11, *The Great Basin,* edited by Watten d'Azevedo. Washington, D.C.: Smithsonian Institution Press.

Fowler, Catherine S., Molly Dufort, Mary Rusco, and the Historic Preservation Committee, Timbisha Shoshone Tribe. 1995. *Residence without Reservation: Ethnographic Overview and Traditional Land Use Study, Timbisha Shoshone, Death Valley National Park, California.* Death Valley: National Park Service.

Francaviglia, Richard V. 1978a. *The Mormon Landscape: Existence, Creation, and Perception of a Unique Image in the American West.* New York: AMS.

———. 1978b. "The Passing Mormon Village." *Landscape* 22 (spring): 40–47.

———. 1981. "Main Street USA: A Comparison/Contrast of Streetscapes in Disneyland and Walt Disney World." *Journal of Popular Culture* 15 (summer): 141–56.

———. 1989. "Main Street: The Twentieth Century." *Timeline* 6 (February–March): 28–43.

———. 1991. *Hard Places: Reading the Landscape of America's Historic Mining Districts.* Iowa City: University of Iowa Press.

———. 1996. *Main Street Revisited: Time, Space, and Image Building in Small Town America.* Iowa City: University of Iowa Press.

Friday, Chris. 1994. *Organizing Asian American Labor: The Pacific Coast Canned-Salmon Industry, 1870–1942.* Philadelphia: Temple University Press.

Friedmann, John, and Goetz Wolff. 1982. "World City Formation: An Agenda for Research and Action." *International Journal of Urban and Regional Research* 6 (September): 309–44.

Fuller, Nancy. 1991. "Ak-Chin Him Dak: A New Model for Community Heritage Management Opens to the Public." *Cultural Resources Management Bulletin* 14, no. 5: 36–37, 43.

Geological Survey of California. 1869. *The Yosemite Guide-Book: A Description of the Yosemite Valley and the Adjacent Region of the Sierra Nevada, and the Big Trees of California.* Sacramento: Geological Survey of California.

George Gallup Organization. 1986. *A Gallup Study of Public Attitudes towards Issues Facing Urban America,* 2 vols. Washington, D.C.: Urban Land Institute.

Getz, Lynn. 1987. "Barneston." In *Cedar River Watershed Cultural Resource Inventory.* Seattle: Seattle Water Department.

Glassie, Henry H. 1968. *Pattern in the Material Folk Culture of the Eastern United States.* Philadelphia: University of Pennsylvania Press.

Goldberger, Paul. 1980. "A Startling Soft, Green Lawn in Central Park." *New York Times,* June 5.

Golden, Tim. 1997. "In Yosemite, Nature May Have Its Way Yet." *New York Times,* 2 February.

Gómez-Peña, Guillermo. 1993. *Warrior for Gringostroika: Essays, Performances, Texts, and Poetry.* St. Paul, Minn.: Greywolf Press.

Gramann, John. 1992. *Visitors, Alternative Futures, and Recreational Displacement at Yosemite National Park.* College Station: Departments of Recreation, Park, and Tourism Sciences and of Rural Sociology, Texas A&M University.

Green, Archie. 1995a. "Labor Landmarks Past and Present." *Labor's Heritage* 6 (spring): 26–53.

———. 1995b. "What Is a Landmark?" *Labor's Heritage* 6 (spring): 54–63.

Greenwood, Roberta S. 1993. "Old Approaches and New Directions: Implications for Future Research." In *The Hidden Heritage: Historical Archaeology of the Overseas Chinese,* edited by Priscilla Wegars. Amityville, N.Y.: Baywood Publishing Co.

Greiser, Sally Thompson, and T. Weber Greiser. 1993. "Two Views of the World." *Cultural Resources Management Bulletin* 16 (special issue): 9–11.

Grossman, James R. 1994. "National Park Service Theme Study in Labor History." *Cultural Resources Management Bulletin* 17, no. 5: 12–13.

Groth, Paul. 1997. "Frameworks for Cultural Landscape Study." In *Understanding Ordinary Landscapes,* edited by Paul Groth and Todd W. Bressi. New Haven: Yale University Press.

Hall, Ansel F., ed. 1921. *Handbook of Yosemite National Park.* New York: G. P. Putnam's Sons.

Hall, Marcus H. 1999. "American Nature, Italian Culture: Restoring the Land in Two Continents." Ph.D. diss., University of Wisconsin-Madison.

Hart, John. 1991. *Farming at the Edge: Saving Family Farms in Marin County, California.* Berkeley: University of California Press.

Haswell, Susan Olsen, and Arnold R. Alanen. 1994. *A Garden Apart: An Agricultural and Settlement History of Michigan's Sleeping Bear Dunes National Lakeshore Region.* Omaha: Midwest Regional Office, National Park Service.

Hattori, Eugene. 1991. "Chinese and Japanese." In *Nevada Comprehensive Preservation Plan,* edited by William G. White and Ronald M. James. Carson City, Nev.: State Historic Preservation Office.

Hawes, Elizabeth. 1982. "Whose Park Is It Anyway?" *New York Times Magazine,* September 5: 18–19ff.

Hayden, Dolores. 1976. *Seven American Utopias: The Architecture of Communitarian Socialism, 1790–1975.* Cambridge: MIT Press.

————. 1995. *The Power of Place: Urban Landscapes as Public History.* Cambridge: MIT Press.

Hayden, Dolores, Gail Dubrow, and Carolyn Flynn. 1985. *The Power of Place: Los Angeles.* Los Angeles: The Power of Place.

Hayward, Gordon. 1993. "A Plan for Agricultural Preservation." *Planning & Zoning News* (Mich.), March, 17–19.

Hayward, Jeffrey (People, Places, and Design Research). 1991. *Recreation and Leisure Time Study Concerning the Users and Non-Users of Lincoln Park.* Chicago: Chicago Park District & Recreation & Leisure Task Force.

Heady, Harold F., and Paul J. Zinke. 1978. *Vegetational Changes in Yosemite Valley.* Washington, D.C.: Government Printing Office.

"Heritage Tourism Defined." 1993. *Heritage Tourism Program Update* 1 (fall): 2.

Hill, C. L. 1916. *Forests of Yosemite, Sequoia, and General Grant National Parks.* Washington, D.C.: Government Printing Office.

Hobsbawm, Eric, and Terrence Ranger. 1992. *The Invention of Tradition.* New York: Cambridge University Press.

Hosmer, Charles B., Jr. 1985. "The Colonial Revival in the Public Eye: Williamsburg and Garden Restoration." In *The Colonial Revival in America,* edited by Alan Axelrod. New York: W. W. Norton for the Henry Francis Du Pont Winterthur Museum.

House, Freeman. 1996. "Restoring Relations: The Vernacular Approach to Ecological Restoration." *Restoration and Management Notes* 14 (summer): 57–61.

Hufford, Mary. 1985. "Culture and the Cutivation of Nature: The Pinelands National Reserve." In *Folklife Annual, 1985,* edited by Alan Jabbour and James Hardin. Washington, D.C.: Library of Congress.

————. 1986. *One Space, Many Places.* Washington, D.C.: American Folklife Center, Library of Congress.

Hunt, John Dixon, and Joachim Wolschke-Bulmahn. 1993. "Introduction: Discovering the Vernacular Garden." In *The Vernacular Garden,* edited by John Dixon Hunt and Joachim Wolschke-Bulmahn. Washington, D.C.: Dumbarton Oaks Research Library & Collection.

Hutchings, James M. 1990 (1886). *In the Heart of the Sierras: To Yosemite Valley and the Big Tree Grove.* Lafayette, Calif.: Great West Books.

Huxtable, Ada Louise. 1992. "Inventing American Reality." *New York Review of Books* 39 (3 December): 24–29.

Ito, Kazuo. 1973. *Issei: A History of Japanese Immigrants in North America,* translated by Shinichiro Nakamura and Jean S. Gerard. Seattle: Japanese Community Service.

Jackson, Donald Dale. 1992. "It's Wake-Up Time for Main Street When Wal-Mart Comes to Town." *Smithsonian* 23 (October): 36ff.

Jackson, John Brinckerhoff. 1976. "'Sterile Restorations Cannot Replace a Sense of the Stream of Time." *Landscape Architecture* 66 (May): 194.

————. 1980. *The Necessity for Ruins and Other Topics.* Amherst: University of Massachusetts Press.

————. 1984. *Discovering the Vernacular Landscape.* New Haven: Yale University Press.

————. 1986a. "The Vernacular Landscape." In *Landscape Meanings and Values,* edited by Edmund G. Penning-Rowsell and David Lowenthal. London: Allen & Unwin.

———. 1986b. "Vernacular." In *American Architecture: Innovation and Tradition,* edited by David G. De Long, Helen Searing, and Robert A. M. Stern. New York: Rizzoli.

———. 1990. "The House in the Vernacular Landscape." In *The Making of the American Landscape,* edited by Michael Conzen. London: Harper Collins.

———. 1994. *A Sense of Place, A Sense of Time.* New Haven: Yale University Press.

———. 1997. *Landscape in Sight: Looking at America,* edited by Helen Lefkowitz Horowitz. New Haven: Yale University Press.

Japanese Agricultural Association. 1918. *The Japanese Farmers in California.* San Francisco: Japanese Agricultural Association.

Japanese American Citizens' League, White River Valley Chapter. 1986. *A Pictorial Album of the History of the Japanese of the White River Valley.* Auburn, Wash.: JACL, White River Valley Chapter.

Johnston, R. J. 1991. *Geography and Geographers: Anglo-American Human Geography since 1945.* 4th ed. London: Edward Arnold.

Kammen, Michael, ed. 1980. *The Past before Us: Contemporary Historical Writing in the United States.* Ithaca: Cornell University Press.

Keller, Genevieve P. 1993. "The Inventory and Analysis of Historic Landscapes." *Historic Preservation Forum* 7 (May–June): 26–35.

Keller, J. Timothy, and Genevieve P. Keller. 1987. *How to Evaluate and Nominate Designed Historic Landscapes.* National Register Bulletin 18. Washington, D.C.: National Park Service.

Kimmelman, Michael. 1997. "By Whatever Name, Easier to Like." *New York Times,* February 17.

King, Anthony D. 1991. *Urbanism, Colonialism, and the World Economy: Cultural and Spatial Foundations of the World Urban System.* London: Routledge.

King, Thomas F. 1993. "Beyond Bulletin 38: Comments on the Traditional Properties Symposium." *Cultural Resources Management Bulletin* 16 (special issue): 60–64.

Kolodny, Annette. 1984. *The Land before Her: Fantasy and Experience of the American Frontiers, 1630–1860.* Chapel Hill: University of North Carolina Press.

Laidlaw, Robert M. 1991. "Federal Agency Management and Native American Heritage Values." *Cultural Resources Management Bulletin* 14, no. 5: 16–18.

Lamme, Ary J., III. 1989. *America's Historic Landscapes: Community Power and the Preservation of Four National Historic Sites.* Knoxville: University of Tennessee Press.

Land and Community Associates. 1977a. *Culture and Environment: A Challenge for the Amana Colonies.* Charlottesville, Va.: Land and Community Associates.

———. 1977b. *A Conservation Handbook for Amana Villages.* Charlottesville, Va.: Land and Community Associates.

———. 1994. *Cultural Landscape Report: Yosemite Valley, Yosemite National Park.* Charlottesville, Va.: Land and Community Associates.

Land Trust Alliance. 1998. *1998 National Directory of Conservation Land Trusts.* Washington, D.C.: Land Trust Alliance.

LANDSCAPES. 1990. *Comprehensive Master Plan: Andrew Jackson Downing Memorial Park, Newburgh, New York.* Newburgh, N.Y.: Downing Park Planning Committee.

————. 1991. *The Lancaster Cemetery and Woodward Hill Cemetery, Lancaster, Pennsylvania: Preservation Needs Assessment.* Lancaster, Pa.: Historic Preservation Trust of Lancaster County.

Lane, Franklin. 1919. Preface to *Yosemite National Park, California,* by United States Railroad Administration. Washington, D.C.: Government Printing Office.

Leone, Mark. 1973. "Archeology as the Science of Technology: Mormon Town Plans and Fences." In *Research and Theory in Current Archeology,* edited by Charles Redman. New York: John Wiley & Sons.

————. 1979. *The Roots of Modern Mormonism.* Cambridge: Harvard University Press.

Lewis, John Newel. 1983. *Ajoupa Architecture of the Caribbean: Trinidad's Heritage.* Trinidad: J. Newel Lewis.

Limerick, Patricia Nelson. 1987. *The Legacy of Conquest: The Unbroken Past of the American West.* New York: W. W. Norton.

————. 1992. "Disorientation and Reorientation: The American Landscape Discovered from the West." *Journal of American History,* December, 1021–49.

Litke, Frederic. 1987. *A Voyage around the World, 1826–1829.* Vol. 1: *To Russian America and Siberia* (transl. by Renee Marshall), ed. Richard A. Pierce. Kingston, Ontario: Limestone Press.

Livingston, D. S. 1993. *Ranching on the Point Reyes Peninsula: A History of the Dairy and Beef Ranches within Point Reyes National Seashore, 1834–1992.* Point Reyes Station, Calif.: Point Reyes National Seashore.

Lockwood, Alice B., comp. and ed. 1934. *Gardens of Colony and State: Gardens and Gardeners of the American Colonies and of the Republic before 1840.* New York: Charles Scribner's Sons for the Garden Club of America.

Lowenthal, David. 1985. *The Past Is a Foreign Country.* New York: Cambridge University Press.

————. 1996. *Possessed by the Past: The Heritage Crusade and the Spoils of History.* New York: Free Press.

Lowenthal, David, and H. C. Prince. 1965. "English Landscape Tastes." *Geographical Review* 55 (April): 196–222.

Lynch, Kevin. 1980. *What Time Is This Place?* Cambridge: MIT Press.

MacDonald, Eric, and Arnold R. Alanen. 1999. *Tending a "Comfortable Wilderness": A History of Agricultural and Cultural Landscapes on North Manitou Island, Sleeping Bear Dunes National Lakeshore.* Empire, Mich.: Sleeping Bear Dunes National Lakeshore.

Mahan, Ingrid. 1999. Untitled article. *MainStreet News,* no. 151 (February): 5, 15.

Malin, James C. 1984. *History and Ecology: Studies of the Grassland,* edited by Robert P. Swierengen. Lincoln: University of Nebraska Press.

Mason, Robert J. 1992. *Contested Lands: Conflict and Compromise in New Jersey's Pine Barrens.* Philadelphia: Temple University Press.

Mathewes, Perry. 1998. "New Documentation for the Tyron Palace Gardens." *Magnolia: Bulletin of the Southern Garden History Society* 14 (spring): 1–6.

Matthes, Francois E. 1950. *The Incomparable Valley: A Geologic Interpretation of the Yosemite.* Berkeley: University of California Press.

McClelland, Linda Flint. 1998. *Building the National Parks: Historic Landscape Design and Construction.* Baltimore: Johns Hopkins University Press.

McClelland, Linda Flint, J. Timothy Keller, Genevieve P. Keller, and Robert Z. Melnick. 1990. *How to Identify, Evaluate, and Register Rural Historic Landscapes.* National Register Bulletin 30. Washington, D.C.: National Park Service, Interagency Resources Division.

McCormick, Kathleen. 1994. "Vaulting the Garden Wall: Preservation Projects Raise New Contextual Questions." *Landscape Architecture* 84 (May): 74–81.

McEnaney, Marla J., William H. Tishler, and Arnold R. Alanen. 1995. *Farming at the Water's Edge: An Assessment of Agricultural and Cultural Landscape Resources in the Proposed Port Oneida Rural Historic District at Sleeping Bear Dunes National Lakeshore, Michigan.* Omaha: Midwest Regional Office, National Park Service.

McKinley, Laura. 1993. *An Unbroken Historical Record: Ebey's Landing National Historical Reserve—Administrative History.* Seattle: Cultural Resources Division, Pacific Northwest Region, National Park Service.

McWilliams, Carey. 1939. *Factories in the Field: The Story of Migratory Farm Labor in California.* Boston: Little, Brown.

Meinig, D. W., ed. 1979. *The Interpretation of Ordinary Landscapes: Geographical Essays.* New York: Oxford University Press.

Melnick, Robert Z., Daniel Sponn, and Emma Jane Saxe. 1984. *Cultural Landscapes: Rural Historic Districts in the National Park System.* Washington, D.C.: Historic Architecture Division, Cultural Resources Management, National Park Service.

Miller, Page Putnam, ed. 1992. *Reclaiming the Past: Landmarks of Women's History.* Bloomington: Indiana University Press.

Miller, Page Putnam. 1993. "The Women's History Landmark Project: Policy and Research." *Public Historian* 15 (fall): 82–88.

Mitchell, Joan. 1987. "Planning at Canyon de Chelly National Monument." *Cultural Resources Management Bulletin* 10, no. 1: 19–21, 30.

Mitchell, Nora. 1995. "Cultural Landscapes in the United States." In *Cultural Landscapes of Universal Value: Components of a Global Strategy,* edited by Bernd Von Droste zu Hülshoff, Harald Plachter, and Mechtild Rössler. Jena: Gustav Fisher Verlag, in cooperation with UNESCO.

Murtagh, William J. 1988. *Keeping Time: The History and Theory of Preservation in America.* Pittstown, N.J.: Main Street Press.

Nash, Roderick Frazier. 1989. *The Rights of Nature: A History of Environmental Ethics.* Madison: University of Wisconsin Press.

National Park Service. 1931. *Yosemite National Park, California.* Washington, D.C.: Government Printing Office.

———. 1979. *Sleeping Bear Dunes National Lakeshore: General Management Plan.* Denver: Denver Service Center, National Park Service.

———. 1980. *Comprehensive Plan for Ebey's Landing National Historical Reserve, Washington.* Seattle: Pacific Northwest Region, National Park Service.

———. 1985. *Land Use Plan, Cultural Landscape Report: Boxley Valley.* Harrison, Ark.: Buffalo National River, National Park Service.

———. 1987. *Development Concept Plan/Interpretive Prospectus, North Manitou Island, Sleeping Bear Dunes National Lakeshore, Michigan.* Washington, D.C.: National Park Service.

———. 1988. *Land Management Plan: Cades Cove Historic District, Great Smoky Mountains National Park*. Gatlinburg, Tenn.: National Park Service.

———. 1990. *Joint Management Plan: Canyon de Chelly National Monument*. Santa Fe, N.M.: Southwest Regional Office, National Park Service.

———. 1991a. *Guidelines for Completing National Register of Historic Places Forms*. National Register Bulletin 16A. Washington, D.C: National Park Service, Interagency Resources Division.

———. 1991b. *How to Apply the National Register Criteria for Evaluation*, rev. ed. National Register Bulletin 15A. Washington, D.C.: National Park Service, Interagency Resources Division.

———. 1992. *Draft Guidelines for the Treatment of Historic Landscapes*. Washington, D.C.: National Park Service, Preservation Assistance Division.

National Trust for Historic Preservation. n.d. "Getting Started: How to Succeed in Heritage Tourism." Washington, D.C.: National Trust for Historic Preservation.

Nevius, Blake. 1976. *Cooper's Landscapes: An Essay on the Picturesque Vision*. Berkeley: University of California Press.

Noah, Timothy. 1995. "Tired of Mountains and Trees? New Park Features Superfund Site, Shopping Mall." *Wall Street Journal,* July 28.

Noguchi, Yone. 1897. *The Voice of the Valley*. San Francisco: William Doxey.

Nomura, Gail. 1993. "Overview." In *The Historic Context for the Protection of Asian/Pacific American Resources in Washington State,* edited by Gail Dubrow, Gail Nomura, et al. Olympia, Wash.: Office of Archeology & Historic Preservation (draft manuscript).

O'Brien, Michael J. 1984. *Grassland, Forest, and Historical Settlement*. Lincoln: University of Nebraska Press.

O'Donnell, Patricia M. 1992. "Cultural Landscape Analysis: The Vanderbilt Estate at Hyde Park." *Association for Preservation Technology (APT) Bulletin* 24, no. 3–4: 25–41.

———. 1993. "The Treatment of Historic Landscapes." *Historic Preservation Forum* 7 (May–June): 26–35.

O'Donnell, Patricia, and Robert Z. Melnick. 1987. "Toward a Preservation Ethic." *Landscape Architecture* 77 (July–August): 136.

Oliver, Paul, ed. 1997. *Encyclopedia of Vernacular Architecture of the World,* 3 vols. Cambridge: Cambridge University Press.

Olmsted, Frederick Law. 1871. "Public Parks and the Enlargement of Towns." *Journal of Social Science* 3:1–36.

Orland, Ted. 1985. *Man & Yosemite: A Photographer's View of the Early Years*. Santa Cruz, Calif.: Image Continuum Press.

Orsi, Richard J., Alfred Runte, and Marlene Smith-Baranzini, eds. 1993. *Yosemite and Sequoia: A Century of California National Parks*. Berkeley and San Francisco: University of California Press & California Historical Society.

Paddock, Eric. 1991. Introduction to *Testaments in Wood: Finnish Log Structures at Embarrass, Minnesota,* by Wayne Gudmundson. St. Paul: Minnesota Historical Society Press.

Page, Robert R., Cathy R. Gilbert, and Susan A. Dolan. 1998. *A Guide to Cultural Land-*

scape Reports: Contents, Process, and Techniques. Washington, D.C.: National Park Service, Park Historic Structures and Cultural Landscapes Program.

Palsson, Gisli, ed. 1990. *From Water to World-Making: African Models and Arid Lands*. Uppsala, Sweden: Scandinavian Institute of African Studies.

Parker, Patricia L., and Thomas F. King. 1992. *Guidelines for Identifying and Evaluating Traditional Cultural Properties*. National Register Bulletin 38. Washington, D.C.: National Park Service.

Porter, Daniel. 1990. "Open Air Museums: At the Crossroads?" *Heritage* 16 (January–February): 9.

Porter, Philip W., and Fred E. Lukermann. 1975. "The Geography of Utopia." In *Geographies of the Mind*, edited by David Lowenthal and Martyn J. Bowden. New York: Oxford University Press.

Price, Andrew, Jr. 1989. *Port Blakely: The Community Captain Renton Built*. Seattle: Port Blakely Books.

Quintero-Rivera, Angel. 1988. *Patricios y Plebeyos: Burgueses, Hacendados, Artesanos, y Obreros: Las Relaciones de Clase en P.R. del Cambio de Siglo*. Rio Piedras, P.R.: Huracán.

Ramírez, Guillermo. n.d. *El Arte Popular en Puerto Rico (En Busca de las Raíces de Nuestra Cultura)*. New York: Colección Montaña.

Rapaport, Amos. 1969. *House Form and Culture*. Englewood Cliffs, N.J.: Prentice-Hall.

"Raw Vision's Definitions." 1993. *Raw Vision* 7 (summer): 18–19.

Rigau, Jorge. 1992. *Puerto Rico, 1900: Turn of the Century Architecture in the Hispanic Caribbean, 1898–1930*. New York: Rizzoli.

Riley, Robert. 1987. "Vernacular Landscapes." In *Advances in Environment, Behavior, and Design*, vol. 1, ed. Ervin H. Zube and Gary T. Moore. New York: Plenum Press.

———. 1992. "Attachment to the Ordinary Landscape." In *Place Attachment*, edited by Irwin Altman and Setha Low. New York: Plenum Press.

Rodríguez Castro, Maria Elena. 1993. "Las Casas del Porvenir: Nación y Narración en el Ensayo Puertorriqueño." *Revista IberoAmericana* 59 (January–June): 33–54.

Rogers, Elizabeth Barlow. 1987. *Rebuilding Central Park: A Management and Restoration Plan*. Cambridge: MIT Press.

Rolston, Holmes, III. 1994. Foreword to *An Environmental Proposal for Ethics: The Principle of Integrity*, by Laura Westra. Lanham, Md.: Rowman & Littlefield.

Rolvaag, O. E. 1927. *Giants in the Earth: A Saga of the Prairie*. New York: Harper & Brothers.

Rosenzweig, Roy, and Elizabeth Blackmar. 1992. *The Park and the People: A History of Central Park*. Ithaca: Cornell University Press.

Rowe, Colin, and Fred Koetter. 1978. *Collage City*. Cambridge: MIT Press.

"Rugby Colony Master Plan." 1986. *Progressive Architecture* 67 (June): 10–13.

Runte, Alfred. 1992 (1990). *Yosemite: The Embattled Wilderness*. Yosemite National Park, Calif.: Yosemite Association.

Russell, Carl Parcher. 1992 (1959). *One Hundred Years in Yosemite*. Yosemite National Park, Calif.: Yosemite Association.

Sancar, Fahriye Hazer, and Theano Terkenli Koop. 1995. "Proposing a Behavioral Definition of the 'Vernacular' Based on a Comparative Analysis of the Behavior Settings in Three Settlements in Turkey and Greece." *Journal of Architectural and Planning Research* 12, no. 2: 141–65.

Sanchez, Korrol. 1994. *From Colonia to Community: The History of Puerto Ricans in New York City.* Berkeley: University of California Press.

Sánchez, Luis Rafael. 1992. "La Guagua Aerea," translated by Diana L. Velez. In *La Casa de Todos Nosotros.* New York: Museo del Barrio.

Sargent, Shirley. 1975. *Yosemite and Its Innkeepers.* Yosemite, Calif.: Flying Spur Press.

Sauer, Carl. 1925 (1969). "The Morphology of Landscape." In *Land and Life: A Selection from the Writings of Carl Ortwin Sauer,* edited by John Leighly. Berkeley: University of California Press.

Schneider, Keith. 1994. "Town Finds Rare Way to Protect Farms: Tax." *New York Times,* September 11.

Schuyler, David. 1986. *The New Urban Landscape: The Redefinition of City Form in Nineteenth-Century America.* Baltimore: Johns Hopkins University Press.

———. 1991. "Belated Honor to a Prophet: Newburgh's Downing Park." *Landscape* 31 (spring): 10–17.

———. 1996. *Apostle of Taste: Andrew Jackson Downing, 1815–1852.* Baltimore: Johns Hopkins University Press.

Schuyler, David, and Jane Turner Censer, eds. 1992. *The Papers of Frederick Law Olmsted.* Vol. 6, *The Years of Olmsted, Vaux & Company, 1865–1874.* Baltimore: Johns Hopkins University Press.

Sebastian, Lynn. 1993. "Protecting Traditional Properties through the Section 106 Process." *Cultural Resources Management Bulletin* 16 (special issue): 22–26.

Segre, Roberto. 1984–85. "Continuidad y Renovación de las Tradiciones Vernaculas en el Ambiente Caribeño Contemporáneo." *Anales del Caribe del Centro de Estudios del Caribe* 4–5:70–108.

Sennett, Richard. 1990. *The Conscience of the Eye: The Design and Social Life of Cities.* New York: Alfred A. Knopf.

Sepúlveda, Anibal. 1989. *San Juan: Historia Ilustrada de su Desarrollo Urbano (1509–1898).* San Juan, P.R.: Centro de Investigaciones CARIMAR.

Sepúlveda, Anibal, and Jorge Carbonell. 1987. *Cangregos-Santurce: Historia Ilustrada de su Desarrollo Urbano (1509–1950).* San Juan, P.R.: Centro de Investigaciones CARIMAR y Oficina Estatal de Preservación Histórica.

Shigemori, F. N. Mirei. 1949. *Gardens of Japan.* Kyoto: Nissha Printing Co.

Shiro, Fujioka, ed. 1953. *The History of the Development of the Flower Market in Southern California.* Los Angeles: Southern California Flower Market.

Shukert, R. D. G. Martin. 1995. *The River Country Heritage Tourism Plan.* Lincoln: Nebraska State Historical Society.

Silos & Smokestacks Board of Trustees, Partnership Management Plan Task Force. 1997. *Silos & Smokestacks Partnership Management Plan: America's Agricultural Heritage Partnership of Northeastern Iowa.* Waterloo, Iowa: Silos & Smokestacks Board of Trustees.

Silver, Timothy. 1990. *A New Face on the Countryside: Indians, Colonists, and Slaves in South Atlantic Forests, 1500–1800.* Cambridge: Cambridge University Press.

Skow, John. 1999. "Scorching the Earth to Save It." *Outside* 24 (April): 66–71.

Smith, Neil. 1992. "New City, New Frontier: The Lower East Side as Wild, Wild West." In *Variations of a Theme Park: The New American City and the End of Public Space,* edited by Michael Sorkin. New York: Hill & Wang.

Smith-Middleton, Holly, and Arnold R. Alanen. 1998. *Images of Indian River: A Landscape History of Sitka National Historical Park.* Anchorage: Alaska Systems Support Office, National Park Service.

Sorensen, Ann A., Richard P. Greene, and Karen Russ. 1997. *Farming on the Edge.* Washington, D.C.: American Farmland Trust.

Sorkin, Michael, ed. 1992. *Variations on a Theme Park: The New American City and the End of Public Space.* New York: Noonday.

Southeastern Arizona Governments Organization (SEAGO). 1982. "Old Bisbee Development Area." In *City of Bisbee Comprehensive Plan: Phase One.* Bisbee, Ariz.: SEAGO.

Stephensen, P. R. 1986 (1936). *The Foundations of Culture in Australia: An Essay towards National Self Respect.* Sydney, Australia: Allen & Unwin.

Stilgoe, John R. 1982. *Common Landscape of America, 1580 to 1845.* New Haven: Yale University Press.

Stokes, Samuel N., A. Elizabeth Watson, and Shelly S. Mastran. 1997. *Saving America's Countryside: A Guide to Rural Preservation.* 2d ed. Baltimore: Johns Hopkins University Press.

Stornoway, Lewis. 1888. *Yosemite: Where to Go and What to Do.* San Francisco: C. A. Murdock & Co.

Takaki, Ronald. 1993. *A Different Mirror: A History of Multicultural America.* Boston: Little, Brown.

Takami, David. 1989. *Shared Dreams: A History of Asians and Pacific Americans in Washington State.* Olympia: Washington State Centennial Commission.

————. 1992. "Executive Order 9066—Fifty Years before and Fifty Years After: A History of Japanese Americans in Seattle." Seattle: Wing Lake Asian Museum.

Thayer, Robert L. 1994. *Gray World, Green Heart: Technology, Nature, and Sustainable Landscape.* New York: John Wiley & Sons.

Theodoratus, Dorothea J. 1993. "A Perspective on Traditional Sites." *Proceedings of the Society for California Archeology* 6:45–47.

Thomas, David Hurst. 1998. *Archaeology.* 3d ed. Fort Worth: Harcourt Brace College Publishers.

Toth, Edward. 1991. *An Ecosystem Approach to Woodland Management: The Case of Prospect Park.* Bethesda, Md.: National Association of Olmsted Parks.

Trustees of Reservations, The (TTOR). 1992. *Conserving the Massachusetts Landscape: 1992 Annual Report.* Beverly, Mass.: TTOR.

Tuan, Yi-Fu. 1984. *Dominance & Affection: The Making of Pets.* New Haven: Yale University Press.

UNESCO (United Nations Educational, Scientific and Cultural Organization): Intergovernmental Committee for the Protection of the World Cultural and Natural Heritage. 1994. *Operational Guidelines for the Implementation of the World Heritage Convention.* Paris: UNESCO.

U.S. Immigration Commission. 1911. *Immigrants in Industries: Part 25. Japanese and*

Other Immigrant Races in the Pacific Coast and Rocky Mountain States: Diversified Industries. Washington, D.C.: Government Printing Office.

Wagner, Philip, and Marvin Mikesell, eds. 1962. *Readings in Cultural Geography.* Chicago: University of Chicago Press.

Waugh, Isami Arifuku, Alex Yamato, and Raymond Okamura. 1988. "A History of Japanese Americans in California." In *Five Views: An Ethnic Sites Survey of California,* by California Department of Parks and Recreation. Sacramento: Office of Historic Preservation.

Webb, Melody. 1987. "Cultural Landscapes in the National Park Service." *Public Historian* 9 (spring): 77–89.

Wei, Fan. 1992. "Village *Fengshui* Principles." In *The Chinese Landscape: The Village as Place,* edited by Ronald G. Knapp. Honolulu: University of Hawaii Press.

Westmacott, Richard. 1994. *Managing Culturally Significant Agricultural Landscapes in the National Park System* (draft). Washington, D.C.: National Park Service.

Westra, Laura. 1994. *An Environmental Proposal for Ethics: The Principle of Integrity.* Lanham, Md.: Rowman & Littlefield.

White, William. 1991. "Operating Plan." In *Nevada Comprehensive Plan,* edited by William G. White and Ronald M. James. Carson City: Nevada State Historic Preservation Office.

Wicklein, John. 1994. "Spirit Paths of the Anasazi." *Archeology* 47 (January–February): 36–41.

Williams, Brenda Wheeler, Arnold R. Alanen, and William H. Tishler. 1996. *Coming through with Rye: Historic Agricultural Landscapes on South Manitou Island at Sleeping Bear Dunes National Lakeshore, Michigan.* Omaha: Midwest Regional Office, National Park Service.

Williams, Raymond. 1985. *Keywords: A Vocabulary of Culture and Society.* New York: Oxford University Press.

Wilson, Alexander. 1991. *The Culture of Nature: North American Landscape from Disney to* Exxon Valdez. Toronto: Between the Lines.

Wilson, Chris. 1997. *The Myth of Santa Fe: Creating a Modern Regional Tradition.* Albuquerque: University of New Mexico Press.

Wilson, Herbert Earl. 1922. *The Lore and the Lure of the Yosemite.* San Francisco: Sunset Books.

Worster, Donald. 1993. *The Wealth of Nature: Environmental History and Ecological Imagination.* New York: Oxford University Press.

Wyatt, Barbara, and Midwest Vernacular Architecture Forum. 1987. *Surveying and Evaluating Vernacular Architecture* (draft). National Register Bulletin 31. Washington, D.C.: National Park Service.

Yagasaki, Noritaka. 1982. "Ethnic Cooperativism and Immigrant Agriculture: A Study of Japanese Floriculture and Truck Farming in California." Ph.D. diss., University of California, Berkeley.

Zukin, Sharon. 1991. *Landscapes of Power: From Detroit to Disneyland.* Berkeley and Los Angeles: University of California Press.

———. 1995. *The Culture of Cities.* Cambridge: Blackwell Publishers.

Contributors

ARNOLD R. ALANEN, who has a B.A. in architectural studies and a Ph.D. in geography from the University of Minnesota, is a professor of landscape architecture at the University of Wisconsin–Madison, where he specializes in landscape history and cultural landscape studies. He has been both a Fulbright Graduate Fellow and a Visiting Research Professor at the University of Helsinki, Finland. Dr. Alanen is co-author of *Main Street Ready-Made: The New Deal Community of Greendale, Wisconsin* (1987). He has conducted numerous studies of historic and cultural landscapes for the National Park Service in Alaska, Michigan, Missouri, and Wisconsin; in 1997 and 1999, respectively, his work at Sleeping Bear Dunes National Lakeshore in Michigan and Sitka National Historical Park in Alaska received national research awards from the American Society of Landscape Architects.

ROBERT Z. MELNICK has a B.A. from Bard College and a master's of landscape architecture from SUNY-Syracuse. He is dean of the School of Architecture and Allied Arts and a professor of landscape architecture at the University of Oregon. Prof. Melnick is a co-author of the National Register bulletin on rural landscapes. A Fellow of the American Society of Landscape Architects, he serves on the board of the National Center for Preservation Technology and Training. He has received several professional awards for landscape preservation projects.

LUIS APONTE-PARÉS has a B.Arch. from Catholic University and an M.S. in architecture and a Ph.D. in urban planning from Columbia University. Currently an associate professor of community planning at the University of Massachusetts–Boston, he previously taught at Pratt Institute and City College in New York City.

GAIL LEE DUBROW is an associate professor of urban design and planning at the University of Washington, where she also serves as director of the Preservation Planning and Design Program. She received a bachelor's degree in architecture from the University of Washington and a Ph.D. in urban planning from the University of California at Los Angeles. Dr. Dubrow's collection, *Restoring Women's History through Historic Preservation,* co-edited with Jennifer Goodman, is forthcoming from the Johns Hopkins University Press.

RICHARD FRANCAVIGLIA, since receiving a Ph.D. in geography from the University of Oregon in 1970, has worked in both public history and higher education. He currently serves as director of the Center for Greater Southwestern Studies and the History of Cartography at the University of Texas at Arlington, where he also is a professor of history.

DONALD L. HARDESTY, who has a Ph.D. in anthropology from the University of Oregon, is a professor of anthropology at the University of Nevada, Reno, where he also has been Foundation Professor. Dr. Hardesty is a past president of the Society for Historical Archaeology and is president of the Mining History Association.

CATHERINE HOWETT is a professor of landscape architecture and historic preservation in the School of Environmental Design of the University of Georgia. Prof. Howett currently is a senior fellow in the Studies in Landscape Architecture program of Dumbarton Oaks, Washington, D.C. She was the recipient of the 1998 Outstanding Educator Award from the Council of Educators in Landscape Architecture.

PATRICIA M. O'DONNELL received master's degrees in landscape architecture and urban planning from the University of Illinois. As a principal of LANDSCAPES Landscape Architecture • Planning • Historic Preservation in Charlotte, Vermont, since 1987, she has developed a specialization in preservation planning and implementation for cultural landscapes. She is a fellow of the American Society of Landscape Architects.

DAVID SCHUYLER, who received his Ph.D. in history from Columbia University, is a professor of American studies at Franklin & Marshall College. He is the author of *Apostle of Taste: Andrew Jackson Downing, 1815–1852* (1996) and *The New Urban Landscape: The Redefinition of City Form in Nineteenth-Century America* (1986) and is co-editor of three volumes of the *Frederick Law Olmsted Papers.*

Index